CW00336239

IDENTIFYING SELFHOOD

Imagination, Narrative,
and Hermeneutics in the
Thought of Paul Ricoeur

Henry Isaac Venema

STATE UNIVERSITY OF NEW YORK PRESS

Published by
State University of New York Press

© 2000 State University of New York

All rights reserved

Printed in the United States of America

No part of this book may be used or reproduced
in any manner whatsoever without written permission.
No part of this book may be stored in a retrieval system
or transmitted in any form or by any means including
electronic, electrostatic, magnetic tape, mechanical,
photocopying, recording, or otherwise without the prior
permission in writing of the publisher.

For information address State University of New York Press,
90 State Street, Suite 700, Albany, N.Y. 12207

Production by Cathleen Collins
Marketing by Anne M. Valentine

Library of Congress Cataloging in Publication Data

Venema, Henry Isaac, 1958–
    Identifying selfhood : imagination, narrative, and hermeneutics in the thought of Paul
Ricoeur / Henry Isaac Venema.
        p.   cm. — (McGill studies in the history of religions)
    Includes bibliographical references (p.   ) and index.
    ISBN 0-7914-4673-5 (alk. paper) — ISBN 0-7914-4674-3 (pbk. : alk. paper)
    1. Ricoeur, Paul. 2. Self (Philosophy) 3. Identity (Philosophical concept) I. Title. II.
Series.
B2430.R55 V46 2000
126'.092—dc21
                                                                                99-059160

10 9 8 7 6 5 4 3 2 1

This book is dedicated to the memory of my father Wietse whose face I see in my children he never knew.

CONTENTS

ACKNOWLEDGMENTS

I would like to express my deep gratitude to three professors who were indispensable for the completion of this book. To Paul Mathew St. Pierre at Simon Fraser University, whose kindness, support, and many hours of discussion were essential to the development of my understanding of metaphor and narrative. To Jim Olthuis at The Institute for Christian Studies, whose friendship and philosophical insight have profoundly affected the direction of my life, teaching, and research. And particularly I like to thank Maurice Boutin at McGill University. Without his charity of thought, incisive criticism, and tireless expectation of excellence this research project would never have seen its way into print.

Most importantly, I would like to thank my wife Margaret whose patience and support have been immeasurable, and my two children, Allisa and Justin, whose interruptions were always welcome.

ABBREVIATIONS

OPR   D. Woods, *On Paul Ricoeur* (1991)
PH   P. Ricoeur, "Phenomenology and Hermeneutics" (1975)
PPR   L. Hahn, *The Philosophy of Paul Ricoeur* (1995)
PS   G. Bachelard, *The Poetics of Space* (1964)
RH   J. Caputo, *Radical Hermeneutics* (1987)
RM   P. Ricoeur, *The Rule of Metaphor* (1977)
SA   P. Ricoeur, *Soi-même comme un autre* (1990)
SE   P. Ricoeur, *The Symbolism of Evil* (1967)
TDI   P. Ricoeur, "The Text as Dynamic Identity" (1985)
TH   P. Ricoeur, "The Task of Hermeneutics" (1973)
TN 1   P. Ricoeur, *Time and Narrative*, Volume 1 (1984)
TN 2   P. Ricoeur, *Time and Narrative*, Volume 2 (1985)
TN 3   P. Ricoeur, *Time and Narrative*, Volume 3 (1988)

INTRODUCTION

"The symbol gives rise to thought" (SE 347). This affirmation opens interesting possibilities. Ricoeur explains that this "sentence, which enchants me, says two things: the symbol gives; but what it gives is occasion for thought, something to think about" (SE 348). Although the giving of this gift facilitates the production of thought, the return to a "primitive naïveté," where the "immediacy of belief" (SE 351) is affirmed without suspicion or doubt, has never been the focus of Ricoeur's philosophical inquiries; however, the pursuit of a "second naïveté," is his constant goal and with his publication of *Oneself as Another* (1992) Ricoeur gives new life to the correlation between commitment and thought. Ricoeur develops his entire philosophy of selfhood on the assumption that hermeneutical inquiry is "attestation" of the being of selfhood. Here, attestation has the meaning of "a kind of belief. . . . attestation belongs to the grammar of 'I believe-in' " (OA 21).

By giving occasion for thought, the symbol neither predetermines the outcome of thought, nor gives opportunity for fideism to rule. What Ricoeur wants to describe is the structure of linguistic reflection on existence. "The consciousness of self seems to constitute itself at its lowest level by means of symbolism and to work out an abstract language only subsequently, by means of a spontaneous hermeneutics of its primary symbols" (SE 9). What begins with a primitive symbolism ends with ontological discourse.[1] To understand the relation between primitive and complex language, Ricoeur employs a hermeneutical methodology rather than a one-directional movement based on a hierarchy of below and above. In what is perhaps Ricoeur's most succinct and earliest[2] formulation of this hermeneutic relation, at least partly based on Augustine's *credo ut intelligam*,[3] he explains that "what we have just called a knot—the knot where the symbol gives and criticism interprets—appears in hermeneutics as a circle. The circle can be stated bluntly: 'We must understand

1

to believe, but we must believe to understand.' The circle is not a vicious circle, still less a mortal one; it is a living and stimulating circle. We must believe to understand: never, in fact, does the interpreter get near to what his text says unless he lives in the *aura* of the meaning he is inquiring after" (SE 351).

Examining the nature of symbols within the context of a "symbolism of evil," Ricoeur suggests a principle applicable to the task of understanding human experience as a whole. Through a descriptive phenomenology of confession, Ricoeur uncovers a level of worldly participation that is prior to abstract reflection and philosophical speculation. Symbols "gather together at one point a mass of significations which, before giving rise to thought, give rise to speech" (SE 11) that is heard before it is spoken (FP 29–30). Our basic orientation and commitment to the world is given shape by a knot of significations focused on a "symbol-thing" such as the "sky, water, moon, . . . tree, stone" (SE 6), which then gives rise to speech in the form of linguistic symbols. Subsequent to the formation of language, a "re-enactment of confession" takes place through ritual and narrative. Telling and retelling re-enacts our symbolic connection to our world. Narration, particularly in the form of mythic tales, offers "an understanding of human reality as a whole . . . through the myth by means of a reminiscence and an expectation" (SE 6). By remembering and looking ahead, narration helps us understand our deepest commitments and confessions of belonging by giving shape to the "opaque" effort to exist. Narrating the past gives hope for the future (TN 3: 258). However, narration is but one part of the hermeneutic of understanding. Rooted in the symbolization of experience, ontological discourse arises from narration and returns in a more abstract manner to what was first symbolized. "It is the whole circle, made up of confession, myth, and speculation, that we must understand" (SE 9). If thinking about existence and selfhood is to take place, the symbolism expressed by confession, commitment, and belief must become an integral part of the effort to understand how we participate in our world.

The circle of commitment and thought is the object of Ricoeur's philosophical explorations; it also documents his own philosophical method. On several occasions Ricoeur reveals the basic philosophical commitments that have animated his research.[4] Undoubtedly, his commitment to meaning is preeminent and characterizes his method as a form of phenomenology. Before the subject can reflect on questions of being, a reduction to the meaning of being must take place.[5] "The reflecting subject in search of meaning, [and] self-understanding" must take a "detour"[6] through the various forms of linguistic meaning, in order, ultimately, to clarify existence and selfhood by means of ontological concepts. Gary Madison points out that for Ricoeur the "subject is a speaking/spoken subject . . . and to the degree that it exists self-understandingly it does so only as the result of the constitutive and critical play of signs, symbols and texts; it is not a natural (or metaphysical) given but the result of a semiosis" (HP 95). Just as symbols give rise to thought, Ricoeur's commitment to meaning calls for the analysis of meaning manifest in language. "It could . . . be said that the preliminary choice in favor of meaning is a sort of philosophical act of faith taking the place of the traditional 'inner light'; but only if, at the same time, it is pointed out that it is in fact a philosophical faith, a new *fides quaerens intellectum*. The initial presupposition of meaning is borne out and validated in the totality of phenomenologico-hermeneutic procedures" (Jervolino 96). The circle of symbol and thought repeats on the level of language what is supposed to take place within the larger circle of linguistic meaning and existence. Just as the philosophical act of faith is tested through method and method is tested by the fruit it bears in the explication of commitment, so too the project of existence is supposed to be tested by the world of meaning it prefigures.

Ricoeur's own commitment to meaningful existence is tested by a three-fold methodology. "I should like to characterize [my] philosophical tradition" or approach, Ricoeur explains, "by three features: it stands in the line of a *reflexive* philosophy; it remains within the sphere of Husserlian *phenomenology*; it strives to be a hermeneutical version of this phenomenology" (OI 12). Elsewhere, in *Oneself as Another*, Ricoeur places this threefold approach in the context of two additional "philosophical intentions" that converge in the question of selfhood: a polarity of "self-sameness" and "selfhood," and a polarity of selfhood and otherness (OA 3, 16).

For Ricoeur the fundamental assumption of reflexive philosophy "considers the most radical philosophical problems as those that concern the possibility of *self-understanding* as the subject of the operations of knowing, willing, evaluating, and so on. Reflexion is that act of turning back upon itself by which a subject grasps, in a moment of intellectual clarity and moral responsibility, the unifying principle of the operations among which it is *dispersed* and forgets itself as subject" (OI 12). At first glance it might seem as though Ricoeur's preoccupation with the "reflexive" philosophical tradition, consumed with the idea of a self-transparent subject, runs counter to the recovery of selfhood from cultural signs, symbols, and texts. Although the tradition of Husserl's phenomenology shares the central intention of "reflexive" philosophy, Ricoeur's transformation of the phenomenological project precludes the possibility of self-transparency. Ricoeur radically alters the very notion of reflection.[7] The desire for "radical grounding" in self-transparency is a quest that is caught in an infinite regress, where the question "Who is conscious of consciousness?" can never be answered. A metaphysical "ground that grounds itself" (OA 11) is forever out of reach. Hence, Ricoeur transforms reflection by way of a hermeneutical variation of phenomenology, not to "posit" a substantive ego in control of the operations of consciousness, or to dispose of the importance of the subject altogether, but to purge subjectivity from idealistic and metaphysical interpretations. Ricoeur eloquently explains that to say *self* is not to say *I*. The *I* is posited—or is deposed. The *self* is implied reflexively [*réfléchi*] in the operations, the analysis of which precedes the return towards this self. Upon this dialectic of analysis and reflection is grafted that of *idem* and *ipse*. Finally, the dialectic of the same and the other crowns the first two dialectics. I shall conclude this preface by underscoring the two features [the polysemy of the question "Who?", and the testimonial character of the answer "The self"] diametrically opposing, not simply the immediacy of the *I am*, but also the ambition of placing it in the position of ultimate foundation. (OA 18; SA 30)

The quest for a nonidealistic interpretation of the self is the central concern of Ricoeur's hermeneutics of selfhood. However, it remains to be seen if Ricoeur does indeed accomplish this goal; for as he readily admits, the orientation in favor of linguistic (semantic) meaning makes nonidealist discourse "difficult" (PH 115). If the tradition of modernity as exemplified by Husserl's attempt to ground meaning in absolute self-consciousness is to be set aside in favor of a reflexive understanding of the self, then not only discourse about the self but the very notion of selfhood must be reshaped.[8]

Ricoeur explains that "no consciousness is self-consciousness before being consciousness *of* something *towards which* it surpasses itself . . . consciousness is outside itself, that is *towards meaning* before meaning is for it and, above all, before consciousness is *for itself*" (PH 115). Meaning and subjectivity are outside consciousness. The task of hermeneutics is to recover a self from the vast diversity of signs, symbols, and texts, which consciousness is intentionally oriented toward. What is recovered, however, is not supposed to be a transparent unifying principle behind the operations of consciousness that only bold methodological precision could reveal, but a self received through the interpretation of various forms of semiotic meaning. The self is not the *archê*, ground, or first thought that secures theoretical reflection; it is that which is aimed at through a long and difficult linguistic detour. As Ricoeur explains, in his "Intellectual Autobiography,"

> I came to the conclusion that, despite the idealist thesis of the ultimate self-responsibility of the mediating subject, subjectivity did not constitute the primary category of a theory of understanding, that it has to be lost as origin if it is to be recovered in a more modest role than that of radical origin. To be sure, there is still a need for a speaking-subject to receive the matter of the text, to make it its own, to appropriate it, in order to balance the correlative moment of *distanciation* of the textualization of experience. The proof that appropriation does not imply the surreptitious return of sovereign subjectivity lies in the necessity that one disappropriate

oneself, a necessity imposed by the self-understanding before the text. I then stated in the 1975 text, "I exchange the ego, master of itself, for the self, disciple of the text." I was anticipating in this way the opposition between the self and the ego [*le soi et le moi*], which would become the basis for my analyses in *Oneself as Another*. (IA 35)

To understand the meaning of selfhood fragmented among the vast array of linguistic works, one must become aware of the interconnective structure of language, not to recover a metaphysical principle of unity, but a self that does not result from an interpretive reflection on the meaning of existence. Selfhood always remains a task modeled in signs, symbols, and texts, but it can never be the accomplishment of the process of linguistic interpretation itself. What Ricoeur seeks in a "world of slippage" are analogously related linguistic patterns of selfhood appropriated from texts that help us to contend with the discordant nature of experience.[9]

The question of humanity is thus an open question that Ricoeur approaches with reference to the series of questions Kant posed. Ricoeur explains that the question, "*What is a human?*, far from constituting the first question that philosophy is able to raise, comes at the end of a series of prior questions such as: *What can I know? What must I do? What am I allowed to hope?* I do not claim that these three Kantian questions are the only ones that can introduce the decisive question: What is a human? My only claim is that, in order not to remain trivial, the answer to this question must appear as the ultimate outcome of a series of preparatory steps" (NP 89–90). In this regard, the hermeneutics of the self can be characterized as an "interrogative" recovery that focuses on the semantics of "Who?" is implied in what I can know, do, and hope for. Rather than the substantive "what" of the modern *cogito*, Ricoeur's hermeneutics of the self is supposed to be a response to the questions, "Who is speaking? Who is acting? Who is recounting about himself or herself? Who is the moral subject of imputation?" (OA 16). Scattered among the "objectivities (discursive, practical, narrative, and prescriptive predicates) in the [reflective] process of the self,"[10] phenomenological hermeneutics searches for attestation of *"the self"* (OA 16). However, according to Ricoeur, this fragmentation of response results neither in an endless plurality nor in despair. As he explains in the introduction to *Oneself as Another*, the self is a concord of discordance held together analogically.

This fragmentation ... has a thematic unity that keeps it from the dissemination that would lead the discourse back to silence. In a sense, one could say that these studies together have as their thematic unity *human action* and that the notion of action acquires, over the course of the studies, an ever-increasing extension and concreteness. . . . But the unity that the concern with human action confers to these studies as a whole is not the unity that an ultimate foundation would confer to a series of derivative disciplines. It is rather a merely analogical unity between the multiple uses of the term "acting," which, as we have just mentioned, receives its polysemy from the variety and contingency of the questions that activate the analyses leading back to the reflection on the self. (OA 20)

For Ricoeur, the question of selfhood, self-identity, and self-understanding is not without coherence. The analyses of the semantic objectifications of self are linked together analogically and, as Ricoeur claims, give ontological testimony of the productive power responsible for this diversity of activities, namely, the self as "*conatus*" (OA 315), as "*homo capax.*"[11]

The consequences of this view of selfhood, however, remain in question. Ricoeur asks if we can "give new value to the meaning of being as act and potentiality, securing in this way the analogical unity of acting on a stable ontological meaning."[12] The difficulties posed by such an ontological question are complicated by the fact that

this reevaluation of a meaning of being, too often sacrificed to being-as-substance, can take place only against the backdrop of a plurality more radical than any other, namely that of the meanings of being. Moreover, it will quickly become apparent that the ontology of act and of potentiality will in turn open up variations of meaning difficult to specify because of their multiple historical expressions. Finally, and most especially, the dialectic of the same and the other, readjusted to the dimensions of our hermeneutic of the self and its other, will prevent an ontology of act and potentiality from becoming enclosed within a tautology. The polysemy of otherness . . . will imprint upon the entire ontology of acting the seal of the diversity of sense that foils the ambition of arriving at an ultimate foundation, characteristic of cogito philosophies. (OA 20–21)

Ricoeur has set for himself an ambitious and difficult task. Compounding the fragmentation of meaning dispersed in cultural works, the self only has analogical unity predicated on a polysemic ontology which is in turn rooted in this fragmentation of semantic meaning.

This task of the hermeneutical discovery of selfhood is made even more problematic when one considers its linguistic structure. According to Ricoeur, the ego, "master of itself," can be "exchanged" for the self, "disciple of the text" (IA 35; PH 113). For Ricoeur the act of interpretation opens a reflective space that takes linguistic distance from experience in order to better understand experience. Ricoeur sets the imagination free to re/construct worlds of possibility where self-identity is put into play. These are imaginative places where new ways of living can be explored, textual worlds that provide "a vast laboratory for thought experiments"[13] about the meaning of self, others, otherness, and the Other (*le tout-autre*). Here the process of interpretation provides linguistic images, metaphorical sight, and fictional configurations that allow the ego/self to see modes of selfhood that might otherwise never have been considered. Through interpretive reading and rereading of texts, the identity of self oscillates between the sedimentation and innovation of this almost infinite variety of meaning.[14] Set in play by the imagination,[15] these alternatives for selfhood can be lived "as if" they were real.[16]

This creation of symbol, myth, metaphor, and narrative opens a virtual reflective space rich with possibilities for self-transformation. The imagination creates literary models *for* selfhood that have the capacity to become models *of* selfhood, that is, the capacity to be transformed from virtual models into living testimony of a self made actual through choice and action. For Ricoeur, the power of imagination to see selfhood as other than it has been received remains incomplete if the self does not become what it envisions: seeing selfhood as . . . , must become being selfhood as . . .[17] The virtual world of the text must be actualized, lived, embodied, appropriated, and incorporated into the process of existing in the mode of selfhood. This is why Ricoeur's analysis of the "narrative arc" (TN 1: 52–87) places narrative configuration between what is prefigured in experience and the narrative refiguration of experience. Without the return movement of language to life, the gap, space, or distance opened by imagination would remain a virtual creation, disconnected from ordinary life, unable to affect a meaningful transformation of the ego, master of itself, into a self discipled by its textual other (LQN 25).

But isn't this precisely the problem? What do these linguistic models offer? If they are models of selfhood, then they identify a particular variation of selfhood, a particular way of living that can only be realized through choice and action. This type of selfhood is always literary selfhood, that is, a self identified within the referential world of the text. It is not selfhood as such but a narrative, poetic, or mythical self. These variations of selfhood are always semantically structured: a self that is talked about, a topic alongside other topics of conversation, a discussion about a character in a novel, an "extra-linguistic" referent of some text or another (RM 75). Does this kind of identification say anything about the relation between these semantic models of identity and those "who" use them for self-identification? How do these particular ways in which the self has been identified affect the intimate experience of selfhood? In other words, if, as Ricoeur argues, selfhood is found in the relationship between the self and the other-than-self (*ipse* selfhood), what kind of relationship does the textual other have with the self, and the self with this literary process of identity formation?

While self-understanding is indeed the result of the critical play of signs, symbols, and texts, and self-identity is structured to a large extent by narrative discourse in particular, is Ricoeur's understanding of the "vast laboratory for thought experiments" adequate for addressing not only the problem of identity but the problem of selfhood as well? If Ricoeur believes that his hermeneutic of selfhood always remains on the level of the "objectivities (discursive, practical, narrative, and prescriptive predicates) in the reflective process [*le procès réflexif*] of the self" (OA 187 n. 22), which only leads indirectly back to the self by way of analogical association between such polysemic identifications, does such hermeneutical analysis collapse the problem of selfhood into that of linguistic identity? Is Ricoeur's philosophy of selfhood able to handle with the appropriate amount of subtlety and care the distinction between the *reflexive structure* of the self (the intimacy of self in relation to the other) and the *reflective process* of identity formation that is indirectly linked to the self that is structured reflexively?[18] Can Ricoeur maintain this difference between identity and selfhood, or does he, as I claim, end up entangling the problem of selfhood (*ipse*) in the semantics of identity (*idem*)? The significance of this question should not be underestimated. Ricoeur bases his entire philosophy of selfhood on the assumption that the construction of linguistic meaning can be expanded from his understanding of the semantics of metaphor, to narrative, to the identity of a character within a narrative, to the refiguration of experience through a transfer of such literary identity from the world of the text to the world of the reader, to the analogical construction of the "thematic unity [of] human action" (OA 19), and finally to the ontological attestation of selfhood as "*homo capax*,"[19] or "*conatus*," the power of "productivity, . . . the actual and potential ground against which selfhood stands out" (OA 315).

It is this cluster of problems that lies at the heart of Ricoeur's philosophy of selfhood: the connection between the self and the imaginative world of the text, between the self and the variations of identity, and between the self and the other. These are the keys not only for unlocking Ricoeur's complex formulation of selfhood, but his philosophical project as a whole. With Ricoeur's 30 books and more than 500 articles spanning a period of more than 60 years, not to mention the 75 books and almost 1,000 articles published about his philosophy in 20 different languages,[20] these questions concerning selfhood help to give thematic organization to this vast and encyclopedic collection. I will use this set of problems concerning Ricoeur's understanding of the self to weave a connecting thread through his most significant publications. From his earliest works, *Freedom and Nature* (F. 1950, E. 1965) and *Fallible Man* (F. 1960, E. 1965) to his most recent treatment of the question of selfhood in *Oneself as Another* (F. 1990, E. 1992), I will show how the question of selfhood has been Ricoeur's abiding concern through all the twists and turns of his hermeneutical detour. Further, I will argue that as productive as Ricoeur's hermeneutic of selfhood is, it collapses selfhood into identity, and in the end, in spite of his best intentions to the contrary, places alterity within the identifying circle of the self-same (*idem* identity). This criticism, however, is only partial. Having been enthusiastically discipled into these difficult problems by way of Ricoeur's texts, I am not entirely unhappy with his hermeneutic of selfhood. It is simply that his detour has not gone far enough, and surprisingly returns in the end to its starting point, to a voluntary *cogito*, albeit broken open by the other, but a *cogito* nonetheless.

To document the development of Ricoeur's philosophy of selfhood I have divided this study into five chapters. In the first chapter, "From Ego to Selfhood: A Question of Method," I set the stage for the placement of the self within Ricoeur's phenomenological hermeneutics. In distinction from Husserl's phenomenology of absolute consciousness, I show how Ricoeur maps out a strategy for purging phenomenology of its idealistic interpretations. Combining a change in emphasis in the later works of Husserl with the hermeneutical thinking of Heidegger and Gadamer, Ricoeur orients phenomenology toward the intersubjective world of linguistic meaning. This world is prior to the formation of individual consciousness and encompasses the subject in the experience of "belonging" (PH 105). It is here that the imagination is at work. Belonging is dialectically[21] linked to a process of distantiation that creates a space for critical reflection on, and imaginative variation of, experience.

In chapter 2, "Imagination: Mediated Self-Constitution," I begin to examine more carefully the relation, in *Freedom and Nature* and *Fallible Man*, between imagination and the process of self-constitution. What becomes clear early on in the philosophy of Ricoeur is the deep connection between the power of creativity and the power of self, so much so that they can easily be confused. For Ricoeur the power that constitutes selfhood is expressed in a duplicate manner by the imagination. The inner structure of the self can be seen through the observation of the imagination in action. Like the imagination, which mediates between the voluntary and involuntary phenomena of consciousness, the self, in *Freedom and Nature*, is lived as the process of decision and action that mediates between what is freely chosen and that which it must accept as its nature. This correlation between imagination and the self is made even more explicit in *Fallible Man*, where the imagination not only structures consciousness but provides the conceptual pattern for self-consciousness and self-constitution. It is here, in *Fallible Man*, that Ricoeur also develops for the first time, albeit in rudimentary form, his hermeneutic of selfhood, which must pass through the reservoir or gift of cultural meaning in order to affirm the correlative worth of the self and the other.

In chapters 3 and 4 I detail the development of Ricoeur's understanding of the creation of meaning in language. By means of metaphor and narrative the imagination opens the text to its referent: a world for the self to inhabit.

What is significant here is the way in which the imagination functions to create an identity between a poetic text and the feeling it generates (an identity between seeing as . . . and being as . . .), as well as an identity between narrative characters within the world of the text and the world of the reader who is supposed to be refigured by that text. Here we are faced with the difficult problem of "appropriation." How is metaphorical seeing as . . . , and narrative identity as . . . , connected to selfhood? What does Ricoeur really mean by the transformation of self by way of metaphor and narrative?

Finally, in chapter 5, "Identity and Selfhood," I explore Ricoeur's formulation of the differences among identity, self-sameness, selfhood, and otherness. Focusing on Ricoeur's book *Oneself as Another*, I show how in some respects his hermeneutical detour returns to its starting point. Here Ricoeur carefully distinguishes self-sameness (*idem* identity) from self-constancy (*ipse* identity) by handling the question "what" or "who" is the subject of language, action, narrative, and the ethical prescription for action. Insisting that self-sameness ought to be clearly distinguished from self-constancy, Ricoeur develops his hermeneutics of selfhood under the assumption that this can be done simply by means of a shift in the interrogative form of analysis. Ricoeur thinks that moving from the question "what is a subject?" to the question "who is the subject?" allows him to uncover a type of selfhood that is not reduced to the identifying structures of self-sameness. However, as I argue, this is not the case. Ricoeur has hopelessly entangled selfhood in the semantics of identity, and has encircled "the pure selfhood of self-constancy" (OA 165) within the power of the self-same.

The consequences of this collapse are significant. In my "Conclusion" I consider some of the implications of this enclosure of the self within the self-same. Arguing that this collapse of selfhood into identity is carried over to Ricoeur's understanding of the other, I suggest that his ethics of reciprocity is less than adequate for dealing with the alterity of the other. Finding that his ontology places the self in a position of power (*conatus*) in relation to a receptive other, I point out that Ricoeur seems to duplicate the self in the figure of the other in order to find reciprocal balance between otherwise disproportionate power. If the other is like me, ready to reduce my power—my selfhood—in order to become a self, and vice versa, then this kind of reciprocal selfhood simply reduces the alterity of the other to holding my power-in-abeyance and preventing it from degenerating into the disfiguring power of violence and evil.

CHAPTER ONE

FROM EGO TO SELFHOOD

A Question of Method

An inquiry into Ricoeur's philosophical method is a complex and difficult endeavor. Although Ricoeur explores the details of his methodology in numerous concisely written articles, his methodological procedures are never divorced from the "understanding" that results from their application. In fact, Ricoeur's entire philosophical project is predicated on the unity of methodological "explanation" and hermeneutical "understanding" of meaning (TH 43–62). Therefore, every conversation about meaning is also about method, and dialogue concerning method is in turn revelatory of meaning. Here lies the difficulty: Ricoeur's method cannot be isolated from meaning and, as I will argue, from life, without betraying its original intent. Focusing on methodological considerations simply gives us an opening onto the much broader landscape of selfhood as a question. Explanation and understanding are intimately connected. Apart from the "world" of meaning, methodological explanation remains lifeless. Ricoeur's method can only be fully understood through careful consideration of the field of application, which for him is the interpretation of selfhood.

Unique to Ricoeur's philosophical method is a critical moment or "space of reflexivity" (HB 89) at the center of his dialectic of explanation and understanding. Ricoeur does not deny the importance of critical analysis and the necessity of methodological precision for understanding the questions of existence. In his insightful exposition of Ricoeur's conception of the *cogito*, Jervolino explains that Ricoeur's "search for a 'methodical' hermeneutics, such as to found and justify in a credible fashion a method or a plurality of methods of interpretation and demystification, corresponds to so deep and pressing a need for clarity, understanding and self-understanding in mankind today that the undertaking must at least be attempted, avoiding any hardening of the

11

Gadamerian opposition between 'truth' and 'method' " (Jervolino 5). By reject-
ing such a dualism of "truth or method," not necessarily found in Gadamer,[1]
Ricoeur attempts to incorporate, at the very heart of the experience of belonging, a methodological moment that he refers to as "distanciation" (TH 60).
Posing a question in relation to Gadamer's philosophy,[2] Ricoeur asks: "*How is
it possible to introduce a critical distance into a consciousness of belonging which
is expressly defined by the rejection of distanciation?*" To which he answers: "It
is possible, in my view, only insofar as historical consciousness seeks not simply
to repudiate distanciation but to assume it" (TH 60). Employing a combination
of Husserlian "imaginative variation" and a quasi-Kantian dialectic of reproductive and productive aspects of the imagination, Ricoeur develops a method that
creates an opening at the core of experience itself where critical reflection can
distance itself from the sedimentation of meaning by exploring imaginative
possibilities for existing in the mode of selfhood offered by the world of the text.

1.1   Distanciation and Phenomenology

The notion of distanciation is perhaps the key feature that distinguishes
Ricoeur's philosophical position from others within the phenomenological-hermeneutical tradition. As Ricoeur himself notes, "the theme of distanciation gives
me the opportunity to mark my personal contribution to the hermeneutical-
phenomenological school; it is quite clearly characterized by the role I assign
to critical distance in all the operations of thought belonging to interpretation"
(FTA xiii–xvi). "Distanciation," however, is more than a mere contribution to
the phenomenological-hermeneutical school. Ricoeur's modest evaluation of
his own position belies the unique transformation of phenomenological hermeneutics that takes place as a result of the insertion of a "space of reflexivity" into
the heart of belonging. Building on the strengths of both the phenomenological
and hermeneutical traditions, Ricoeur develops a position that avoids their
weaknesses.

The notion of distanciation addresses the demand for methodological
clarity while avoiding the idealism associated with the phenomenological tradition. Likewise, by rooting thought in an interpretative process that pays homage
to textual autonomy in conjunction with the appropriation of the referential
world of meaning up front in the text, Ricoeur avoids the hermeneutical ex-
cesses of both subjectivism and objectivism. By positioning the imaginative play
of critical reflexivity at the center of his methodology, Ricoeur in fact places the
two philosophical traditions in service of each other, where "*phenomenology
remains the unsurpassable presupposition of hermeneutics* . . . [and where] phenomenology cannot constitute itself without a *hermeneutical presupposition*"
(PH 101). This dialectic of phenomenology and hermeneutics, mediated or

bridged by a "third term" characterized as a "space of reflexivity," brings us to the methodological and epistemological core of Ricoeur's project. Repetition of this pattern on a variety of levels of analysis opens existence for an interpretive examination.

Ricoeur's most explicit and detailed account of his methodology is found in an article entitled "Phenomenology and Hermeneutics" (1975).[3] Here Ricoeur attempts to reinterpret phenomenology in the light of hermeneutics without giving up the central phenomenological description of intentionality. Rather than eliminating phenomenology as a relic of the modern philosophical project, Ricoeur wishes to strip phenomenology of the "*idealistic* interpretation [given] by Husserl himself."[4] Although each tradition presupposes the other, Ricoeur's credo that "*phenomenology remains the unsurpassable presupposition of hermeneutics* . . . [and conversely] phenomenology cannot constitute itself without a *hermeneutical presupposition*," implies a foundational role for phenomenology even though phenomenological description has "a hermeneutical presupposition." However, as is evident from Ricoeur's threefold arc of mimetic representation,[5] which begins with phenomenological description and then gives way to hermeneutical reflection as a means for offering a poetic solution to the aporetic character of historical consciousness, the interpretive process takes precedence over and above phenomenological description. Although phenomenology provides a preliminary foundation that structures hermeneutics, hermeneutical reflection qualifies and completes the phenomenological quest for meaning. To clarify this hermeneutical qualification, I need to explore in some detail Ricoeur's appropriation of both phenomenology and hermeneutics.

In "Phenomenology and Hermeneutics," Ricoeur discusses a number of themes that are characteristic of Husserlian idealism. Taking the "1930 'Nachwort'" to the *Ideen* as a typical document of Husserlian idealism," Ricoeur explains that the "Nachwort," "together with the *Cartesian Meditations* . . . constitutes . . . the most advanced expression of this idealism" (PH 102). This designation of the "most advanced expression" of Husserl's idealism is of considerable debate. It is of particular importance for our examination of Ricoeur's conception of selfhood that we include within the category "most advanced," the first part of Husserl's *Ideas*. Essential to the development of my argument is the manner in which Ricoeur contrasts his own position with the philosophies of the "*cogito* and *anticogito*." In order to understand this contrast more clearly, it will be beneficial to detail Husserl's descriptions of absolute consciousness found in the first part of *Ideas*.

One might argue, however, that it is somewhat inappropriate to utilize *Ideas* as paradigmatic of Husserlian idealism, due to the fact that Ricoeur himself stipulates that the promise of the transcendental reduction is not fulfilled in *Ideas*, and that the reduction Husserl discussed in *Ideas* remains only a psychological *epochè*, without the presence of the full transcendental reduction.

Further, Ricoeur states that *Ideas* "is a book whose sense lies hidden; one is inevitably inclined to search for this sense elsewhere. At every turn one gets the impression that the essential is not being said, that the effort is to impart a new vision of the world and of consciousness, rather than to say something definitive about the world and about consciousness, something which perhaps could not be understood at all without the acquisition of the new vision."[6] Yet, as Ricoeur points out, the speed with which the reduction is performed in Husserl's *Cartesian Meditations* is in stark contrast with the "interminable preparations and precautions of *Ideas*" (HL 87). To understand the full meaning of Husserl's description of absolute consciousness, I will have to detail the development of the reduction that Ricoeur wishes to pass by in haste.

Aside from my desire to contrast Ricoeur's understanding of selfhood and identity with Husserl's reduction of reality to absolute consciousness, there are additional reasons for focusing on *Ideas*. In this regard Theodore De Boer's work is particularly insightful. Disagreeing with Ricoeur's interpretation of *Ideas*, De Boer explains that Husserl does say at the end of the second chapter "that his meditation has 'reached a climax.' All that comes later is simply addition and elaboration." De Boer continues, however, and argues that "Husserl does speak of these chapters as a 'transcendental preliminary consideration,' which is something different from the 'pre-transcendental consideration' that Ricoeur makes of them. Husserl speaks of a 'preliminary consideration' (*Vorbetrachtung*) because we can grasp the possibility of transcendental reduction only after this analysis" (De Boer 383). In either case, the question is not when Husserl's phenomenology is idealistic or not, but rather when Husserl fully initiates the reduction of the real to the ideal. The point is that idealism remains a theme throughout Husserl's philosophical project. In fact, De Boer notes that "the doctrine of the relativity of the world and the absoluteness of consciousness remained the central point in Husserl's phenomenology even in his very last works. It is the heart of his transcendental idealism" (De Boer 358).

This is also stated by Ricoeur: "In Husserl himself the [phenomenological] method was mixed with an idealistic interpretation which takes up a major portion of the published work and tends to place phenomenology on a plane with turn-of-the-century Neo-Kantianism" (HL 4). Further, "the phenomenology elaborated in *Ideas 1* is incontestably an idealism, even a transcendental idealism" (HL 24). But Ricoeur goes on to explain that confusion of interpretation has arisen due to the discrepancy found between Husserl's phenomenological theory and practice: "The fact is that the idealistic interpretation of the method does not necessarily coincide with its actual practice, as many of his disciples have pointed out" (HL 7). Confusion reigns due to the various levels at which Husserl's use of idealist language can be interpreted. "Finally, 'pure consciousness,' 'transcendental consciousness,' 'the absolute being of consciousness,' and 'originary giving consciousness' are names for a consciousness that fluctuates among several levels or, as it might be said, is described as different phases of the spiritual discipline. Hence issue the errors of interpretation of which Husserl complained so constantly and bitterly" (HL 24). Although Ricoeur never denies the presence of the transcendental reduction in *Ideas*, he questions whether one should not look elsewhere for its full implementation, particularly the "Nachwort" and the *Cartesian Meditations*.

It is my intention, however, not to debate the origin of the implementation of the reduction, but to lay bare Husserl's contrast between the absolute character of consciousness and the relativizing of everything else that results from the reduction. Other problems involved in the interpretation of the development of Husserl's transcendental reduction fall outside the scope of this study. In spite of some disagreement between Ricoeur and De Boer, the features of that which can be characterized as Husserl's transcendental method are held in common by both.

Ricoeur asserts that "the central thesis of Husserlian idealism" can be reduced to the following claims: "The place of plenary intuition is subjectivity. All transcendence is doubtful; immanence alone is indubitable" (PH 103). All the other features of Husserl's phenomenology are founded on this distinction between the indubitability of absolute consciousness and the doubtfulness of all else. Husserl's quest for a science of a different order, characterized as a "radical beginning" grounded within itself (*Selbst-begründung*) (PH 103), is dependent on an egology that seeks to ground all meaning on an absolutely indubitable foundation. Therefore, when Husserl proclaims that "transcendental phenomenology is not a theory, devised merely as a reply to the historic problem of Idealism, it is a science founded in itself, and standing absolutely on its own basis; it is indeed the one science that stands absolutely on its own ground" (*Ideas* 13), such a proclamation can only be made if one clearly understands what transcendental phenomenology rests on. To state it otherwise: What is this ground that has its ground within itself and gives phenomenology a radical beginning?

More than of mere methodological concern, Husserl's phenomenology reorients the ego's connection to the world and is therefore of ontological significance as well. Husserl explains that

> the result of the phenomenological clarification of the meaning of the manner of existence of the real world (and, eidetically, of the real world generally) is that only transcendental subjectivity has ontologically the meaning of Absolute Being, that it only is non-relative, that is relative only to itself; whereas the real world indeed exists, but in respect of essence is relative to transcendental subjectivity, and in such a way that it can have its meaning as existing (*seiende*) reality only as the intentional meaning-product of transcendental subjectivity. (*Ideas* 14)

To understand how the world is relativized in relation to transcendental subjectivity, particularly in view of Ricoeur's rejection of foundational subjectivity, careful explanation of Husserl's transcendental reduction is needed.

Husserl's phenomenological idealism can be given a preliminary characterization as an act of consciousness that reduces "natural" reality considered as "present to hand" (*vorhanden*) into a phenomenon essentially related to me. In the first part of *Ideas*, Husserl begins to show how such an act of consciousness is possible by contrasting his position with that of Brentano's phenomenological psychology. For Husserl, Brentano never moved beyond the "natural attitude." Phenomenological psychology's mistake was to examine the "I" reality as any other science might examine its object of investigation, hence, to take the "I" as something given and described in the manner in which reality is purportedly given for any other science. What Husserl wishes to describe is the "I" reality after a shift in attitude has taken place, a shift away from a natural standpoint which sees the self as a thing in a world of things, to a transcendental standpoint. Husserl calls this shift the phenomenological reduction. To move beyond reality as given, one must restrict one's gaze to the manner in which reality is given for me, to the act of consciousness in which the object has been made conscious to me. In other words, one must reduce reality from its existence apart from my own, to its meaning for me in the conscious act where that meaning occurs. Reality must be "bracketed," phenomenologically reduced, its validity canceled, in order that consciousness can have a *Wesenschau* of its essential nature, free from the distractions of the ever-changing shapes of the visible world.

It could easily be said that phenomenological psychology wishes to isolate the ego and grasp an essential glimpse of its structure, but for Husserl phenomenological psychology fails to transcendentalize the "I" reality. The "I" must no longer be construed as an actual existent among others, because it is "no longer a human Ego *in* the universal, existentially posited world, but exclusively a subject *for* which this world has being, and purely, indeed, *as* that which appears to me, is presented to me, and of which I am conscious in some way or other, so that the real being of the world thereby remains unconsidered, unquestioned, and its validity left out of account" (*Ideas* 8). The psychological ego, through a shift in attitude, is transformed into a transcendental ego. Just as reality to which I belong becomes that which exists for me, the transcendental reduction transforms the subjectivity of the ego from a "person living among others in the world" (*Ideas* 7) into the ego of intentional acts for which the world is a meaning correlate.

The transcendental reduction, or *epochè*, transforms the being of the world into a kind of nonbeing. The world is not annihilated, it is there in all its fullness, but only as meaning in relation to consciousness for which it is meaning. This change in attitude manifests the ego as transcendental consciousness, as that which cannot be thought away or doubted. The ego is the act of consciousness grounded in itself without which the transcendental reduction cannot occur. Rather than the ego construed as a subject "among others in the natural world," the ego becomes the reality to which the phenomenological world is subject. The transcendental ego, although it lacks reality as a being among others, becomes the focal point of unity and the absolute foundation on which all meaning rests. Husserl writes:

> I now also become aware that my own phenomenologically self-contained essence can be posited in an *absolute* sense, as I am the Ego who invests the being of the world which I so constantly speak about with existential validity, as an existence (*Sein*) which wins for me from my own life's pure essence meaning and substantial validity. I myself as this individual essence, posited absolutely, as the open infinite field of pure phenomenological data and their inseparable unity, am the "transcendental Ego." (*Ideas* 11)

The investment of the ego with the quality of absoluteness is a curious notion similar to Descartes' *cogito ergo sum*, although the "absolutely indubitable sphere of Being" (*Ideas* 97), sought by Descartes, remains within the natural attitude. Husserl's notion of consciousness with its intentional meaning correlates is not the same as the residue left behind after an exercise in Cartesian doubt. The Cartesian denial of all but consciousness was still understood as a substance present to hand (*vorhanden*) that stands over against everything else that is changeable and doubtful. Cartesian doubt renders the foundation of science indubitable, but on the level of a being among others. Husserl writes: "he who attempts to doubt is attempting to doubt 'Being' of some form or other, or it may be Being expanded into such predicative forms as 'It is,' or 'It is this or thus,' and the like. The attempt does not affect the form of Being itself" (*Ideas* 97). The absoluteness of Cartesian consciousness is still on the level of the natural or general thesis of the being of the world; it cannot serve as the foundational goal for science; "we cannot at once doubt and hold for certain one and the same quality of Being. It is likewise clear that the *attempt* to doubt any object of awareness in respect of it *being actually there necessarily conditions a certain suspension (Aufhebung) of the thesis*; and it is precisely this that interests us" (*Ideas* 97).

Husserl cannot accept Cartesian doubt as a revelation of absolute consciousness, for one cannot hold the thesis and the antithesis of the reality of the world to be true at the same time and in the same respect.[7] What needs to be done is to suspend, or put out of action, the entire thesis of the world altogether. This, however, does not cancel the thesis of the world. There is no way in which one can undo the passive synthesis[8] of consciousness; rather, what takes place is a transformation of the world of being into meaning. Husserl explains that the suspension of the natural thesis

is not a transformation of the thesis into its antithesis, of positive
into negative; it is also not a transformation into presumption, sug-
gestion, indecision, doubt (in one or another sense of the word);
such a shifting indeed is not at our free pleasure. *Rather it is something quite unique. We do not abandon the thesis we have adopted,
we make no change in our conviction.* . . . And yet the thesis under-
goes a modification — whilst remaining in itself what it is, *we set it
as it were "out of action,"* we *"disconnect it," "bracket it."* It still
remains there like the bracketed in the bracket, like the disconnected outside the connexional system. We can also say: The thesis
is experience as lived (*Erlebnis*), *but we make "no use" of it* . . . we
are dealing with indicators that point to a definite but *unique form
of consciousness,* which clamps on to the original simple thesis . . . and
transvalues it in a quite peculiar way. (*Ideas* 97–98)

Phenomenological reduction refrains from positing the natural world as the
world of being in which I am a part, in order to isolate the essence of the act
which performs the reduction by which the world is made relative as meaning.
The phenomenological reduction reduces the world to an intended meaning
(*noema*) correlate of the intentional act (*noesis*) of an absolute consciousness.
However, this can only be assumed if the "putting out of action" of the natural
world is not equated with the destruction of the world as being, but simply the
free act of placing it within brackets (*Ideas* 99–100).

The act of consciousness that performs the phenomenological reduction
is precisely what Husserl wishes to isolate. By "reducing" the natural thesis of
the world to an intentional field of meaning, what remains is "a new region
of Being, the distinctive character of which has not yet been defined, a region
of individual being," a region "which we refer to on essential grounds as 'pure
experiences (*Erlebnisse*),' 'pure consciousness' with its pure 'correlates of consciousness,' and on the other side its "pure Ego' " (*Ideas* 101). Transcendental
consciousness, or the absolute "pure ego," to which the pure "correlates" of
consciousness are subject, is thus both the residue of the phenomenological
reduction and the act performing the reduction.[9]

Consciousness, as the "new" found "region of Being," is qualified as *absolute* consciousness in three different ways: (1) presence in contrast to absence,
(2) independence in contrast with dependence, (3) existence as necessary and
indubitable, in contrast to contingency. These three different qualifications of
consciousness exemplify the central features of phenomenological idealism and
the modern idea of the *cogito* as the foundation of meaning, which Ricoeur
wishes to set aside. Therefore, these three features of Husserl's conception of
the ego will be explored in greater detail.

1.1.1 *Presence in Contrast to Absence*

Husserl begins to describe the absolute character of consciousness by making a distinction between inner and outer perception, that is, between perceiving a thing and the act of perception as such. The very possibility of a "reflexive" act of consciousness that can make the distinction between turning inward away from the thing intended to the act of intending transforms the act itself into an "inner" object of consciousness. This act of turning inward is the gaze of consciousness directed on its own conscious acts. Therefore, the act of consciousness is the reflexive act itself. This is referred to by Husserl as immanent perception.

> Under *acts immanently directed*, or, to put it more generally, under *intentional experiences immanently related*, we include those acts which are *essentially* so constituted *that their intentional objects, when these exist at all, belong to the same stream of experience as themselves*. . . . Consciousness and its object build up an individual unity purely set up through experiences. Intentional experiences for which this does not hold good are *transcendently directed*, as, for instance, all acts directed towards essences, or towards the intentional experiences of other Egos with other experience-streams; likewise all acts directed upon things, upon realities generally, as we have still to show. (*Ideas* 112)

Here immanent perception does not mean that in addition to transcendent objects there are immanent objects that now become the focus of description. Immanent perception does indeed view acts as objects, but it too is an intentional act and therefore composed of the correlates intention and intended. What interests Husserl is the immanent act that intends an act as its object. These are two acts within the same stream of consciousness but they are not identical, they are different. Whereas an act of perception has its object "outside" the stream of consciousness or has a transcendent intentional object, the object of immanent perception is found within the very same stream of the psychic reality that I am now living through. This, however, raises a peculiar problem. An act of reflection upon an act is always a *new* act of consciousness, because no act can be its own object. It is not possible to describe an act of immanent perception without making it the object of that description, and this reduction of the act to an object requires another act by which this object is perceived. Such an act of description cannot be perceived without another, and another, ad infinitum. Hence, Husserlian phenomenology must find rest or be grounded on something that prevents the human subject from succumbing to this peculiar form of dissipation usually called infinite regress.

Husserl attempts to resolve this problem by claiming that transcendental subjectivity is absolute, or self-contained. By distinguishing between inner and outer, or immanent and transcendent perception, Husserl is in fact making what he calls "a basic and essential difference . . . between *Being as Experience* and *Being as Thing*" (*Ideas* 120).[10] Outer or transcendent being is characterized as phenomenon, given as a temporal-spatial thing, and thereby only given to consciousness through the incomplete perspectives of the thing perceived. But: "*An experience has no perspectives—Ein Erlebnis schattet sich nicht ab*." Husserl goes on to say that

> it follows from the essential nature of spatial thinghood . . . that Being of this species can, in principle, be given in perceptions only by way of perspective manifestation; and it follows likewise from the essential nature of *cogitationes*, of experiences in general, that they exclude these perspective shadings; or otherwise stated, when referring to that which has being in this region, anything of the nature of "appearing" or self-revealing through perspective variations, has simply no meaning. (*Ideas* 121–122)

The object of the act of immanent perception is, in contrast to the object of transcendent perception, completely present with regard to space and time. Rather than given through perspectives and thereby never fully complete, the object of immanent perception is fully present without the spatial limitation of the adumbrations of the object, nor the temporal limitation of the compilation of perspectives. The *object* of the act of immanent perception and the *act* of immanent perception coincide completely, and therefore, this act is absolute, self-contained in its mode of givenness. This is what distinguishes the two types of being: immanent being is given *as* fully present to itself, transcendent being is given *as* absence (*Ideas* 121). In section 44 of *Ideas* Husserl explains that "whereas it is an essential mark of what is given through appearances that no one of these gives the matter in question in an 'absolute' form instead of presenting just one side of it, it is an essential mark of what is immanently given precisely to give an absolute that simply cannot exhibit aspects and vary them perspectively" (*Ideas* 126–127).

Even though the experience of immanent perception is fully present, it cannot be described as temporally complete. Although at the moment of the experience, it is fully present in a temporal and spatial sense, consciousness itself is always linear. Consciousness is a stream, a flow of anticipation and retention, of future, present, and past. Therefore, immanent perceptions change, but this type of change differs from that characteristic of transcendent perception and does not diminish the absoluteness of immanent consciousness.

> Even an experience (*Erlebnis*) is not, and never is, perceived in its completeness, it cannot be grasped adequately in its full unity. It is essentially something that flows, and starting from the present moment we can swim after it, our gaze reflectively turned towards it, whilst the stretches we leave in our wake are lost to our perception. Only in the form of retention or in the form of retrospective remembrance have we any consciousness of what has immediately flowed past us. . . . But *this* incompleteness or "imperfection" which belongs to the essence of our perception of experience is fundamentally other than that which is of the essence of "transcendent" perception, perception through a presentation that varies perspectively through such a thing as appearance. (*Ideas* 127)

Contrasting immanent incompleteness and the perspectival incompleteness of temporal transcendence,[11] Husserl opens a gap that Ricoeur uses to advance the notion of narrative identity which looks for the unity of temporal experience not within consciousness but rather within the object toward which consciousness is intentionally linked.

1.1.2 *Independence in Contrast to Dependence*

The priority of immanent consciousness over transcendent consciousness gives way to the second characteristic of the absolute being of consciousness, namely, its independence in relation to transcendent being. Husserl explains that

> it is a mark of the type of Being peculiar to experience that perceptual insight can direct its immediate, unobstructed gaze upon every real experience, and so enter into the life of a primordial presence. This insight operates as a "reflection," and it has this remarkable peculiarity that that which is thus apprehended through perception is, in principle, characterized as something which not only is and endures within the gaze of perception, but *already was before* this gaze was directed to it. (*Ideas* 128)

"Presence" is primordial; it nonspatially, or transcendentally, grounds consciousness within itself by virtue of the fact that the objects of immanent perception are "already" there "before" we engage in the act of immanent perception. Since the act of immanent perception has the acts of consciousness as its objects, the objects of immanent perception are completely *independent* from the perception of them, for such act-objects constitute the very flow of consciousness and therefore cannot be separated from consciousness itself. Immanent perception as fully

present cannot be *dependent* on the perspectival perception of transcendent objects of consciousness. The object of inner perception is an act that constitutes the
very stream of consciousness and is therefore independent from the perception of
it, whereas the object of transcendent perception is dependent on the act of the
perception of it for its completeness because it is only given in varying perceptual
slices.

1.1.3 *Necessity and Indubitability in Contrast to Contingency*

The characterization of consciousness as necessary and indubitable is the
ultimate expression of Husserl's transcendental idealism. Reflecting on the advances achieved by the transcendental reduction, Husserl states at the beginning of section 46 of *Ideas* that

> [f]rom all this important consequences follow. Every immanent
> perception necessarily guarantees the existence (*Existenz*) of its
> object. If reflective apprehension is directed to my experience, I
> apprehend an absolute Self whose existence (*Dasein*) is, in prin-
> ciple, undeniable, that is, the insight that it does not exist is, in
> principle, impossible; it would be non-sense to maintain the possi-
> bility of an experience *given in such a way not* truly existing. . . . I
> say forthwith and because I must: *I am*, this life is, I live: *cogito*.
> (*Ideas* 130)

Here we see the foundational role of absolute consciousness. Because "all experiences are conscious experiences" (*Ideas* 128), and since the objects of
immanent perception are constitutive of the very stream of consciousness, to
turn one's gaze back onto the stream of conscious experience necessitates the
existence of the stream of consciousness prior to any immanent act of reflection.
This is the ultimate meaning of the term *absolute*. Transcendental reflection
reveals the objects of immanent consciousness to exist out of necessity. What
Husserl in fact describes is an absolute self whose essence and existence necessarily coincide: "the possibility of a perceiving reflection which lays hold on
absolute existence belongs to its essence as it does to every experience" (*Ideas*
128). Therefore, the ego of immanent perception is fully present to itself in the
temporal moment of experience, and within the primordiality of the nonspatial
space of conscious reflection. It is completely independent, free from the perspectival change of transcendent being, and it is that which necessarily exists.
Thus, the existence of the ego, or self, is completely indubitable.[12]

In contrast with absolute consciousness existing out of necessity, the transcendent world, which has already been defined as "absent" and "dependent,"
is now also described as "contingent." With an authoritarian note, Husserl

claims that "it is an essentially valid law that *existence in the form of a thing is never demanded as necessary by virtue of its givenness*, but in a certain way is always *contingent* " (*Ideas* 131). He goes further, declaring that transcendent being is "presumptive reality." In other words, without the absolute being of the conscious experiences we are now living through, all transcendent reality loses its meaning. Transcendent being *presumes* that which gives it meaning.

> In every way, then, it is clear that everything which is there for me in the world of things is on grounds of principle *only a presumptive reality*; that *I myself*, on the contrary, for whom it is there . . . I myself or my experience in its actuality am *absolute* Reality (*Wirklichkeit*), given through a positing that is unconditioned and simply indissoluble. *The thesis of my pure Ego and its personal life, which is "necessary" and plainly indubitable, thus stands opposed to the thesis of the world which is "contingent." All corporeally given thing-like entities can also not be, no corporeally given experiencing can also not be*: that is the essential law, which defines this necessity and that contingency. (*Ideas* 131)

Hence, there is an order of being with regard to the priority of immanent being in relation to "mere" transcendent being. De Boer explains it this way: "[c]onsciousness is the 'ontic presupposition' (*Seinsvoraussetzung*) of the world. Transcendental phenomenology is 'presuppositionless' for exactly this reason, for it is aware that the world cannot be accepted as ground since consciousness is the true ground and basis" (De Boer 357). That is not to say that the world's being is created by immanent consciousness.

> Husserl does not make the classic mistake of rationalism . . . namely, deriving being from thought. . . . The phenomenological point of departure, the principle of all principles, is that every intuition given in an ordinary way is a proper source of knowledge. . . . the existence of the world presupposes the existence of consciousness, but . . . the reverse is not the case. Thus consciousness is described as a necessary condition for the existence of the world. This does not yet imply that it is also a sufficient condition. (De Boer 353–354)

Even though we do not create the world of being among beings, the phenomenological reduction places the world as meaning for me in absolute dependence on the intending act of consciousness. In other words, the transcendental subject is the transparent master of his or her own soul. The self has become the indubitable self-contained creator and ground of all meaning. "With this conclusion," Husserl states, ". . . our study has reached its climax. We have won the knowledge we needed" (*Ideas* 132). With this "sure" foundation, meaning is secure. However, if transcendental reduction transforms reality into meaning and becomes inconceivable apart from the being of absolute consciousness, is not the inverse also true, that phenomenal reality and meaning exist because it is intended by consciousness? Absolute consciousness is therefore an act of constitution or founding. The reduction has shown that the transformation of things, present to hand in the natural attitude, into phenomena in relation to the intentional acts of consciousness, is really an act of constitution for and by consciousness. *Absolute consciousness is really a meaning-giving, meaning-accomplishing being, which has the world as its accomplishment. Consciousness is the ground of the world, the foundation on which being and meaning rest.*

1.2   Ricoeur's Critique of Phenomenological Idealism

Ricoeur rejects this idealistic interpretation of phenomenology. He combines a change in emphasis in the later works of Husserl with the hermeneutical thinking of Heidegger and Gadamer, to orient phenomenology toward the intersubjective world of linguistic meaning that precedes all transcendental attempts to ground meaning in absolute consciousness. This shift Husserl makes toward the *Lebenswelt* is, according to Ricoeur, an inevitable result of the failure of the transcendental reduction to found meaning within itself. It is indicative of a fundamental dualism at the very core of Husserl's phenomenological project, one which Ricoeur seems to repeat in his early phenomenological studies on voluntary and involuntary consciousness, as well as those on the antinomical structure of human fallibility.[13] Therefore, if Ricoeur appropriates significant portions of Husserlian phenomenology in the development of his own hermeneutic of selfhood, does he overcome this dualism or replace it with a hermeneutical variation that has moved the problem from a transcendental identification of selfhood to an identification of selfhood within the language of self-sameness (*idem* identity) and self-constancy (*ipse* identity)? This is a significant problem that is taken up again in the final chapter, which deals explicitly with Ricoeur's most recent formulation of selfhood in *Oneself as Another*.

In spite of this dualism within Husserl's philosophy, Ricoeur is confident that he can use this shift toward the life-world to his own advantage. He explains that

> in becoming more and more existential the phenomenology of the late Husserl became more and more empirical, for the whole order of the understanding . . . henceforth proceeds from "passive synthesis" initiated on the very level of perception. Thereafter it is clear that this progression toward an ever more originary original destroys every claim of constituting the world "in" consciousness or "begin-

ning from" consciousness. The idealistic tendency of transcendental phenomenology is thus compensated for by the progressive discovery that one does not constitute the originary but only all that
one can derive from it. The originary is just what could neither be
constituted nor reduced. (HL 205)

By following Husserl's lead, Ricoeur adopts a methodology that focuses on the
constituting power of *originary meaning outside consciousness* which constitutes
self-consciousness, rather than being constituted by consciousness. For Ricoeur,
transcendental subjectivity ultimately fails to place subjectivity on the firm
foundation that motivates the project of transcendental phenomenology in the
first place. Ricoeur puts into question the clarity of the apprehension of consciousness. Although transcendental phenomenology places all transcendence
in doubt, it is remarkable that transcendental phenomenology seems unable to
grasp the possibility that "transparent subjectivity" is a ruse constructed to satisfy
the dreams of metaphysicians for a being whose existence coincides with its
essence. If all objects of appearance and the philosophical systems used to
construct them are susceptible to doubt, could not the consciousness of lived
experience be the product of forces outside of, or more primordial than, consciousness itself? Citing Heidegger's question, "Who is *Dasein?*" Ricoeur states:
"Insofar as self-knowledge is a dialogue of the soul with itself, and insofar as the
dialogue can be systematically distorted by violence and by the intrusion of
structures of domination into those of communication, self-knowledge as internal-
ized communication can be as doubtful as knowledge of the object, although for
different and quite specific reasons" (PH 109–110). The chiaroscuric play of
ideological, structural, social, psychological, religious, and economic forces within
the self gives testimony to the vanity of transparent self-consciousness.

Although transcendental phenomenology fails in mastering one's own
destiny, Ricoeur remains committed to the employment of phenomenology for
describing what is closest to human existence. Rather than an exercise in
foundationalism, phenomenology must become an invitation to live in and
receive from the world meaning and one's identity as a task. Referring to Husserl's
transcendental phenomenology, Ricoeur argues that in spite of its idealism, the
phenomenological project remains a valid enterprise if taken up on the level of
existence. "I think that each of us is invited to rediscover for himself this act of
transcendence. Thus I will risk an outline of the 'existential' sense of the thesis
of the world;" a life-world in which I discover myself through an interpretation
of the originary original of "actual life."[14]

Ricoeur catches sight of this existential and hermeneutical reorientation
of phenomenological meaning in Husserl's most explicit formulation of transcendental idealism. "The *Cartesian Meditations* are the most radical expression of the new idealism for which the world is not only 'for me' but draws all

of its being-status 'from me.' The world becomes the 'world-perceived-in-the-reflective life.' . . . Phenomenology is the unfolding of the ego, thereafter termed 'monad' in the Leibnizian manner. It is the 'explication of self' (*Selbstauslegung*)" (HL 10). Note the term *explication*, or *Auslegung*. Combined with an increasing emphasis on that which constitutes the ego rather than a constituting ego, Ricoeur sees within Husserl the possibility for the development of a phenomenology that focuses on the interpretation of the originating world of meaning instead of some originating act that founds all meaning. Ricoeur explains that in the *Cartesian Meditations*

> the reduction less and less signifies a "return to the ego" and more and more a "return from logic to the antepredicative," to the primordial evidence of the world. The accent is placed no longer on the monadic ego; instead the accent is placed on the totality formed by the ego and the surrounding world in which it is vitally engaged. Thus, phenomenology tends toward the recognition of what is prior to all reduction and what cannot be reduced. . . . The being of the world is manifest in such a manner that all truth refers back to it.[15]

If Ricoeur heralds Husserl's "progressive abandonment" of phenomenological idealism, why then does he continue to refer to his method as phenomenology, albeit hermeneutically qualified? Rather than dismissing phenomenology outright, Ricoeur wishes to embrace its original insight.

> The first act of consciousness is designating or meaning (*Meinen*). To distinguish signification from signs, to separate it from the word, from the image, and to elucidate the diverse ways in which an empty signification comes to be fulfilled by an intuitive presence, whatever it may be, is to describe signification phenomenologically. The empty act of signifying is nothing other than intentionality. If intentionality is that remarkable property of consciousness to be a consciousness of . . . of moving out from itself toward something else, then the act of signifying contains the essence of intentionality. (HL 5–6)

This "remarkable property" sets Ricoeur's critique of Husserlian idealism in perspective. Rather than looking for the ground or foundation of meaning, phenomenology must follow the aim of its original discovery: the intentionality of consciousness. Transcendental subjectivity, or consciousness thinking itself, betrays the intentional aim by turning away from the intended to that which intends. Ricoeur concludes that this attempt to establish self-knowledge on such an interior foundation is removed from the fundamental structure of intentionality.

> The phenomenology which arose with the discovery of the univer-
> sal character of intentionality has not remained faithful to its own
> discovery, namely that the meaning of consciousness lies outside
> itself. The idealist theory of the constitution of meaning in con-
> sciousness has thus culminated in the hypostasis of subjectivity. . . .
> Such difficulties attest that phenomenology is always in danger of
> reducing itself to a transcendental subjectivism. The radical way of
> putting an end to this constantly recurring confusion is to shift the
> axis of interpretation from the problem of subjectivity to that of the
> world. That is what the theory of the text attempts to do, by subor-
> dinating the question of the author's intention to that of the matter
> of the text. (PH 112)

Hermeneutical phenomenology is interpretive description of what *lies outside* the intending ego. That which is outside the phenomenological ego is the focus of Ricoeur's entire philosophical project. However, never significant for its own sake, meaning is the place from and in which self-understanding occurs. By focusing on language, discourse, and texts, Ricoeur wants to "exchange the *me, master* of itself, for the *self, disciple* of the text" (PH 113). The self that is retrieved is a work of the world of meaning projected by the text.

The transformation of the transcendental ego into a "self" disciplined by the world of intersubjective meaning becomes the central task of hermeneutical phenomenology. Through the use of a nonidealistic concept of intentionality, Ricoeur wishes to take into account "the various aspects of man's insertion in the world" (HL 203). Thus, the self received from the world of meaning is multidimensional, a collection of activities linked to their respective fields of meaning whose principle of unity remains to be established, if at all. Therefore, Ricoeur's hermeneutical variation of phenomenology is employed to under-stand the fundamental features of lived experience, features that find the self first and foremost in an originating source of meaning that precedes conscious-ness of it. "Consciousness defined by its intentionality is outside, beyond. It ties its own wandering to the 'things' to which it can apply its consideration, its desire, its action. Correlatively, the world is 'world-for-my-life,' environment of the 'living ego'" (HL 205). Ricoeur goes on to explain that because the "world" precedes consciousness, it must become the basis for all reflection on human experience. "The 'world' is prior to every 'object.' It is not only presupposed in the intellectualistic sense of a condition for possibilities, it is pre-given in the sense that every present activity surges into a world already there. Moreover, this world is the totality which, not being composed from parts and by means of addition, is inaccessible to doubt. It is the 'passive pre-given universal of all judgmental activity,' the 'one basis of belief upon which every experience of particular objects is erected.' "[16] The concept of the "world" is thus indicative of the repositioning of a methodological foundation no longer located in an indubitable absolute ego, but in a world of diverse meaning full of competing stories that precede self-consciousness.

By shifting from a "ground grounded within itself " behind the intentional acts of consciousness, to the world of meaning in front of consciousness, is Ricoeur not discarding one form of foundationalism for another? Is Ricoeur's insistence on the closure of the idealistic ground of phenomenology, in view of the opening offered by the world of meaning, not a grounding of a different sort? This might be the case if our attention simply focused on Husserlian phenomenological resources without elaborating the second term of the couplet *phenomenological hermeneutics*.

1.3   A Hermeneutical Variation of Phenomenology

As early as 1957, in an article entitled "Existential Phenomenology," Ricoeur displays a propaedeutic interest in phenomenology as a means for uncovering or describing the structures of existence: "existential phenomenology makes the transition between transcendental phenomenology, born of the reduction of everything to its appearing to me, and ontology, which restores the question of the sense of being for all that is said to 'exist' " (HL 212). This early formulation of Ricoeur's methodology lacks the programmatic decentering of the ego that characterizes his later works. Although Ricoeur's early phenomenological studies include a nascent hermeneutic,[17] their preoccupation with eidetic structure forgoes the degree to which Ricoeur's later works are attuned to the deceptive strategies of consciousness that hide, distort, and cloud the dialogue of the soul. Even though Ricoeur does look to "the examples of Hegel, Kierkegaard, and Nietzsche," as philosophers of existence who offer "sufficient indication that description is effective only in the service of a great plan: to denounce an alienation, to rediscover the place of man in the world, or on the other hand, to recover his metaphysical dimension, and so on" (HL 208), it is only in his middle and later works that Ricoeur develops the notion of the critical space of reflexivity that counters the idealism of the self-transparent ego.

Ricoeur, however, employs key elements of phenomenology only by way of a "hermeneutical" critique. In "The Task of Hermeneutics" (1973), Ricoeur traces the essential historical features and figures of the hermeneutical tradition. Beginning with the philological origins in the work of Schleiermacher and ending with Gadamer's magnum opus, *Truth and Method*, Ricoeur concludes that hermeneutics should be defined as "the theory of the operations of understanding in their relation to the interpretation of texts." The central problem of such a theory is "the opposition, disastrous in my view, between explanation and understanding" (TH 43). Hermeneutics thus becomes an attempt to resolve the seemingly divergent concerns of methodological explanation and participatory understanding, in order to ultimately clarify existence by means of concepts that are methodologically responsible and existentially true.

Employing the notion of ontologized understanding, Ricoeur echoes the Heideggerian quest for the recovery of a sense of belonging that is prior to any fragmentation of a subject over against an object. "The first declaration of hermeneutics is to say that the problematic of objectivity presupposes a prior relation of inclusion which encompasses the allegedly autonomous subject and the allegedly adverse object. This inclusive or encompassing relation is what I call belonging" (PH 105). Ricoeur sharpens this declaration by referring to belonging as the *"hermeneutical experience itself,"* which can be understood in Heideggerian terms as "being-in-the-world" with its emphasis on care, or the priority of belonging "which precedes reflection." I belong to the world as *Dasein* before I can objectify it as an epistemological subject (PH 106).

Here a deeper understanding of the meaning of interpretation is revealed. Since belonging is the hermeneutical experience par excellence, interpretation is *co-primordial* with the world to which I and everybody else belongs, it is the "universal concept of interpretation which has the same extension as that of understanding and, in the end, as that of belonging" (PH 107). Referring to Heidegger, Ricoeur points out that interpretation is the "development of understanding." It reveals the "as"-structure of reality, that is, "being" as something. Therefore, "explication does not transform understanding into something else, but makes it become itself" (PH 107). Because belonging is the act of interpretive understanding that "precedes reflection," I am predisposed to an orientation in and by means of the world to which I belong. Hence, being-in-the-world "anticipates" or expects the world to be configured in a certain fashion. Interpretive understanding is characterized "by the 'structure of anticipation,' which prevents explication from ever being a presuppositionless grasp of a pregiven being [*étant*]; explication precedes its object in the mode of the *Vor-habe*, the *Vor-sicht*, the *Vor-griff*, the *Vor-meinung*" (PH 107). By utilizing these Heideggerian concepts, Ricoeur wishes to make clear that the "vast" universality of interpretation is co-extensive with hermeneutical understanding. Ricoeur states: "What is important to emphasize is that it is not possible to implement the structure of the 'as' without also implementing the structure of anticipation. The notion of 'meaning' obeys this double condition of the *Als* and the *Vor-*."[18] Therefore, interpretation as the explication of belonging is predicated on participation in a world that precedes any objectification of the intended objects of consciousness, but also reveals the power of belonging to configure being *as* something.[19]

For Ricoeur, worldly participation provides the means by which I "shatter the pretension of the knowing subject to set itself up as the measure of objectivity. What must be reaffirmed in place of this pretension is the condition of inhabiting the world, a condition which renders situation, understanding and interpretation possible" (TH 56). Conditioned possibility becomes one of the central themes in Ricoeur's appropriation of the hermeneutic tradition. The "hermeneutical experience itself " can be described as the "power to be . . . [which] orientates us in a situation. So understanding is not concerned with grasping a fact but with apprehending a possibility of being" (TH 56). Existence is structured so that the act of living calls for an act of interpretation and understanding that envisions possibilities to be more than and other than what has already been received.

Coupling the Heideggerian concept of ontologized understanding with the Gadamerian "*Sprachlichkeit* of all experience" (PH 115), Ricoeur looks to language to give testimony of the possibilities for being. All experience or existence "has an expressibility in principle. Experience can be said, it demands to be said. To bring it to language is not to change it into something else, but, in articulating and developing it, to make it become itself" (PH 115). Understanding and interpretation, the fundamental structures of belonging to a world, take place in and by means of language. " 'Discourse is the articulation of what understanding is.' It is therefore necessary to situate discourse in the structures of being, rather than situating the latter in discourse: 'Discourse is the 'meaningful' articulation of the understandable structure of being-in-the-world' " (TH 58). Language, however, is not supposed to be objectified discourse about being, about what is; it is in language, by means of the referential function of language codified in textual form, that the *possibilities* of being take shape. "We must not lose sight of this point when we draw the methodological consequences of this analysis: to understand a text, we shall say, is not to find a lifeless sense which is contained therein, but to unfold the possibility of being indicated by the text. Thus we shall remain faithful to the Heideggerian notion of understanding which is essentially a projection or, to speak more dialectically and paradoxically, a projection within a prior being-thrown" (TH 56). Language, particularly symbolic, metaphorical, and fictional language, becomes for Ricoeur the place where being is manifest, but also where self-consciousness and identity are formed.

The revelatory power of language is indicative of the universality of hermeneutical understanding. This is most evident in the "polysemic value of words" that characterizes language use. Before any methodological and hermeneutical reflection can take place, the prescientific use of language already involves hermeneutic understanding; hence, there is a "spontaneous process of interpretation which is part of the most primitive exercise of understanding in any situation" (PH 108). To live, as Ricoeur has said, is to live by means of interpretation. Life is a mediation between oneself and the world in which language "is the medium through which we understand ourselves" (HFD 142). For Ricoeur conversation is paradigmatic of this interpretive process "by which, in the interplay of question and answer, the interlocutors collectively determine the contextual values which structure their conversation" (PH 107). Language mediates meaning face to face, or "*vis-à-vis*" (HFD 143), and therefore is determined by the specific context and purpose of the conversation. To understand the other is to interpret the meaning of the words used. Without this universal fact of interpretation the world would only echo the voice of an absolute and solitary ego.

Such a claim for hermeneutical universality, which is significant in the immediate moment of conversation, fails if it cannot take into account the *history of dialogue* or the "long intersubjective relations . . . sustained by an historical tradition" (PH 108). Language use is rarely the transparent exchange of clearly defined words with univocal meaning; it is the product of long traditions that have developed around a body of texts. Although understanding a conversation requires one to sift through and interpret a vast array of linguistic meanings, the possibilities for being *as* another that are revealed through language have a great deal of baggage in tow, not to mention the unconscious or even the deliberate work of miscommunication and deceit. The universality of the hermeneutical experience itself is the experience of belonging to a world revealed through a language exchange that has *multiple* meanings on a variety of conscious and unconscious levels. Therefore, all understanding, because it takes place through language, is hermeneutical.

The hermeneutical orientation of Ricoeur's phenomenology places the signification of meaningful worldly participation in the linguistic dialectic of sense and reference. Through "the meaning of the act of discourse, or the *noema* of the *saying*" (HFD 135)—that is, the correlate of the phenomenological *noesis*, or intention—textual interpretation opens the phenomenological aim to a multiplicity of articulated meaning that gives testimony of the experience of belonging and to the possibilities for new being. The world of participation is therefore not shrouded in some deep, ineffable mystery; it can be understood when one travels along the phenomenological aim of "intentional exteriorization" (HFD 135) to a world of meaningful belonging signified and articulated in a vast and seemingly infinite number of texts. But whose vision of belonging is understood, and which testimony is true?

Ricoeur addresses this problem not by closing down the multiplicity of meaning, but by giving it a semantic rather than a subjective context. Each author, by giving linguistic shape to experience, proposes meaningful possibilities for living through the reference of the text. Thus Ricoeur explains that phenomenological hermeneutics "give[s] the word 'meaning' a very broad connotation that covers all the aspects and levels of the *intentional exteriorization* which, in turn, renders possible the exteriorization of discourse in writing and in the work" (HFD 135–136). In writing, discourse becomes fixed through its semantic structure, becoming a textual work among other cultural works.[20] The transition from conversation to written text gives the textual form a kind of autonomy or "emancipation" from its historical context and the authorial intention. Since the transcendental ego operative behind experience has been set aside as philosophically untenable, any attempt to recover the original intention of the author from the textual world of meaning would reinstate the necessity of a transcendental ego in control of transcendent meaning. Writing, however, places articulated experience into the shared world of belonging, thus separating it from the life and control of the author. Textual autonomy removes the constraints of authorial intention, freeing the text for multiple interpretations inherent in its polysemic structure. Ricoeur explains that

> this common feature, which constitutes the text as text, is that the meaning contained therein is rendered *autonomous* with respect to the intention of the author, the initial situation of discourse and the original addressee. Intention, situation and original addressee constitute the *Sitz-im-Leben* [site-in-life] of the text. The possibility of multiple interpretations is opened up by a text which is thus freed from its *Sitz-im-Leben*. Beyond the polysemy of words in a conversation is the polysemy of a text which invites multiple readings. (PH 108)

Textual meaning shifts from the world of the original author to the world of the reader by means of the internal dialectic of sense and reference which forms the basic structure of texts.

Here lies one of the fundamental differences between Ricoeur's hermeneutic phenomenology and transcendental idealism. Interpretation is an open understanding of the meaning and significance of existence that takes place here and now in the ambiguous flux of real-life situations by real people. Appropriation of meaning does not take place in the rarified sterility of an absolute consciousness exerting control over the constitution of meaning; it is a risky business of handing control over to the dialogical exchange between the reader and the world of *possibilities* presented by a text. "So understanding is quite different from a constitution of which the subject would possess the key. In this respect, it would be more correct to say that the *self* is constituted by the 'matter' of the text" (HFD 143–144). We live in the middle of life; therefore, beginning from a signification and working backward to the *ultimate* foundation of transcendental subjectivity denies the hermeneutic reality of existence. The world of meaning is something into which we are born, it precedes us and gives us the tools of reference for understanding ourselves. Meaning is always larger and infinitely more diverse than the consciousness of it, and thus the interpretation of meaning is always incomplete. Ricoeur eloquently explains that we suddenly arrive, as it were, in the middle of a conversation which has already begun and in which we try to orientate ourselves in order to be able to contribute to it. Now the ideal of an intuitive foundation is the ideal of an interpretation which, at a certain point, would pass into full vision. . . . Only a total mediation would be equivalent to an intuition which is both first and final. Idealist phenomenology can therefore sustain its pretension to ultimate foundation only by adopting, in an intuitive rather than a speculative mode, the Hegelian claim to absolute knowledge. But the key hypothesis of hermeneutic philosophy is that interpretation is an open process which no single vision can conclude. (PH 108–109)

Therefore, since the interpretation of meaning sheds light on life and self, it continually calls for reinterpretation. Understanding is an ongoing process, centered in the act of creative living. Meaning and existence form a *dynamic* spiral that only moves forward through the continual oscillation of the interpretation and reinterpretation of existence.[21] To be without a concluding "vision" does not mean that hermeneutical phenomenology is without sight. To say that the dynamic spiral of meaning and existence is an "open process" does not mean it is a futile process. Total mediation is indeed passed by, but so too is a vision of being that is completely consumed by the efficacy of history.

1.4   A Dialectic of Phenomenological Hermeneutics

Ricoeur steers a careful course between the extremes of complete domination of meaning by consciousness and the domination of consciousness by meaning. The relation of meaning and existence is for Ricoeur a dialectic of distanciation and belonging that produces a creative tension that makes it possible for him to form a unified method out of the divergent aims of hermeneutical interpretation and phenomenological constitution. Meaning, Ricoeur insists, is always "coextensive with the concept of intentionality," and the extension of consciousness by means of intentionality outside itself toward meaning emphasizes a "priority of meaning over self-consciousness" (PH 116). Between the *experience* of belonging and linguistic *meaning* Ricoeur opens a gap that allows him to take distance from "lived experience" by means of textual signification. This is the phenomenological presupposition of hermeneutical reflection.

The distance from experience that Ricoeur seeks is the distance provided by language. By reinstating a nonidealistic version of Husserl's phenomenological *epochè*, Ricoeur does not want to control and dominate meaning, but to accept the temporality, the birth and death of human existence, and thus the fragmentation of all understanding. However, the hermeneutical appropriation of the meaning of existence is not irresponsible, as if understanding experience would be ultimately unintelligible. By joining the phenomenological and hermeneutical projects into a single, albeit complex method, Ricoeur passes over the rationalism of modern philosophy without accepting the irrationalism of romanticism.[22] The focus on language provides him with a productive means of mediation between critical reflection and historical understanding, where one presupposes the other. The interconnections between these two philosophical attitudes, that is, phenomenological explanation and hermeneutical understanding, forms a unified method. Phenomenology provides the means for taking distance from lived experience, but only because what comes to language is the intelligibility of experience itself. Language does not produce experience; it opens experience to an interpretive understanding. Ricoeur, therefore, explains that "the interplay of distance and proximity, constitutive of the historical connection, is what comes to language rather than what language produces. . . . The reference of the linguistic order back to the structure of experience (which comes to language in the assertion) constitutes, in my view, the most important phenomenological presupposition of hermeneutics" (PH 117–118).

This, however, presents only half of Ricoeur's methodology. The fact that experience is prior to language, that "the constitution of the *complete noema* precedes the properly linguistic plane upon which the function of denomination, predication, syntactic liaison and so on come to be articulated" (PH 118), does not mean that language is the Platonic image of a more primordial presence. Experience, rather than being produced by language, is given configuration by language. Language arises from experience in order to signify and interpret experience; but this signification is not simply the duplication of experience. Language is the repetition of existence, that is, the production of what is repeated, and not the recollection of a self-contained prior experience (RH 15). Through an act of *configuration*, language can also *reconfigure* experience by appropriating latent potentialities and new possibilities. Thus, language is for Ricoeur not the duplication of experience but a signification of the vast possibilities of existence, a revelation of the "surplus"[23] of meaning constitutive of all experience. Therefore, "experience can be said, it demands to be said. To bring it to language is not to change it into something else, but, in articulating and developing it, to make it become itself" (PH 115). The life-world, the gift into which we are born, is not a meaningless and futile process of birth and death; it is a superabundant gift overflowing with meaning that can be understood.

The experience of belonging is the hermeneutical presupposition of phenomenological distance that reshapes the phenomenological project into an interpretive description of the surplus of meaning externalized in textual form. However, the mutual dependence of hermeneutics and phenomenology makes hermeneutical belonging unintelligible without the critical distance of the phenomenological *epochè*. Ricoeur explains that "the *Lebenswelt* is not [to be] confused with some sort of ineffable immediacy and is not identified with the vital and emotional envelope of human experience, but rather is construed as designating the reservoir of meaning, the surplus of sense in living experience, which renders the objectifying and explanatory attitude possible" (PH 119). Ricoeur employs both the phenomenological reduction and the life-world, or of constitution and intuition, in such a way that "the 'lived experience' of phenomenology corresponds, on the side of hermeneutics, to consciousness exposed to historical efficacy. Hence hermeneutical distanciation is to belonging as, in phenomenology, the *epochè* is to lived experience. Hermeneutics similarly begins when, not content to belong to transmitted tradition, we interrupt the relation of belonging in order to signify it" (PH 116–117).

By focusing on the codification of language, Ricoeur joins the phenomenological reduction of being to textual meaning with a hermeneutical appropriation of the referential "world" of meaning revealed in front of the text.[24] Ricoeur mediates between what is passively received as experience, or what he refers to as the involuntary character of existence, and the active or voluntary creation of meaning,[25] by coupling the divergent philosophical projects of phenomenology and hermeneutics in a mutually dependent dialectic of distanciation and belonging. In this sense Ricoeur appears to overcome Husserl's dualism of constitution and intuition that situates one ego in the life-world and another ego in transcendental solitude (HP 55). Ricoeur's vision of hermeneutical phenomenology moves beyond these divergent aims by looking to the works of the imagination, or the testimonies of being, not for a new metaphysic of presence, but for dialogue that will exchange the ego for a self discipled by another. In a sense one could say that Ricoeur's position is a productive resolution of the "paradox [that] is inescapably connected with the equivocal co-presence of two conflicting philosophical projects: a project of describing transcendence versus a project of constituting in immanence. The role of interpretation is precisely to occupy a midpoint between a speculative constructivist philosophy and a philosophy of intuition such as Husserl's phenomenology apparently insists on being" (Jervolino 99).

Does, however, such a mediation between speculative distance and intuitive belonging not create a dualism of a different sort? After all, does not the signification of experience create an "empty" space, or a nonspatial space, out front of itself by means of its world of reference? And does not the linguistic distance from experience create a gap between the experience signified and the signification as such?

There appears to be a breach on two different levels: the *first* appears as a gap between language and experience that opens linguistic meaning to something more than can be phenomenologically described. A *second* gap appears within language itself between the explanatory procedures that detail the "sense" of language and the linguistic "reference" that allows for the signification of the "something more," or "surplus" of meaning proper. In other words, there is a doubling of the gap that creates distance on two different, but related levels: the epistemological, involving explanatory and hermeneutical procedures that reveal a world of meaning in front of the text, and the ontological, involving the proximity and distance that comes to language in the epistemological dialectic of sense and reference.

These two different openings and/or gaps reveal a third one. As noted at the beginning of this chapter, Ricoeur never divorces method from life: the epistemological and ontological levels are linked. Although he begins on the methodological level and works toward the ontological, truth and method remain the presupposition of each other by virtue of a connecting matrix of activity Ricoeur calls the imagination. The creation of distance by means of the phenomenological reduction is in fact the result of the work of the imagination. Ricoeur points out that "the *epochè* is the virtual event, the imaginary act which inaugurates the whole game by which we exchange signs for things and signs for other signs. Phenomenology is like the explicit revival of this virtual event which raises to the dignity of the act, the philosophical gesture. It renders thematic what was only operative, and thereby makes meaning appear as meaning" (PH 116).

Employing a combination of Husserl's "imaginative variations" and Kant's reproductive imagination, Ricoeur develops the idea of the "space of reflexivity" as a *creative center* that mediates between the "efficacy of history" and the openness toward new possibilities for *being more* or *other than* what has been received. Through the power of the imagination Ricoeur not only mends the breach between the divergent aims of phenomenology and hermeneutics, but also provides the means for historical and existential transcendence. The work of the imagination, however, does not step outside history, nor is it a Platonic gaze at the heavenly vault of truth; it is primarily a linguistic act that can take distance *from* "reality" in order to understand the "deep structures *of* reality to which we are related as mortals who are born into this world and who *dwell* in it for a while" (MP 151). The imagination is an activity that provides a "look," ruled by our historical horizon, of the possibilities of belonging and the means for appropriating them.

The imaginative "look" echoes the phenomenological *Wesensschau* of meaning; yet the idea of a "vision" of reality is perhaps a misnomer. Since the hermeneutic connection to existence is linguistic in character, Ricoeur's understanding of imagination is first and foremost a "hidden art" that reveals the possibilities of being by means of language rather than perception. For Ricoeur the Platonic view of imagination as false image-maker, or the Aristotelian faculty by which we make judgments about unclear perceptions and pass along sensory information for the rational mind to consider, is at best a secondary type of imagining, because "we only see images in so far as we first hear them" (IDA 9). The creative imagination envisions possibilities for being primarily through linguistic forms, through symbols, metaphors, historical and fictional narratives. Thus, the imaginative center of Ricoeur's methodology is revealed in the work of the imagination, which binds together the paradoxical claims of phenomenological distance and hermeneutical understanding.

CHAPTER TWO

IMAGINATION

Mediated Self-Constitution

Considering the methodological importance Ricoeur gives to the work of the imagination, it is not surprising to hear him cast his lifelong philosophical inquiries into a grand category of "the formidable question of creativity" (HHS 38). The creative imagination, however, not only mediates between the competing philosophical aims of hermeneutics and phenomenology, but it is rooted in the most basic of human activities as well: living. "The mediating role of imagination is forever at work in lived reality (*le vécu*). There is no lived reality, no human or social reality, which is not already *represented in some sense*" (*Dialogues* 24). Therefore, the work of the imagination, structured as the dialectical relationship of sense and reference, has methodological significance but also reaches the ontological depth of human existence. Through the creative work of imagination, life is both represented and understood; through discourse that is close to the creative power of the imagination life and self are most clearly revealed. The hermeneutical "detour of countless mediations—signs, symbols, texts and human praxis itself" (*Dialogues* 32)—is a detour through works that are not separated from life and closed in on themselves, but say something meaningful about the world we live in. In doing so, the hermeneutical detour gives a reflexive response to the question: "Who is this that we call human?" Here Ricoeur identifies the core meaning of human existence as fundamentally textual or narrative in character. "I would say, borrowing Wittgenstein's term, that the 'language-game' of narration ultimately reveals that the meaning of human existence is itself narrative" (*Dialogues* 17). Ricoeur's investigations into the various works of the creative imagination not only reveal the significant and referential features of such works, but point to a collection of creative-imaginative activity that is instrumental in the formation of human selfhood and identity.

Important as it appears, what is remarkable about Ricoeur's treatment of
the relation between the imagination and the cultural reservoir of linguistic
meaning is the abundance of philosophical inquiries into symbol, myth, metaphor, and narrative, into the *works* of the imagination, in contrast to the relative
absence of a detailed description of the imagination as such. This, however,
should not be too surprising given Ricoeur's interpretation of consciousness as
consciousness of something, that is, as intentional, directed outside itself, connected to that which is other, and thus decentered. An *interpretation* of the
productive works of imagination, rather than a phenomenological analysis of
transcendental subjectivity, is supposed to be more revealing of an imagination
at work engendering consciousness with a self-consciousness originating from
that which is other-than-my-consciousness. The activity of the imagination is to
be understood in a fragmentary manner through the vast diversity of what it
produces, thus avoiding, on the one hand, the route of direct reflection on the
imagination, and on the other, the complete dispersal of an activity responsible
for the reception and creation of meaning. Ricoeur explains that "the formidable question of creativity" is one that "always seemed to me to be too easy or
too difficult: too easy, insofar as it invites waffle devoid of rigor; too difficult, as
Kant himself said of the schematism which he called 'a mechanism hidden in
the depths of the soul, which it is impossible to extricate from nature.' However,
if the problem of creativity cannot be approached directly and as a whole,
perhaps it can be treated in a lateral and fragmentary fashion" (HHS 38–39).
The works of imagination are not the shattered remains of an idealist ego
responsible for the constitution of linguistic images, but reveal an analogous,
"open-ended, incomplete, imperfect mediation" (TN 3: 207) or pattern common to the various forms of creativity that provides a fragile view of a creativity
that can be called human. The focus on the linguistic creation of meaning in
symbol, metaphor, and narrative opens language to the question of humanity
and selfhood, which in turn allows and calls for ontological reflection.

What is at stake for Ricoeur in his studies on symbolism, metaphor, and
narrative is the very core of the relation between meaning and existence. The
process from creative discourse to questions of selfhood and to ontological discourse opens the self-contained ego to an ever-enlarging landscape: first through
the world of textual reference, then as the voice of the other calling for recognition, finally as the very possibility for initiating action in the social world on
the grand scale of time and history.

Ricoeur's philosophical inquiries into the works of imagination open a
door to the meaning of human existence by tracing out a pattern of imaginativity
amid the vast polysemy of imaginative discourse. Far from reestablishing a
unifying transcendental subjectivity, and thereby closing down linguistic plurality in an authoritarian act of violence, Ricoeur's quest for "a general philosophy
of the creative imagination . . . [or] the constantly postponed project of a 'Poet-

ics of the Will' " (HHS 39) addresses the pressing need to truly hear the voice of the "other" without losing the possibility of selfhood in radical plurality, but on the other hand to refuse to enclose all otherness in the circle of the "same," or to identify otherness with self-reference. Ricoeur explains that "the philosophical task is not to close the circle, to centralize or totalize knowledge, but to keep open the irreducible plurality of discourse."[1] For Ricoeur it is the imagination understood as a decentered meaning-receiving meaning-creating collection of activities, that performs this task.

2.1   Creative Imaginativity

Ricoeur offers some rather concise parameters within which the question of the imagination should be addressed. In several articles, particularly "Imagination in Discourse and in Action" (1978) and "The Function of Fiction in Shaping Reality" (1979), Ricoeur develops a "conception of imagination, first set out in the context of a theory of metaphor centered around the notion of semantic innovation," and expands it "outside the sphere of discourse to which it originally belonged" (IDA 3). Ricoeur goes on to say that the "[t]ie between imagination and semantic innovation . . . [is] the core of our entire analysis" (IDA 3). Metaphoric creativity reveals something fundamentally constitutive about human imagination, and all subsequent elaboration of various creative activities displays an analogous similarity by virtue of the repetition of the pattern of metaphoric creation.

One may think that the tie between imagination and semantic innovation, since it is the "core" of Ricoeur's "entire analysis" and the key to understanding his work on metaphor and narrative, is a relatively late conception in the overall historical development of Ricoeur's hermeneutical-phenomenology. This, however, is not the case. Ricoeur, reflecting on the development of his notion of the imagination, ties the work of the imagination to the symbolization of experience at "*its cultural level*" (HHS 39). Further, Ricoeur recalls how the imagination "was already situated, in the period of *Fallible Man*, at the fragile point where the voluntary and the involuntary are articulated and where fallibility insinuates itself into the ontological structure of man," which is antedated by the quest, in *Freedom and Nature*, for a " 'Poetics of the Will' . . . [or] a general philosophy of the creative imagination" (HHS 39).

Throughout Ricoeur's publications the imagination can be seen in different stages of development. The imagination in combination with the notion of semantic innovation is simply the latest reorganization of the imaginative core of human existence. Although the conceptual apparatus Ricoeur employed in his earliest publications, such as eidetic analysis, empirics, and the focus of hermeneutics on symbolism, has been set aside in favor of reflective hermeneutical phenomenology, the significance of the imagination as a work of mediation has remained a constant feature of his writings. Further, the initial conceptual pattern of the work of the imagination Ricoeur employed, particularly evident in *Freedom and Nature* (1966) and *Fallible Man* (1967), is refigured and repeated with an ever-increasing degree of nuance and sophistication throughout his published works. Therefore, despite the essentialist nature of the discussion of the work of imagination in Ricoeur's early works and his recent proclamation of the "new" manner in which the self is understood (OA 120 n. 5, 124 n. 11), the mediating work of the imagination seen in these early investigations of voluntary consciousness and human fallibility displays several vectors of continuity with his more recent studies in *The Rule of Metaphor* (1977), *Time and Narrative* (1984–1988), and *Oneself as Another* (1992). This development of Ricoeur's notion of the mediating role of the imagination will be examined as a propaedeutic for the investigation of the creative imagination at work in semantic innovation, narrative configuration, and identity.

2.2   Freedom and Nature

Ricoeur's first major publication, *Le Volontaire et l'involuntaire* (1950), translated under the title *Freedom and Nature* (1966), is an attempt to "reveal . . . man's structures or *fundamental possibilities*" (FN 3) by means of a phenomenological reduction, which from the outset is dissociated from Husserl's transcendental reduction. "In contrast we shall see that all our considerations drive us away from the famous and obscure transcendental reduction which, we believe, is an obstacle to genuine understanding of personal body" (FN 4). Yet, Ricoeur is nevertheless concerned with the elucidation of *essential meanings*, although reinterpreted "simply as meanings or principles of intelligibility of the broad voluntary and involuntary functions" (FN 4), they still are the result of a *Wesensschau*, a direct and "immediate understanding" by means of a phenomenological reduction.

The most "immediate" *Wesensschau* for Ricoeur is the revelation of the human "situation" as "*the reciprocity of the involuntary and the voluntary*" (FN 4), where all that is involuntary lacks meaning apart from its relationship to voluntary will. In direct contrast with the phenomenology of Maurice Merleau-Ponty,[2] description starts from "the top down and not from the bottom up" (FN 5). There can only be one "I will," one "central function" with many "partial functions" or involuntary components that limit voluntary power. Hence "the involuntary refers to the will [only] as that which gives its motives and capacities, its foundations, and even its limits" (FN 5). Ricoeur construes the central phenomenological intuition as a reciprocity between two poles that are related to each other in terms of unity and diversity: the unifying or organizing pole of the voluntary "I will," and the diversity of involuntary capacities in conjunction with an intractable necessity that stands in need of order and cohesion. Ricoeur's remarkable phrase that "the will is the one which brings order to the many of the involuntary" (FN 5) is the core intuition of the meaning of existence that is laid bare through the careful application of descriptive phenomenology.

The centrality of the *cogito*, understood as the unifying function of the "I will," is in marked contrast to Ricoeur's disavowal of the philosophies of the *cogito* in *Oneself as Another*. Yet, in *Freedom and Nature*, despite the unmediated eidetic picture of the *cogito*, we see the beginnings of Ricoeur's vision of selfhood as open to the Other. The voluntary "I will" is given limits or a foundation of potentiality for enacting a voluntary choice; it is connected to a level or dimension of affectivity that opens the self-contained ego to that which is outside its control. By initiating a phenomenology of the will, Ricoeur reinterprets the intentional thrust of consciousness as essentially volitional, as an active process that begins with decision but ends in consent to all that is involuntary. Mohanty underscores Ricoeur's volitional reorientation of the Husserlian concept of intentionality by explaining that for Ricoeur "volition is intention *par excellence*, for every intention is attention and every attention 'reveals an 'I can' at the heart of the 'I think.' Every act, whether specifically volitional or not, is an intentional act in so far as it expresses a power in us which we exercise, so much so that the analysis of volition places us at the very heart of the intentional function of consciousness" (Mohanty 1972: 144).

By reformulating the "I think" in terms of an "I can," and thereby placing the intentionality of consciousness in a context of what can and cannot be willed, that is, in a context of the potentialities and limits that condition what can actually be willed, Ricoeur opens the entire intentional thrust of consciousness to that which is other than *cogito*. By following the intentional thrust of the *cogito* through the power of decision and the project of action, we see the *cogito* extended beyond itself and confronted by the need for "acquiescence to the necessity which it can neither propose nor change" (FN 7). The intentional thrust of the *cogito* is confronted with its own involuntary necessity, its own functional capacities necessary for the completion of its task as well as the absolute involuntary realities of birth, death, character, the unconscious, and other people. However, voluntary decision and choice must give way to "consent" and accept these limitations that are other than the "I will," yet nevertheless *my* limitations which comprise a fundamental involuntary dimension that is reciprocally bound up with the very possibility for willing. The description of the "human situation" is one of a split ego, of a self divided between the inherent otherness of its affective necessity and that which is centered within the voluntary will.

By extending the phenomenological reduction beyond immanent consciousness, Ricoeur transforms the initial Husserlian project into a "task of describing the voluntary and involuntary," where the goal "is in effect one of becoming receptive to Cogito's *complete* experience, including even its most diffuse affective margins" (FN 7). All dimensions of affective experience need to be taken into account, but only in relation to the "I can" which gives affective experience its meaning. For Ricoeur,

> the reconquest of the Cogito must be complete: we can only discover the body and the involuntary which it sustains in the context of the Cogito itself. The Cogito's experience, taken as a whole, includes "I desire," "I can," "I intend," and, in a general way, my existence as a body. A common subjectivity is the basis for the homogeneity of voluntary and involuntary structures. Our description, yielding to what appears to the consideration of the self, thus moves into a unique universe of discourse concerning the subjectivity of the integral Cogito. The nexus of the voluntary and involuntary does not lie at the boundary of two universes of discourse, one of which would be reflection concerning thought and the other concerning the physical aspects of the body: Cogito's intuition is the intuition of a body conjoined to a willing which submits to it and governs it. It is the meaning of the body as a source of motives, as a cluster of capacities, and even as necessary nature. Our task will in effect be one of discovering even necessity in the first person, as the nature which I am. (FN 9–10)

Ricoeur's attempt to take ownership within the *cogito* of all that is involuntary and to include "otherness" within a circle of the "I can," that is, within the circle of the "homogeneity . . . [of] a common subjectivity," must be counterbalanced by his insistence that "the Ego must more radically renounce the covert claim of all consciousness, must abandon its wish to posit itself, so that it can receive the nourishing and inspiring spontaneity which breaks the sterile circle of the self's constant return to itself" (FN 14). Ricoeur, therefore, asks us to balance the phenomenological task of describing and including all experience within the purview of a unifying *cogito* over and against an otherness that breaths life into the *cogito* by drawing it outside itself. What in effect Ricoeur is insisting on is the need for, and the limitation of, an eidetic description of an all-encompassing reciprocity of the voluntary and involuntary. If that which is *other* is not to be reduced to the *same*, description "need[s] to pass from objectivity to existence . . . It requires that I participate actively in *my incarnation as a mystery*" (FN 14).

Ricoeur's effort to describe the reciprocal structure of the "voluntary" and "involuntary" is juxtaposed with the unfathomable depth of experience. Phenomenological discourse of the "I can" is always open to the "mystery" of existence. However, mystery needs to be clarified by eidetic meaning so that the "*distinctive understanding* of subjective structures of the voluntary and an *encompassing sense* of the mystery of incarnation mutually complete and limit each other" (FN 15). From the very outset, Ricoeur views phenomenological description as an eidetic abstraction necessary for the clarification of existence; but such a reduction of existence to essential meanings must not be understood as the masterful control over existence nor its "objective" or "transcendental" constitution (FN 16). Because existence escapes complete description, phenomenology can only construct signposts amid the temporal flux of experience but can never exhaust the ontological depth of the mystery of living. For Ricoeur the

> philosophy of man appears . . . as a living tension between an objectivity elaborated by a phenomenology to do justice to the Cogito . . . and the sense of my incarnate existence. The latter constantly overflows the objectivity which in appearance respects it most but which by its very nature tends to eschew it. That is why the concepts we use, such as motivation, completion of a project, situation, etc., are *indications* of a living experience in which we are submerged more than signs of mastery which our intelligence exercises over our human condition. But in turn it is the task of philosophy to clarify existence itself by use of concepts. (FN 17)

The structures of the voluntary and involuntary must be set off from the lived reality of human existence. In this manner, Ricoeur places the description of essential meanings over against existence as "indications" of the structure of life that are beyond the control of the *cogito*.

The relationship between this phenomenology of essential structures and the mystery of existence has for Ricoeur an interpretive quality. As a diagnosis of lived reality, the essential meanings of the voluntary and involuntary can be viewed as an interpretive pattern whose chief purpose is to clarify the mystery of existence without reducing mystery to descriptive sterility.[3] However, to place "essential meanings" in juxtaposition with existence is puzzling if existence has no discernible characteristics aside from phenomenological reductive essences. If the mystery of existence has no intelligible familiarity apart from phenomenological meaning, apart from its recognizable and "intelligible essential structures," existence as such would be unrecognizable. Therefore, the interpretation of existence by means of a phenomenological reduction must presuppose some recognizable outline to which we attribute the phrase *the mystery of existence*. Even if phenomenology describes essential contours, existence is understood as lived experience before it is described. The epistemic interpretive relevance of the reciprocity of the voluntary and involuntary, if it is to be "mutually complete" and limited by existence, must correlate with a deeper and more fundamental level of experienced reciprocity. Eidetic description must be tuned to and reflect the ebb and flow of existence.

Ricoeur explains that "to participate in the mystery of incarnate existence means to adopt the internal rhythm of *drama*" (FN 17). The duality of the voluntary and involuntary, held together through the reciprocal mutuality of the "I can," is predicated on a *dramatic* dualism experienced at the heart of existence. "A new dualism, a dualism of existence within the experienced unity, replaces epistemic dualism and suddenly endows it with a radical and, we might say, existential significance which goes singularly beyond the demands of method. Existence tends to break itself up. In effect the advent of consciousness is always to some degree the disruption of an intimate harmony" (FN 17).

The duality of the voluntary and involuntary is founded on the radical possibility of denial, on the dramatic refusal of the will to live as "harmonious self." This lets

> a dream of purity and integrity take . . . hold of consciousness which then conceives of itself as ideally complete, transparent, and capable of positing itself absolutely. The expulsion of the personal body beyond the circle of subjectivity, its ejection into the realm of objects considered at a distance, can from this viewpoint be interpreted as a savage revenge of a subjectivity which feels exposed, abandoned, thrown into the world, and has lost the naïveté of the original compact. (FN 18)

Lived reality is characterized as the episodic movement and opaque fragmentation of egological distance from and proximity with incarnate otherness. By casting the drama of existence in an objective phenomenology of the voluntary and involuntary, Ricoeur is in effect prescribing a unifying interpretive discourse, rooted in a fundamental ontology, for the existential rift of anthropological fragmentation.[4] The purpose of *Freedom and Nature*, Ricoeur explains, "is to understand the mystery as reconciliation, that is, as restoration, even on the clearest level of consciousness, of the original concord of vague consciousness with its body and its world. In this sense the theory of the voluntary and involuntary not only describes and understands, but also restores" (FN 18). By clarifying the conflicting mystery of existence through the interpretive diagnostic of the voluntary and involuntary, phenomenology gathers together the diversity of involuntary necessity into the unifying discourse of "I can" in order to reestablish "an original concord" that seems absent in lived reality.

Beyond the possibility of restoration, Ricoeur's phenomenology of the voluntary and involuntary reveals the necessity for an ontological ground despite the fact that "there is no *system* of nature and freedom" (FN 19). The unification of the involuntary and voluntary, or of the passive and active dimensions of consciousness, points to a more fundamental "paradoxical ontology" which assumes that existence is somehow "covertly reconciled." For Ricoeur, "the juncture of being appears in a blind intuition reflected in paradoxes; it is never what I observe, but rather what serves as occasion for the articulation of the great contrasts of freedom and nature . . . [which] can be reconciled only in hope and in another age" (FN 19).

This poses an interesting problem. If hope for reconciliation is in fact a real possibility by virtue of the reciprocity or "original concord" of the voluntary and involuntary, then essentially the "great contrasts" are unified, but on the level of existence they oppose each other. This paradoxical unity of essential reciprocity gives existence its meaning. In other words, the link between essence and existence is understood as original meaning in relation to actual existence. The latter is ordered by the essential structures of the reciprocity of the voluntary and involuntary, although it is experienced as a mysterious conflict. Ordered through a "blind intuition" of paradoxical unity, existence is in a sense finished beforehand. "What we shall then become" is predicated on the preconceived idea of a "homogeneity" of a common subjectivity or selfhood that is formed behind the back of the existing subject. Accordingly, the mystery of existence is the failure to express such fundamental unity; therefore, Ricoeur waits in hope for the day when essence and existence will coalesce. If existence escapes complete description and has more depth than mere ethical refusal, then the essential "completeness" implied by the paradoxical ontology of eidetic reciprocity between the voluntary and the involuntary opens to a level of otherness that cannot be enclosed within a descriptive or ontological circle. To conclude that Ricoeur is arguing for a metaphysical determination of the mystery of existence would trivialize the dramatic character of existence. If life is indeed a texture of plots, events, and characters, then it is unfinished and without closure.[5] No single phenomenological, ontological, or metaphysical determination can inscribe lived reality. We are in the middle of a life that has not been concluded. "The medium of human unity is duration, living motivation, the history of the union of soul and body . . . is a drama, that is, an internal action which takes time" (FN 136). For Ricoeur, existence is ultimately a constant production through reproduction, a project carried out *but always and only in relation to an intersubjective world that impinges on it and continually redefines existence.*

Ricoeur's preoccupation, in *Freedom and Nature*, with the fundamental reciprocal structures of the *cogito* reduces the vast variety and complexity of experience to one of two types: voluntary or involuntary. By offering a unifying discourse in order to heal the dualism of existence, Ricoeur's phenomenology becomes, to use a Derridean phrase, a *pharmakon*, having both medicinal and poisonous qualities. As a possible description of anthropological unity Ricoeur's phenomenology moves beyond Husserlian transcendental subjectivity by connecting in a more radical manner the notion of the *cogito* to affective otherness. However, by prescribing unity in doses of unmediated essentialist language, he holds the notions of subjectivity, selfhood, and identity captive by a methodology that determines them beforehand.[6] Ricoeur's *Freedom and Nature* is an

early attempt to break free from a self-constituting transcendental subjectivity by
including all levels of affectivity within the reciprocity of the voluntary and
involuntary, without sacrificing the notion of the *cogito*. However, the unmediated character of the phenomenological reduction produces a deep ambivalence with regard to the origin and unity of subjectivity or selfhood. It is only
through a hermeneutical reorientation of phenomenology that the question of
subjectivity can be transformed from one of an original essential unity constituting selfhood prior to existence into a question of selfhood that always remains
a task to be accomplished. Despite its ambivalent character, *Freedom and Nature*
initiates an important investigation into the problem of subjectivity. Even though
Ricoeur eventually abandons the phenomenological clarity of a unified subjectivity in favor of a hermeneutic of selfhood, in *Freedom and Nature* he develops
a conceptual pattern or model of the relationship between meaning and existence mediated by the imagination that persists in various forms throughout his
later publications.

Ricoeur situates the imagination between voluntary singularity and involuntary diversity, at the critical junction between an active voluntary center of
consciousness and the inherent passivity of consciousness that is open to involuntary affectivity. With reference to the specific structures of voluntary decision,
Ricoeur explains that his phenomenological description has led him "to seek
the crossroads of need and willing in imagination—imagination of the missing
thing and of action aimed towards the thing" (FN 95). By mediating between
involuntary need and an appropriate satisfying action, the imagination straddles
two fields of discourse: cognitive and practical.

On a cognitive level, the imagination performs a quasi-hylemorphic function by transforming affective sensual "matter" into an appropriate conceptual
"form" to be considered by the will as a possible motive for a decision.[7] Imagination changes affective matter or felt need into an *image* suitable for the
cognitive process of deliberation. The raw affective need or the "blind" and
undefined intentional lack pressing on voluntary consciousness is given by the
imagination the specific form of an appropriate object for satisfying a need. In
other words, the imagination presents a representation of the affective involuntary diversity of needs by producing corresponding images with a level of cognitive clarity and definition that is otherwise absent from raw need.

This mediating function of imagination, if we follow Ricoeur's example
of hunger, is primarily perceptual or visional in character.[8] The initial involuntary impulse to satisfy hunger is only given specific form, or made concrete in
relation to the perception of an appropriate object such as bread. The sight of
bread gives an immediate corresponding form to the affective matter of involuntary hunger. In the absence of such immediate presence, however, the imagination functions by passively receiving and transforming sensual matter into a
conceptual image to be utilized by the will for the deliberation of an appropri-

ate course of action that would result in satisfying the need for food. The initial perception of bread gives imagination the image with which it can create and re-create a motive for willful action. This, Ricoeur explains, is not only true of hunger, but all forms of involuntary affective need since they, too, can be re-created and represented in motive form for cognitive deliberation. Although imagination "is the heir of the perceived," the creation and re-creation of represented images frees objects from their actual presence and reduces them to motives for action. Therefore, the cognitive quality of imaginative representation is not to be confused with a mental presence of something absent because it is the creation of an absence that is made present only through action. Ricoeur states that "if imagination can play such a role, it is because, contrary to common psychological opinion, it itself is an intentional design projected into *absence*, a product of consciousness within actual nothing and not a mental *presence*. Intentional as perception, it can, like perception, play such a role as it completes the virtual intentionality of need: absence gives a vivid, non-actual form to lack" (FN 97).

Such motivational image construction brings about a *clarification* of the opaque intentionality of involuntary affectivity through a "quasi-representation" or "quasi-observation of the object . . . [that] is the light of need just as the actual presence of the object would be" (FN 52). It also reveals the necessity of a decisive projection and action, by voluntary consciousness, into this illuminating "absence" in order to bring about need's satisfaction. Image construction not only provides motives for cognitive deliberation, but also is tied to the practical acquisition of goods that will satisfy the vast diversity of involuntary need. Utilizing the imagination's ability to open a meaningful, or cognitively clear space or "absence" within consciousness, Ricoeur expands the meaning of imaginative consciousness to include an anticipatory structure that fundamentally reorients his description of voluntary consciousness. For him

> imagination is also, and perhaps primarily, a militant power in the service of a diffuse sense of the future by which we anticipate the actual-to-be, as an absent actual at the basis of the world. As such it can mediate need and willing, each in its way directed towards the future of the world: the latter in order to open up new possibilities within it, the former in order to await there the fruit of achievement and encounter. Both carry us ahead of ourselves into a world which is at the same time indeterminate and full of promises and threats. Imagination focuses the double anticipation of project and concern. . . . It is a lamp we point ahead to light up lack in terms of an entirely worldly absence.[9]

Imagination is always "*anticipating imagination*" (FN 105) which opens a space ahead of consciousness for appropriate action.

Imagination is seated at a vertical and horizontal, or cognitive and prac-tical, crossroad.[10] On a cognitive level, imagination mediates in service of an interior hierarchy of needs and motives that forms the basis of a projected course of action. However, on the practical level of temporal fulfillment of a projected course of action, the imagination mediates between absence and presence of actual fulfillment. Imagination calls for deliberation to come to a close in a choice that moves from interior to exterior and "constitutes me as existence" (FN 167).

The consequences of such a view of anticipatory imagination are significant for understanding subjectivity and selfhood. Deliberation culminates with pro-jection into a future by a specific choice coupled with action that seals the compact of meaning and existence. Through choice the projected and provi-sional or potential self is transformed into an actual existing self who must take responsibility for his or her insertion into the intersubjective world of others. Ricoeur explains that the formation by means of deliberation of a project for action is a "projecting of the self ahead of itself " (FN 171). Choice brings all involuntary diversity under a single voluntary determination, making actual the potential self projected by the deliberative process. In voluntary choice "I choose *myself* in determining *what* I shall be in my doing." Ricoeur goes on to explain that

> the projected myself gives consistency to my self, to the self which is at present projecting. Before the choice, I was only the unity of a wish to choose and the unity of painful consciousness of my intimate division. I create myself as an actual living unity in my act: in that moment of choice I come to myself, I come out of the internal shadows, I irrupt as myself, I ek-sist. Finally, in the choice the constellation of motives itself is fixed in its definitive order . . . [but] we have to dare: freedom is always a risk.[11]

The transition from essence to existence, from potential to actual selfhood, takes place through the mediating work of imagination, which anticipates a possible self through the projection of an absence, an opening into which free choice takes a risk and makes selfhood actual.

Such phenomenological description, Ricoeur points out, seems to frag-ment the *cogito* into deliberative self, projected self, acting self, and so on. It is nevertheless predicated on the initial insight of the unified connection between the voluntary and involuntary, which in turn is rooted in the ontological affirmation that subjectivity is indeed essentially whole. Ricoeur therefore ex-plains that such "a primordial identification resists the temptation to exile my self into the margins of my acts: an identification of the projecting and the projected myself. I am the myself which now wills (and projects) just as I am he who will do (and is projected). 'This action is myself' means that there are no two selves, one projecting and one in the project; I affirm myself as the subject precisely in the object of my willing."[12] Selfhood is to be found in the oscillation of the projecting self and the projected self, or in the deliberative cognitive self and the practical acting self. Although the self "ek-sists" through choice that gives a "definitive order" to it, I am no less a self in the deliberative mode that considers what "order" is to give me definition. In fact, the self that is projected and chosen soon becomes part of the involuntary order of necessity, a historical self accountable for its past and in need of imaginative mediation with a new voluntary projection and choice of self.

The projecting self and the project that becomes myself is a historical process that oscillates between deliberation and choice. To choose my projected self is not to conclude the project, but to keep the project of selfhood alive. However, giving order and stability to subjectivity through choice brings about a sedimentation of self, a historical necessity that involuntarily limits future choice. To "ek-sist" is a spiral process that dramatically unfolds in time. It is not a matter of identifying the essence of self with one or the other. Subjectivity comprises both the projecting and the project, the voluntary and the involuntary. It is the dramatic process itself, continually oscillating between determination and indetermination, form and matter, singularity and diversity, which constitutes subjectivity. This is why Ricoeur continually reaffirms his commitment that "the medium of human unity is duration, living motivation," that "the history of the union of soul and body . . . is a drama, that is, an internal action which takes time" (FN 136). To "ek-sist" is to continually mediate via the productive work of the imagination. Phenomenological description reveals the general structure of the self at work; but it can only be identified as a particular self (me, you, him, her) through markers left behind by the historical process of self-determinative action in the intersubjective life-world.[13]

Freedom and Nature offers a description of the mediating work of the imagination that combines a hierarchical cognitive structure with a practical actualization of selfhood. The drama of existence is in essence a mediation performed by the imagination, which first reduces involuntary diversity to the singularity of voluntary form, and then opens the way for choice to give actual determination to imaginative absence. These two functions of the work of the imagination, although they give testimony to an essential model *of* human existence, testify to a prescriptive power for determining the success of actual mediation. Ricoeur's phenomenology of essential structures is not an innocent description, merely recording inherent potentialities within lived reality. Description of the reciprocal structures of involuntary diversity entails a determination not only of a unified self, but the determination of failed unity or fragmented subjectivity. Essentially, phenomenology describes the power of imagination, choice, and action to continually establish selfhood; but in order for Ricoeur's phenomenological diagnosis to have existential validity it must also be

able to account for the possibility of failure and fragmentation, since the historical drama of existence is one of conflict rather than unity (FN 20). Therefore,
Ricoeur's essential model *of* existence is also a model *for* existence.

2.3   Fault and Failure

In the introduction to *Freedom and Nature* Ricoeur discusses the
significance of anthropological failure under the heading "Abstraction of the
Fault" (FN 20–28). Despite the conflictual nature of existence in which we see
"the tendency of the 'I' to close a circle with itself" (FN 20), the fault as actually
experienced failure is not necessitated by the essential duality of the voluntary
and involuntary. Ricoeur writes:

> The fault is not an element of fundamental ontology homogeneous
> with other factors discovered by pure description, like motives,
> powers, conditions, and limits. It can be conceived only as an acci-
> dent, an interruption, a fall. It does not constitute a part of a system
> together with the fundamental possibilities contained in willing and
> the involuntary. There can be no genesis of the fault starting with
> the voluntary or the involuntary, even though each aspect of the
> circular system . . . constitutes an invitation to the fault. Rather, the
> fault remains an alien body in the essential structure of man. There
> is no principle of intelligibility of such disruption, analogous to the
> *mutual intelligibility* of involuntary and voluntary functions, in the
> sense that their essences complete each other within the human
> unity. The *fault is absurd*. (FN 24)

However, the fact remains that failure, fault, and evil are part of lived reality. While
the fault is "absurd," the possibility for its occurrence must be taken into account.
Since the invitation to failure is presented by "each aspect of the circular
system" of the voluntary and involuntary, it is not surprising to find Ricoeur
placing the imagination at center stage. Unity results from a successful forward
projection mediated by the imagination. But the imaginative "power of showing
the object whose appeal is nothing but the echo of our needs echoed by the
world" can be transformed into an abnormal "fascination with the image" (FN
98–99). The will can "enslave" itself to "the charm of the imagination . . . [and
its] magic power of absence" (FN 98). Although "there is no power within man
capable of enslaving him, all the involuntary is for freedom, and consciousness
can only be its own slave," the imagination is nevertheless a "privileged point
of entry of . . . the fault" (FN 98). Imaginative mediation, while not responsible
for failure, is a fragile and weak link that provides a possibility for the fault.
Hence Ricoeur explains that

the power of imagination to fascinate, to dupe, and to deceive . . . the very imagination which seals the compact of our freedom and our body is also the instrument of our bondage and the occasion for corruption. To the guilty consciousness imagination does not simply show thing and value, but fascinates it by their very absence or rather by the image of absence which thereafter functions as the snare of a false presence. There must be a lie already ingrained at the heart of consciousness. Here we stand at the source of a psychology of temptation: imagination tempts and seduces by the absence it represents and depicts. Through it need in turn not only demands, but also tempts and seduces. Starting with this seduction, imaginary pleasure can be uprooted from need and pursued for itself, endlessly refined in quantity, duration, intensity. (FN 102–103)

For Ricoeur, imagination performs a fundamental mediation between the voluntary and involuntary, and it also shares the burden with voluntary consciousness for the occasion and possibility of failure.

Such is the essential composition of the drama of existence. The voluntary will brings meaning and order to involuntary otherness and affectivity by continually moving from the projecting self to the projected self by means of decision, choice, and action. The dialectic of the voluntary and involuntary is a fragile mediation that presents the possibility for failure. The conflictual nature of existence is predicated on an inherent weakness in its essential structure which, while not necessitating fragmentation, provides the occasion for choices that result in the loss of freedom.

Failure is not the simple transgression of a deontological code; beyond moral failure lies a fault at the core of the mediating process of living which results in a conflict that either moves to inscribe all of reality within an originating self-sufficient *cogito*, or to completely subject the *cogito* to the lure of affectivity and thereby lose all voluntary initiative. For Ricoeur, living well is a single process that combines a receptive proximity or openness with an active distance from affective otherness. To live is to engage in a mediation between the voluntary and involuntary aspects of existence, but to live well is to do so successfully by producing a unified self through the mediating power of the imagination. Essential subjectivity always remains a task to be accomplished. Anthropological unity is a momentary product and work of the cycle of motivation, decision, choice, and action. To be a subject, a self, is the repetition of "ek-sist"ence, a distention of subjectivity toward the future through the reception of the past. Time stretches the momentary self into an episodic, dramatic self. The unity of this "internal action" and drama "which takes time" Ricoeur explores only later, through a hermeneutical transformation of the work of imagination from a projection of internal absence to that of the intersubjective world of the text and the narrative enterprise. *Freedom and Nature* only offers an essential unity of existence that ultimately concludes in compound descriptions of paradox. "Choice," Ricoeur states,

> appear[s] to us as a paradox, a paradox of initiative and receptivity, or irruption and attention. In some respects it is an *absolute*, absolute irruption, in other respects it is *relative*: relative to motives in general and through them to values in general, relative to bodily motives in particular and through them to values of organic life. The grandeur and misery of human freedom . . . [are] joined in a kind of dependent independence. (FN 483)

Only with *Fallible Man* (1967), where the question of anthropological unity is set within the grand dialectic of finitude and infinitude, will this paradoxical unity be replaced by an emphasis on the fundamental disproportion of selfhood as a primordial act of freedom over and above the indeterminate obstinacy of the involuntary. While the intention of *Freedom and Nature* is to exhibit the mutuality of the voluntary and involuntary, *Fallible Man* seeks to affirm a "primordial self beyond its acts" (FM xlviii) that can only be accounted for by means of a philosophical reflection that begins with disproportion rather than mutuality.

2.4   Fallible Man

In *Fallible Man* the concern for mutual reciprocity of the voluntary and involuntary is no longer treated in isolation from the question of human fallibility. Ricoeur removes the phenomenological brackets placed around the "fault" in *Freedom and Nature*, and expands his investigation of the structure of subjectivity in order to develop a philosophical anthropology that can take into account human existence in its "totality." Human existence is still considered as a mediation of dialectically intertwined opposites, but Ricoeur now removes the phenomenological constraints and opens his investigation to a dialectic of sweeping *dis*proportions. Ricoeur explains that

> the theory of fallibility represents a broadening of the anthropological perspective of the first work, which was more closely centered on the structure of the will. The elaboration of the concept of fallibility has provided an opportunity for a much more extensive study of the structures of the human reality. The duality of the voluntary and involuntary is brought back into a much vaster dialectic dominated by the ideas of man's disproportion, the polarity within him of the finite and the infinite, and his activity of interme-

diation or mediation. Man's specific weakness and his essential fallibility are ultimately sought within this structure of mediation between the pole of his finitude and the pole of his infinitude. (FM xliv)

The removal of the phenomenological brackets, and the consideration of the fault as part of the essential structure of human reality, is not simply a grand redescription of mutual reciprocity. Rather than beginning with a description of the essential unity of voluntary and involuntary structures of the *cogito*, Ricoeur employs a transcendental reflective method that is initiated on three levels of disproportion in order to reveal human existence as a necessary "third term," a work of mediation par excellence that is ultimately constituted in relation to others.

Like *Freedom and Nature*, *Fallible Man* is ambivalent with regard to the status of the subject. It remains unclear whether Ricoeur wishes to uncover "a notion of being which is *act* rather than *form*, living affirmation, the power of existing and making exist," that is, a self which is a task opened in front of consciousness, or whether he wants to establish a primordial link through the notion of selfhood to that which would serve as a metaphysical ground of human reality.[14] While Ricoeur has already disavowed the radicality of a Husserlian ego in control of the constitution of reality, and calls for an understanding of selfhood that is linked with the other, he nevertheless seems to inscribe otherness within an identifying self-reference that reduces difference to an original affirmation of "Joy" where "I am it, you are it, because we are what it is" (FM 137). Through the participation in the infinite quest for self-affirmation, the individuality of self and others, or the other-than-self, seems to disappear. By identifying "Being" with the affirmation of selfhood, in which "I am it and I participate in it" (FM 137), and in which all humanity participates, does Ricoeur close the door to the voice of the other? Is not Ricoeur's recourse to the transcendental third term an attempt to find a universal commonality that overcomes difference through a higher unity by enlarging the circle until all difference disappears? While this appears to be a valid conclusion, Ricoeur argues that this is but one side of a dialectical coin:

> thus we speak of "several" consciousnesses, this is not to be taken as a simple arithmetic plurality; the otherness of consciousnesses is relative to a primordial identity and unity that makes possible the understanding of language, the communication of culture, and the communion of persons. Thereby another is not only an other, but my like. Conversely, this fundamental unity of *logos* is relative to the difference of *legein*. This difference signifies that the unity of humanity is realized nowhere else than in the movement of communication. Thus, difference is not absolute, as if the multiplicity of

consciousnesses were purely numerical and their coexistence merely
contingent, nor is the unity of the being of man absolute.... Man
is this plural and collective unity of destination and the difference
of destinies are to be understood through each other. (FM 138)

Ricoeur's vision of selfhood is one that must be able to affirm both the self and
other than self. It remains to be seen whether Ricoeur can maintain such
dialectical mutuality when the connection between the self and the other-than-
self is made through the transcendental synthesis of a passive receptivity to
otherness and a rationality that transcends otherness by naming it.

Unlike *Oneself as Another*, where Ricoeur asserts that his hermeneutic of
selfhood has "superseded" the "philosophies of the subject" (OA 4), *Fallible
Man* develops an idea of the subject as a necessary "third term" or synthetic
unity through the application of a form of transcendental reflection characterized by epistemological "trans-parency" (FM 144). Ricoeur's elaboration in
Oneself as Another of a hermeneutic of selfhood that calls for analogous self-
identification without metaphysically grounding the *cogito* as first principle,
seems to be at odds with the clarity of the concept of human fallibility that
Fallible Man transcendentally reveals. Despite a fundamental difference of
approach between this early publication and Ricoeur's latest work, there remain
some remarkable similarities that are important for our investigation of identity.
For the first time, Ricoeur makes a connection in *Fallible Man* among language, imagination, and selfhood that opens a door for the transformation and
reorientation of the entire question of selfhood as found in *Oneself as Another*.
Through a careful examination of *Fallible Man* the essential features for map-
ping the lines of continuity and discontinuity between transcendental subjectivity and the hermeneutics of selfhood will be exposed.

In *Fallible Man* Ricoeur seeks to clarify existence through a consciousness of fault and evil. The purpose of such reflection is not theological. Rather,
Ricoeur's goal is to follow a chain of connections between the consciousness of
fault and a primordial affirmation of a self that is more than the sum total of
individual acts. For Ricoeur, although "we have no access to this self outside
of its specific acts, ... the consciousness of fault makes manifest in them and
beyond them the demand for wholeness that constitutes us. In this way, this
consciousness is a recourse to the primordial self beyond its acts" (FM xlviii).
In other words, Ricoeur seeks to affirm the presence of the "self" beyond the
enumeration of individual acts that is prior to an ethic of good and evil. Such
self-presence must account for the diversity of individual acts without necessitating the occurrence of evil, and also provide the opportunity or possibility for
evil to occur. Primordial selfhood is for Ricoeur a universal "keyboard," or
philosophical anthropological structure, which is revealed as a primal unity on
which all human acts can be predicated. "Man's humanity is that discrepancy

in levels, that initial polarity, that divergence of affective tension between the extremities of which is placed the [fragile] 'heart' " (FM 92), which can account for the totality of human existence without relinquishing a primary affirmation of innocent fragility. By proposing the concept of "fallible man," Ricoeur is on a mythical quest to show that "however primordial badness may be, goodness is yet more primordial" (FM 145).

What is remarkable about Ricoeur's approach to the human question in *Fallible Man* is the claim of transcendental reflection to reach beyond individual acts and uncover an anthropological structure that makes these acts possible in their very diversity. The fact that Ricoeur gives a mythic qualification to this diversity does little to hinder the ability of transcendental reflection to access the primordial. Even though existence is "fallen" and "man 'finds himself subject' to err" (FM 1), the testimony of this state of "weakness" or the "rhetoric of misery" does not shroud primordial selfhood in darkness. If lived misery can be expressed with the passionate force of mythical language, transcendental reflection can bring the hidden depth of the primordial soul into the light of a philosophical anthropology. "If that pathos was already mythos, that is, speech, it must be possible to reconstruct it in the dimension of philosophical discourse" (FM 83). Rather than encumbering reflection, the consciousness of fallen existence provides transcendental analysis with the best means of discovering the primordial unity of selfhood, because

> we have access to the primordial only through what is fallen. In return, if the fallen denotes nothing about that *from which* it has fallen, no philosophy of the primordial is possible, and we cannot even say that man is fallen. For the very idea of downfall involves reference to the loss of a certain innocence that we understand sufficiently to name it and to designate the present condition as a lapse, a loss or a fall. I cannot understand treason as evil without judging it by an idea of trust and loyalty in relation to which it is evil. (FM 76)

Transcendental reflection can move beyond the fault lines of human reality by uncovering a unifying "third term" that provides the possibility for a mediation of disparate extremes that is truly human. Ricoeur begins his investigation of human fallibility on a transcendental level in order to provide a formal philosophical model that is connected to the primordial from the very outset and can be utilized for further investigations of the practical and affective levels of disproportion. Ricoeur is convinced that transcendental reflection "is merely the 'natural light' in which something can appear and sustain determination. In short, transcendental reflection is on the primordial level at the very outset. It does not have to reach it through a depraved condition. That is why

it has been able to serve as a guide for the exploration of the 'practical' disproportion that is more primal than the ethical duality, and *to uncover a principle
of limitation that would not already be radical evil"* (FM 78–79). Transcendental reflection provides a model of the primordial that has application beyond
epistemic objectivity, to include practical consciousness, self-consciousness, and
a grounding ontological structure.

2.4.1 *The Transcendental Synthesis*

In order to initiate philosophical reflection on the nature of self-consciousness, Ricoeur begins with an investigation of the objectivity of the world.
Before individuated self-consciousness can be examined, a formal model of
consciousness must be developed to serve as a neutral and universal means for
making possible genuine philosophical inquiry into the disproportion that constitutes personal existence. In other words, although transcendental reflection
begins with the structure of consciousness, "it is not yet the unity of a person
in itself and for itself; it is not one person; it is no one. The 'I' of I think is
merely the form of a world for anyone and everyone. It is consciousness in
general, that is, a pure and simple project of the object" (FM 46). By focusing
on the objectivity or the synthetic unity of the object, Ricoeur seeks to transcendentally recover that which makes such objective unity possible in the first
place, thereby providing a philosophical avenue toward the very core of self-
consciousness via the consciousness of objectivity.

The consequences of Ricoeur's transcendental starting-point for the elaboration of a philosophical anthropology are such that reflection must begin with
the duality inherent in the constitution of the objectivity of objects. For "it is
one thing . . . to *receive* the presence of things, it is another to *determine* the
meaning of things. To receive is to give oneself intuitively to their existence; to
think is to dominate this presence in a discourse which discriminates by denomination and connects in articulate phrasing" (FM 19).

Transcendental reflection begins with a disproportionate duality. Reception of "the presence of things" is combined with a determining domination of
presence by language. While one is intuitively open to passively receive the
presence of things, it is only by means of language, specifically the noun and
verb, that things can be given universal designation. The formal model of
consciousness that transcendental reflection reveals is a duality of a passively
received immediate presence of particular objects, and a linguistic determination of finite presence through the universal infinitude of noun and verb. Transcendental consciousness is thus a duality of the finitude of passive reception
and the infinite quest for active determination of all reception.

Ricoeur explains that the finitude of reception is limited by the perspective of the viewer. Although consciousness is found in the reception of a world correlative with its determination, it is always received from a particular vantage point, from a "perspectival limitation of perception" (FM 20). The objects correlative with reception are never given to me completely; transcendental reflection must account for that which centers the flow of ever-changing perceptions (FM 21). Through a change in bodily position or a change in the manner in which an object is presented, transcendental reflection accounts for the unity of the object by means of a " 'here from where' the thing is seen" (FM 21). In contrast to the *otherness of the silhouettes*," Ricoeur "regressively" uncovers a pole of "absolute" placement that links the objectivity of objects to a unifying subjective center. "When I break up the identity of the object into the otherness of its silhouettes, and these into the otherness of the active and passive positions of the body, I ascribe the diversity of the operation to the identity of a subject pole: these diverse silhouettes appear *to me*, that is, to this unity and to this identity of the subject pole which is, as it were, behind the diversity of the flow of silhouettes, behind the flow of positions" (FM 22). On the level of transcendental consciousness the finitude of unifying perspective is correlative with the otherness of indeterminate presentation. Despite Ricoeur's insistence that "our primary relation to the world . . . is to receive objects and not create them" (FM 24), the intuitive passivity characterized as the openness and reception of otherness is in "essence . . . inadequate, [and] to the essence of this inadequacy to refer back to the onesided character of perception, and to the essence of the one-sidedness of the thing's profiles to refer back to the otherness of the body's initial positions *from where* the thing appears . . . [its] zero origin. To perceive *from here* is the finitude of perceiving *something*. The point of view is the ineluctable initial narrowness of my openness to the world" (FM 23).

Ricoeur's characterization of the finitude of receptive openness as a unifying subject passively linked to the vast diversity of inadequate perceptual otherness is only one part of transcendental consciousness. The finitude of perception and absolute placement that gives perception its "zero origin," and "the original 'here' " from where the world is perceived, must be open to a

> "view-on" finitude, a dominating look which has already begun to transgress the finitude. . . . In order for human finitude to be seen and expressed, a moment that surpasses it must be inherent in the situation, or state of being finite. This means that every description of finitude is abstract, i.e., separated and incomplete, if it neglects to account for the transgression that makes discourse on finitude possible. The complete discourse on finitude is a discourse on the finitude and the infinitude of man. (FM 24–25)

Transcendental consciousness is found in the relation between passive reception and the act of transcending the finite perspective. If otherness and diversity
are to be named, an active determination must accompany the objectival silhouettes of the thing's appearance. The inadequacy of reception is linked with
another movement or intentional "aim" of fulfillment "which penetrates it
through and through, which literally passes right through it, and to which
speech is originally linked" (FM 27). For Ricoeur, the limiting finitude of
reception can be transcended through the act of meaningful signification that
unifies the diversity of appearance. Although things present themselves as incomplete relative to my perspective,

> I anticipate the [complete] thing itself by relating the side which I
> see to those which I do not see but which I *know*. Thus I judge the
> entire thing by going beyond its given sides into the thing itself.
> This transgression is the intention to signify. Through it I bring
> myself before a sense which will never be perceived anywhere by
> anyone, which is not a superior point of view, which is not in fact
> a point of view at all but an inversion into the universal of all point
> of view. (FM 26)

Transcendental consciousness is the "absolutely primal" combination of not
just "saying and seeing" (FM 27), but the determination of the meaning of
perceptual otherness through a linguistic act of denomination. The limitation
and inadequacy of perception is transcended or *overcome*, Ricoeur contends,
through the act of saying.

This duality of limitation and fulfillment provides Ricoeur with the opportunity to develop his trademark conception of the "surplus of meaning." By
placing the dialectic of saying and seeing within that of finitude and infinitude,
saying not only presents more than can be perceived, but refers to a "power of
affirmation" (FM 35) that reaches beyond mere verbalization. "What is said,
the *lekton* of my *legein*, the *dictum* of every *dictio*, transcends, as an ideal
meaning-unity, the simple experience of the statement" (FM 28). By "say[ing]
more than I see when I signify," language reaches for the universal point of view
that gives perceptual fragmentation a cohesive "self-identity" (FM 28). Saying
determines the identity of otherness through an act of denomination. However,
since the act of designation aims at an ideal linguistic meaning-unity, the narrowness of my own act of naming is transcended through the intersubjective
universality that language possesses. "We need the 'name,'" explains Ricoeur,
"to give a ground to the meaning-unity, the non-perspectival unity of the thing,
the one which is announced to and understood by another and which he will
verify in his turn and from his position in a sequence of converging perceptions" (FM 29). The activity of naming escapes and exceeds the limitation of
individuated perspective. It opens my narrow receptiveness to a surplus of

meaning by "convert[ing] my 'here' from an absolute placement into an any-place-whatever, which is relative to all the others, in a geometrical and social space in which there is no privileged emplacement" (FM 31). The transcending aim of language thus makes a fundamental connection between speech and the otherness of perceptual presence. Otherness is overcome through the intersubjective universality of language.

Ricoeur characterizes linguistic transcendence as a dominating denomination "*over* perception" and as "speaking *over* perspective" (FM 31 emphasis mine). The dialectic of seeing and saying is weighted in favor of the linguistic determination over the inadequate presentation of perceptual otherness. Contrary to the reciprocal nature of Ricoeur's description of consciousness in *Freedom and Nature*, transcendental consciousness is a disproportionate mode of consciousness.

Ricoeur intensifies the disproportionate nature of transcendental consciousness through a further elaboration of the infinite nature of speech. The infinitude of language is not only a relation of the universality of a name that accompanies the perceptual diversity of objects. The transcending "truth intention" of the noun is transcended from within speech itself by a "power of affirmation" linked to the verb. Following Aristotle, Ricoeur explains that "the verb . . . is a noun-meaning shot through with an added meaning . . . and even by a twofold supra-signification" (FM 32). The verb has the ability to transcend its own primary function of designating the thing as a subject, through a second or higher function that provides the possibility for the "affirmation and negation" of the thing's being. Inherent in the sentence is a possibility "to affirm and deny the presence of what is absent and to affirm and deny the presence of what is present" (FM 34). Thus the infinite moment of speech anticipates a deeper voluntary level of consciousness that can not only transcend the receptive passivity of finite perspective, but also designate more than is possible through naming. Corresponding to the transcending movement of the verb over the noun is the subjective ability of volition to make an infinite variety of assertions that transcend what is involuntarily received as presence. Ricoeur explains that "we may say that the supra-signification of the verb is the correlative noema of the noesis which we now see to be constituted by the volitional moment of affirmation" (FM 35).

The transcendental model of consciousness, even though it is an objective form of universal consciousness, is nevertheless linked to the anthropological substrate of the power of the will. Ricoeur's reference to active naming and passive reception repeats on a transcendental level what has already been described on the phenomenological level. In *Freedom and Nature* volition defines the essence of consciousness. However, with the addition of the dialectic of the *finitude* of reception and the *infinitude* of determination in *Fallible Man*, consciousness is no longer characterized by the mutuality of the voluntary and

involuntary. By indicating that it is one thing to receive and another to determine the meaning and affirm or deny the being of objects, transcendental
consciousness reconfigures the phenomenological relation of mutuality as developed in *Freedom and Nature*, into one characterized by a disproportion of
two opposing aims: a transcending aim that dominates reception through "the
verb that gives expression to being and the truth, at the risk of falling into error,"
and its counteraim of "the passive look riveted to appearance and perspective"
(FM 37), which is overcome by the former linguistic aim.

Since this fracture is discovered through the act of intentional reflection
on the *objectivity* of objects, that is, on "the indivisible unity of an appearance
and an ability to express" the unity (FM 37), the noetic correlate of transcendental consciousness must also be synthetic in nature: a disproportionate *unity*
of reception and determination. Just as the objectivity of the object is a composition of two elements, so too the consciousness of objectivity is a blend of
the finitude of reception and the infinitude of the "power of affirmation." Ricoeur
refers to the intentional correlate of objectivity as the necessary third term that
"makes this synthesis *on* the thing possible . . . by projecting in advance the
objectivity of the object, i.e., the mode of being proper to it and in virtue of
which it can appear and be expressed" (FM 39). In reference to Kant, Ricoeur
proposes that it is the transcendental imagination, and by way of analogy the
empirical imagination, which provides the "medium" for the "mixture" of the
objective synthesis.

The link Ricoeur establishes between the transcendental imagination as
medium and the mixture of the objectivity of objects attempts to capture the
unique character of transcendental consciousness. In the production of the
objectivity of objects, the imagination "does not exist *for itself*: it completely
exhausts itself in the act of constituting objectivity; for itself the imaginative
synthesis is *obscure*" (FM 41). The imagination is thus the medium of consciousness, a medium, Ricoeur notes, that can be compared to light as the
means by which something is illuminated, not the object of illumination: "we
do not see the light but in the light" (FM 40). The imagination as the intentional counterpart of the objectivity of objects is likened to the medium that
produces the mixture of the "space of expressibility" and the "point of view"
without revealing its mysterious ability to mix such pure intelligibility with the
shifting silhouettes of sensation. The imagination always "remains an enigma,"
and yet a transcendental necessity to account for the unity of the fundamental
disproportion of the objectivity of objects.

Transcendental consciousness can therefore be further characterized as a
disproportionate domination of seeing by saying mediated through the work of
the imagination, which is only discovered through reflection on the objective
unity of objects. Transcendental reflection makes a connection between the
objective dialectic of language and perception and the hidden depth of the

subjective source of objectivity. Language, perception, and imagination constitute a formal model of consciousness that is able to reach beyond the opacity
of fallen existence, to uncover the even more hidden mediated disproportion,
that is, human existence. Ricoeur's analysis of transcendental consciousness
provides a *linguistic avenue* which, when followed, opens universal consciousness to self-consciousness and the lived reality of affective consciousness. Through
a hermeneutic focusing on the objectivity of linguistic objects, reflection can
pass from the objective explanations of syntax to an understanding of the mediating process of human existence that the creative imagination reveals through
its linguistic determinations of experience.

2.4.2 *From Transcendental Consciousness to Self-Constitution*

The goal of *Fallible Man* is to uncover a universal anthropological "keyboard" on which all human action can be predicated. Transcendental consciousness, while providing a means for examining the human condition, is not
yet self-consciousness, that is, "the unity of a person in itself and for itself; it is
not one person; it is no one. The 'I' of I think is merely the form of a world
for anyone and everyone. It is consciousness in general, that is, a pure and
simple project of the object" (FM 45–46). Transcendental consciousness simply
provides an epistemological or theoretical model for uncovering further mediations of human existence with greater philosophical rigor. In order for the
model of consciousness to be complete Ricoeur progressively deepens his
reflection to include not only the practical task of *self-consciousness*, but also the
response of human feeling generated through participation in the *actual* work
of *self-constitution*. Ricoeur's goal is to capture the very act of being human
simultaneously on all three levels of disproportion by means of the initial model
of transcendental consciousness.[15]

In order to duplicate on a practical level the pattern established in epistemological consciousness, Ricoeur explains that the "notions of perspective,
meaning, and synthesis . . . will be the melodic germ of all the subsequent
developments" (FM 49). The transition from abstract universal consciousness to
reflection on "human reality will appear to us as a progressively richer and more
complete dialectic between more and more concrete poles and in mediations
that become progressively closer to life" (FM 49). Therefore, Ricoeur repeats
the initial model of reflection by superimposing it on the concrete practical
elements of the task of being human.

> All the aspects of "practical" finitude that can be understood on the
> basis of the transcendental notion of perspective may be summed up
> in the notion of character. All the aspects of "practical" infinitude

> *that can be understood on the basis of the transcendental notion of*
> *meaning may be summed up in the notion of happiness. The "prac-*
> *tical" mediation that extends the mediation of the transcendental*
> *imagination, projected into the object, is the constitution of the per-*
> *son by means of "respect." This new analysis aims at showing the*
> *fragility of this practical mediation of respect, for which the person is*
> *the correlate.*[16]

Although Ricoeur maintains a similarity between the structure of theoretical and practical consciousness, the advent of self-consciousness brings about a
dynamic progression of the initial "melodic germ." While transcendental consciousness provides an entree to the fundamental questions of human existence,
it remains a static model of consciousness focused on the objectivity of objects;
self-consciousness opens the universality of linguistic meaning to the linearity
of "events" that mark one's participation in the project of humanity. Self-
consciousness is therefore a "consciousness of direction" mobilized by the representation "of an ideal of what the person should be. The Self is aimed at
rather than experienced. Indeed, the person is not yet consciousness of Self for
Self; it is consciousness of self only in the representation of the ideal of the
Self. There is no experience of the person in itself and for itself" (FM 69). Self-
consciousness is a form of consciousness directed outside itself, focused on
some imaginative representation or ideal project of what selfhood should be
like. The progression from transcendental to practical consciousness combines
both forms of consciousness into a single process. The project of humanity calls
for an objective representation to serve as a guide for reflective analysis on the
practical mediation of human existence.

Since the combination of practical and transcendental consciousness is
rooted in the objective representation of a task, both the image and the task
share a common composition: the unity of a reception and transgression brought
about by a third term. For Ricoeur, "what we must first establish is that the
person is primarily a project which I represent to myself, which I set before me
and entertain, and that this project of the person is, like the thing but in an
entirely irreducible way, a 'synthesis' which is effected" (FM 69–70). This project
combines an infinite aim with its finite realization into a synthetic representation that serves as a means to reveal substantially more than was possible through
the third term of transcendental consciousness. Practical consciousness uncovers the "heart" or "feeling" that generates the project of humanity which Ricoeur
defines as the reciprocal quest to find one's own self through the representation
of another as "an end in itself, that is, one whose value is not subordinated to
anything else" (FM 71).

This new object of practical consciousness is also a composite of two
divergent poles: reception and transgression. Here, reception and transgression

are concerned with the project of human freedom rather than with the universal constitution of the objectivity of objects. The practical synthesis is one where "I posit actions only by letting myself be influenced by motives"—in other words: "I *constitute* my actions to the extent that I *gather in* reasons for them" (FM 52). Reflective analysis on the practical synthesis of consciousness shifts away from the linguistic determination of perceptual reception to the active determination of the passive reception of motives that incline without necessitating the active fulfillment of the project of humanity. The object of practical consciousness is a representation of a dynamic infinite activity bound up with the finite passivity of inclination, passion, and desire.

The passivity of inclination and desire, like the perceptual reception of transcendental consciousness, is the recognition that practical consciousness is first and foremost open to the world. Recapitulating his analysis of the motivated project in *Freedom and Nature*, Ricoeur explains that the finite passivity of desire "is an experienced lack of . . . , an impulse oriented toward . . . In desire I am outside myself: I am with the desirable in the world. In short, in desire I am open to all the affective tones of things that attract or repel me. It is this attraction, grasped on the thing itself, over there, elsewhere, or nowhere, which makes desire an openness onto . . . and not a presence to the self closed on itself" (FM 53). Practical consciousness is thus a consciousness of being affected by and open to a world qualified by its ability to motivate without necessitating the human project.

Being open to this practical world of images, which gives clarity to an otherwise undifferentiated opacity of desire, reveals a point of closure. Openness to the world takes place from a particular existential vantage point. To be affected by the world is to feel oneself oriented toward the world by means of "the body's dumb and inexpressible presence to itself" (FM 55). The finitude of practical consciousness consists in "the 'here' of my body," the place where openness has its point of orientation and closure to the otherness of the world. The fundamental difference between transcendental consciousness and practical consciousness consists in finding oneself *affected* by a *field of motivation* that generates bodily feeling that belongs to a specific individual: oneself. Practical consciousness passes from universality to individuality. Here, Ricoeur locates "the primal difference between the I and all others" (FM 55). He explains that "to find oneself in a certain mood is to feel one's individuality as inexpressible and incommunicable. Just as one's position cannot be shared with another, so also the affective situation in which I find myself and feel myself cannot be exchanged" (FM 55). Therefore, while infected with the "melodic germ" of perspectival limitation and "zero origin" of transcendental consciousness, Ricoeur's analysis of practical consciousness reveals the dialectical pole of finitude as the "primal" origin of "self-attachment" (FM 55) that results in the differentiation of self from others.

The consciousness of individuality is not a reference to some sort of physical substrate; rather it refers to what Ricoeur calls "character," which is only given through "the adumbrations of an expression" correlative with the project of humanity (FM 60). Character is not a "thing," but the individualization of the totality of humanity. "It is in this sense that 'each' man is 'man' " (FM 61). Individual acts and feelings designate my participation in the project of humanity; "my character is that humanity seen from somewhere, the whole city seen from a certain angle, the partial totality" (FM 61). While practical consciousness marks the advent of the consciousness of individuality, the primal origin of self-differentiation is connected to my participation in the project of humanity. To understand oneself or one's character can only be done in relation to the openness of the infinite aim of humanity; for Ricoeur, this is a *relation of analogy*. "I read my character and designate it only through allusion, in the feeling of otherness that makes me different from all others; or rather, different from those like me, for another is a like man but a different character" (FM 61). Consciousness of individuality calls for an analogous transference from "my place" to "every place." To understand oneself as the "narrowness of the 'whole soul,'" whose humanity is openness" (FM 61), requires that I put myself in the place of another, that I share in not his or her point of orientation, but the universal aim "for whose sake everything else is done" (FM 64). To be conscious of myself requires that I transgress or transcend my point of orientation by means of the "total aim of all facets of transgression" (FM 64). Individual action is not simply the fulfillment of desire, but a choice that fulfills the aim of all desire.

Consciousness of individuality takes place through a teleological determination that functions as "the horizon from every point of view" (FM 65). To be open to the project of humanity links the passivity of desire to "a totality of meaning and contentment," which Ricoeur calls "happiness" (FM 65). All individual actions are set over against an infinite aim for happiness, which serves as a "termination of destiny" common to every action. Just as the transcendental quest for rational totality of meaning determines the finitude of perceptual reception, the universal quest for happiness determines the purpose of the finite fulfillment of all desire. "The idea of a complete volition and the destination of reason hollow an infinite depth in my desire, making it the desire for happiness and not merely the desire for pleasure" (FM 67). The infinite quest for happiness orients desire toward a goal that transcends the limiting boundaries of individual character and perspective that differentiate my individuality from that of others. Happiness gives more than the immediate satisfaction of fulfilled desire. Desire is finite, but happiness sets consciousness on route toward the infinite, toward an "order in which we already are" (FM 66). Although "no act gives happiness . . . the encounters of our life that are most worthy of being called 'events' indicate the direction of happiness . . . .The events that bespeak happiness are those which remove obstacles and uncover a vast landscape of existence. The excess of meaning, the overflow, the immense: that is the sign that we are 'directed toward' happiness" (FM 68). Practical consciousness combines the infinite universality of the surplus of meaning with a universal goal for all human action. Meaning and happiness are "coeval" (FM 69), counterparts connected to the closure of individual self-differentiation.

Ricoeur takes the juxtaposition and disproportion of happiness and character as indicative of the task of self-consciousness. To know oneself requires a representational image of one's own individuality analogously linked to the goal of humanity as a whole. Such a synthesis must be an "end in itself . . . whose value is not subordinate to anything else" (FM 71). This image of humanity must subordinate all individual values and means of affecting its realization. The "project of the person . . . to which all the means and calculations of means are subordinate" (FM 71) combines the abstract idea of a person as an end in itself with the concrete individuality revealed by self-differentiation. Ricoeur develops an image of the person as both infinite goal and finite "existence that one apprehends, or, to be more precise, a presence with which one enters into relation of mutual understanding, exchange, work, sociality" (FM 71). The project of the person, by subordinating the individuality of self and others to the infinite goal of humanity, determines finite existence with a form of reciprocity that overcomes differentiation and otherness. The idea of the person thus becomes a way of understanding oneself as another *through the synthetic unity* of a common goal and its individual realization.

To complete the model of practical consciousness, Ricoeur points out that "it should be possible to go back from this idea to the experience in which it is constituted" (FM 72). Again following Kant, Ricoeur explains that the condition of possibility for the synthesis of the person is found "in a specific moral feeling . . . called respect" (FM 72). Like transcendental imagination, the affective work of feeling is "an art concealed in the depths of the human soul" (FM 73) and exhausts itself in the act of synthesis. The feeling of respect is revelatory of the act of self-constitution in which "I am an obeying subject *and* a commanding sovereign" (FM 75). The feeling of respect opens practical consciousness to a "twofold mode of *belonging*" constitutive of the consciousness of my existence (FM 75). Thus the *practical* model for selfhood gives way to an examination of the *affective* model of selfhood, to the act in which the project of humanity is transformed from a representational image into the passion-filled quest that makes the aim toward happiness one's own lived reality.

2.4.3 *Self-Constitution*

If the feeling of respect accounts for the birth of mediated self-consciousness, then "feeling manifests what life aims at" (FM 91). The "heart" of the "twofold mode of belonging" is a center of affection where one's individuality is felt in distinction from others, simultaneously with feelings of community and sameness generated through participation in the human quest for happiness.[17] The affective heart is a synthesis of "*Eros* and *Bios*," feelings characterized by either their infinite aim or their finite orientation. Here, Ricoeur reveals the central duality of his philosophical anthropology. "Formless moods" or spiritual feelings of belonging are opposed but dialectically related to the immediate needs of finite "Care" (FM 104–105). Spiritual belonging manifests the transcending ability to participate in the project of humanity. Spirituality is indicative of our connection to the project of Reason, that is, to the totality of meaning opened by language, and therefore of that which sustains the effort of self-constituting existence. Affective consciousness is that moment in which the project of humanity taken up through finite action is *felt as belonging to* "the excess of meaning, the overflow, the immense," to a superabundance of being felt through "formless moods" particularized in feelings of "delight, joy, exultation, and serenity" (FM 105).

Affective consciousness is more than consciousness of the immediateness of care or the finitude of pleasurable feeling; it is a form of ontological consciousness where openness to the infinite quest for meaning and happiness is felt as "man's very openness to being" (FM 105). To belong to the totality of meaning and happiness of the project of humanity a transformation is needed of their objective representations into a fundamental feeling that assures us of their deep connection to the lived reality of actual self-constitution.

> This fundamental feeling, this Eros through which we are in being, is particularized in a diversity of feelings of belonging that are, as it were, the schematization of it. These feelings, called "spiritual," are no longer adaptable to any finite satisfaction; they make up the pole of infinitude of our whole affective life. This schematization develops in two directions, that of interhuman participation in the various forms of "We," and that of participation in tasks of supra-personal works that are "Ideas." (FM 103)

Through participation in this "excess" of the "We" and "Ideas," individuality is experienced as a dialectic of otherness and sameness. To be oneself is to mediate the closure of individuality and openness to an ontological universality, and overcome the limitation of perspective and character. The ideal of humanity as "an end in itself" is therefore transmuted from an imaginative task that I set before myself in an objective manner into a living reality of "being-with . . . being-for and . . . being-in" that reveals itself as "an order in which, alone, we can continue to exist" (FM 104). By opening individuality to "the Unconditioned that is demanded by reason and whose inwardness is manifested by feeling" (FM 106), affective consciousness shows my individuality as ontologically connected to others, to the project of humanity, and to the totality of reason aimed at through language. In other words, meaning and action are fundamentally connected in the moment of affective self-constitution; they are "not something alien but . . . rather a part of our very nature" (FM 103–104).

The ontological connection between feelings of openness toward being and feelings of the immediateness of finite care is at best tenuous. Self-constitution, like the transcendental imagination and the formal feeling of respect, aims at the infinite through finite means. Self-constitution internalizes an infinite goal but is only able to affect a finite realization that falls short of its demand for totality. The heart of this dual mode of belonging is felt as conflict, as a dynamic transition and fragile mediation between the demands of living and thinking. Belonging to and participating in the "excess" ("We" and "Ideas") instills a deep conflict between the demands of *eros* and *bios*. To be oneself is a process in which the call for selfhood outstrips the possibility for fulfillment. The constitution of self is a passionate quest filled with conflict to meet the demand of "an order in which, alone, we can continue to exist" (FM 104).

Self-constitution is a repetition of the process of aiming at full participation in the "excess" of the "We" and "Ideas" through the finite limitation of one's individuality. Selfhood is a mediation in which the goal of living must culminate in participation in an ontological order that not only affirms my individuality but that of others as well. For Ricoeur, the affirmation of self is dependent on the affirmation of others. Spirituality does not end in solipsism; it is open to the immense and "surplus" in which all others participate. For how could the spiritual feelings of belonging be indicative of one's own participation in the goal of humanity and totality of meaning, and not that of others? So the quest for self-constitution is in reality a quest of "reciprocal" affirmation "which no will to live can account for, it is the true passage from consciousness to self-consciousness. . . . My existence for myself is dependent on this constitution in another's opinion. My 'Self,' it may be said, is received from the opinion of others that establishes it. The constitution of subjects is thus a mutual constitution through opinion" (FM 121). Belonging to the totality of meaning and the happiness of humanity can only take place through a reciprocal relationship that ultimately affirms my own being at the same time as it affirms that of others.

But this quest for self-constitution places the self in a disproportionate relation over the other by means of a determinative model of consciousness; it is a triple quest or threefold passion of "having, power, and worth," which gives specific "interhuman, social, and cultural" configuration to the act of self-constitution. Since Ricoeur's transcendental model or "melodic germ" is on a primordial level from the outset, it is capable of "discover[ing] an authentic *Suchen* behind the triple *Sucht*, the 'quest' of humanity behind the passional 'pursuit,' the quest that is no longer mad and in bondage but constitutive of human praxis and the human Self" (FM 111). Continued reflection on the affective heart of self-constitution is not only in fundamental continuity with previous stages of transcendental reflection; it also reveals the primordial anthropological keyboard on which all human acts are predicated.

Unique to Ricoeur's analysis of affective consciousness is the employment of "imaginative variation," of the "economic, political, and cultural" objective configurations that the quest for self-constitution sets up between one's own Self and another Self. In order to "manifest the essence" of each of these configurations, one must "break the prestige of the fact" through "a kind of imagination of innocence or a 'kingdom' wherein the quests for having, power, and worth would be what they are in fact" (FM 112). The imaginative variation of the objective configurations of self-constitution provides the innocent vision necessary to recover the primordial heart.

Ricoeur begins his application of imaginative variation with the most rudimentary quest for self-affirmation. To distinguish one's own self from that of another is to make a distinction between "mine and yours" in which "the 'I' constitutes itself . . . by founding itself on a 'mine' " (FM 113). By transforming "simple need" into desire for an economic object "available" to and over against me, "it creates the whole cycle of feelings relative to acquisition, appropriation, possession, and preservation" (FM 114) of that object. The innocent quest for having is an essential "fact" that results from the imaginative variation of "passions of having—greed, avarice, envy, etc." (FM 113). Utilizing language similar to the linguistic determination over perspectival receptiveness, Ricoeur characterizes this initial differentiation of the self from the other than self as an experience of

> both my control over the having of which I can avail myself and my dependence with regard to that which is other than myself and on which I make myself dependent; I avail myself of it insofar as I am dependent on it; and I am dependent on it as a thing that can escape from me, degenerate, be lost, or be taken away: the possibility of no-longer-having is inherent in the tendency to avail oneself of. . . . The otherness of the mine, which is the breach between the I and the mine, is made up of the threat of losing what I have that is mine as long as I hold on to it. Possession is thus the ensemble of forces that hold out against loss. (FM 114)

Innocent having results from a control over that which I seek to receive through possession. Although the otherness of the economic object delineates the "I" from the mine, thus making self-constitution dependent on the other than self, Ricoeur expresses this relationship in terms of passive reception and active control by which I make myself dependent. While the objective economic dimension is essential to self-constitution where "I cannot imagine the I without the mine, or man without having" (FM 115), having is in continuity with the transcendental model of determinative consciousness that is characterized by domination and control rather than mutuality.

The self is further constituted through a second quest for affirmation. The relations of having are tied to "relations of power" that exhibit even more keenly self-constitution as a domination over the other. The acquisition of goods through labor is a natural extension of the quest for having. Such "work calls into play the power relations of man over man within the context of the relations of force between man and nature. . . . Man's presence among things is a phenomenon of domination that makes man a force subjugating other forces" (FM 116). These relations of power become objectified in collective institutions that are "sanctioned by an authority that is ultimately political" (FM 117–118). Objective political institutions serve as the means to recover feelings of domination and control that are "a necessary 'differentiation' between men and [are] implied in the essence of the political sphere" (FM 118).

Although political power that "perverts itself into *Herrschsucht*" is unquestionably a form of self-affirmation through the control and domination of others, Ricoeur nevertheless construes the innocent quest for power as "intersubjective feelings that modulate indefinitely on the theme of commanding—obeying" (FM 118), and calls for a work of imagination to "conceive of an authority which would propose to educate the individual to freedom, which would be a power without violence; in short, I can imagine the difference between power and violence; the utopia of a Kingdom of God, a City of God, an empire of minds, or a kingdom of ends" (FM 120). Such imaginative variation looks for "pure feelings . . . at the root of the passions of power" that are in essence feelings rooted "in the command-obey relationship" (FM 120). The innocence of political self-affirmation seems to be devoid of any form of mutuality and, like the quest for having, displays a fundamental continuity with the model of transcendental consciousness.

It is only with the third quest that Ricoeur's understanding of self-constitution transcends the relationships of domination and control over the other in favor of dual mutual self-constitution. This is the quest for esteem. Ricoeur's entire explanatory tone changes once he has crossed the threshold from the *determination of otherness* into that region where "the self is constituted" via the "belief" of worthiness *received from the other*. Disowning the attempts for self-affirmation through the quests for having and power, Ricoeur relinquishes his model of control and looks to the fragile opinion of the other for the true affirmation of self.

> The quest for reciprocity, which no will to live can account for, is the true passage from consciousness to self-consciousness. Now this demand is not satisfied by the interhuman relations in the context of having, which are relations of mutual exclusion, nor by the

relations in the context of power, which are asymmetrical, hierarchical relations, and therefore non-reciprocal ones. This is why the
constitution of the *Self* is pursued beyond the economic and political spheres in the realm of interpersonal relations. It is there that I
pursue the aim of being esteemed, approved, and recognized. My
existence for myself is dependent on this constitution in another's
opinion. My "Self," it may be said, is received from the opinion of
others that establishes it. The constitution of subjects is thus a mutual
constitution through opinion. (FM 121)

This form of mutual self-constitution lacks the objective clarity associated with
economic goods or political institutions that characterize the two previous levels
of self-constitution. The essence of self-constitution is based on "the possibility
of being no more than the word of another" (FM 122). Yet, this does not break
with Ricoeur's preoccupation with the objective configurations of this quest for
self-constitution. The quest for "recognition" is founded rather on a different
level of objectivity to which self-affirmation is primordially linked.

Dividing the objectivity of the quest for worth into formal and material
categories, Ricoeur reconnects feeling with the practical "*idea* of humanity."
Citing Kant, Ricoeur explains that "*what* I esteem in others and for which I
expect confirmation from others in myself, is what may be called our existence-
worth, our existing worth. . . . Thus esteem indeed involves a representation,
the representation of an end that is not merely an 'end to be realized,' but and
'end existing by itself' " (FM 122). Formal objectivity is the representation of
worth "not merely *for* us, but in *itself*" (FM 122). Not a good to be possessed,
or an object to exercise power over, the objectivity of worth "consists in that I
cannot use another merely as a means, nor utilize persons like things" (FM
122–123). Through the opinion of worth understood in such a nonutilitarian
manner, which I receive from another and the other receives from me, the idea
of humanity as end in itself takes formal objective shape. In other words, the
idea of humanity expressed by others for me and which I express about others
has a recognizable objective stability that gives consistency not only to the
human quest for esteem but to the very recognition of self as self. The objective
essence of self-constitution focuses on the expression of mutual worth, and
Ricoeur's formalization of selfhood brings his investigation full circle: what
began as a transcendental model of consciousness through the linguistic determination of otherness returns to this level of linguistic objectivity.

Coupled with the formal category of objectivity is that of material objectivity. The mutual exchange of the opinion of worthiness formally expressed as
an idea of humanity as end in itself, is represented materially in the works of
culture. Through the creative and imaginative activity of the mind the very
meaning of humanity is symbolized. " 'Works' of art and literature, and, in

general, works of the mind, insofar as they not merely mirror an environment and an epoch but search out man's possibilities, are the true 'objects' that manifest the abstract universality of the idea of humanity through their concrete universality" (FM 123). Self-worth in the mind of another is a "testimony" to the idea of humanity. Through "monuments existing in the world," particularly textual works, a form of objective stability is available to guide the ego into true mutual affirmation. Ricoeur looks to the works of culture for imaginative variations of the essence of self-affirmation. Cultural works provide a vast laboratory for exploring the inner dynamic of true self-constitution where "my own self-esteem that I search for by means of the esteem of others is of the same nature as the esteem I experience for others. If humanity is what I esteem in another and in myself, I esteem myself as a thou for another. I esteem myself in the second person . . . I love myself as if what I loved were another . . . I believe that I am worth something in the eyes of another who approves my existence; in the extreme case, this other is myself" (FM 124). Works of culture offer a rich and varied testimony of the very possibility for self-constitution. To say "I" is to receive through cultural symbol systems imaginative possibilities that would affirm one's own self-worth simultaneously with the existence-worth of another.

Reciprocal esteem of oneself as another returns to the universal linguistic determination of verb and noun over the finite limitation of individual self-perspective. The *formal* or transcendental imagination first encountered as the necessary third term of transcendental consciousness now reappears with a more specific *material* purpose. Imagination is not just the medium and mixture of epistemological necessity; it provides the means by which selfhood is affirmed through the medium and mixture of cultural works. To achieve true self-consciousness, one must pass through the gift of cultural meaning where one receives from another the opinion of worth as an end in oneself. And this reception of worth is a reception by means of language, which Ricoeur has already explained as a determination of otherness through the universalizing aim of the totality of meaning. The objective configurations of mutual self-constitution offered by cultural works are the products of an imagination characterized by a relationship of determination rather than mutuality.

Mutual self-constitution is the true passage from consciousness to self-consciousness. It is also the passage from the initial model of determinative consciousness, which is the "melodic germ of all the subsequent developments" (FM 49), to a more interactive model free from receptive domination. In other words, the tenuous disproportionate mediation of the infinite and finite feelings of belonging that characterize the act of self-constitution reveals a paradigmatic disproportion and contradiction as well. While Ricoeur is very careful in the development of his philosophical anthropology to maintain the uniformity of reflective style, it is puzzling to find that once he arrives at the point of true self-constitution he shifts to a different conceptual model, when all the while he has insisted that

because transcendental consciousness is on a primordial level from the outset it
is capable of revealing the essence of the act of self-constitution. If we follow the
development of Ricoeur's anthropology, the other has always been a distinction
determined through acts of domination by either linguistic meaning or universal
value. With the advent of affective consciousness the conquest of the other is
transformed into a quest to affirm the other through the affirmation of the other
directed toward me. While the opinion of worth is received from the other and
is therefore indicative of a degree of passivity, Ricoeur no longer speaks of the
need to determine the other. His affirmation of the true moment of self-constitution
as *mutual* self-constitution is a conclusion that seems out of step with patterns
methodically developed and maintained through the analysis of the transcendental, practical, and affective modes of consciousness.

Although the transcendental imagination is given content and life by the
quest for true self-worth, the use of a linguistic model that determines the other
in order to name it begs the question of its appropriateness for giving philosophical clarity to the notion of mutual self-affirmation. Doesn't this reveal a
fundamental difference between two incompatible conceptual models? Although
there is an ontological difference among the objects of Ricoeur's three levels of
investigation, what is the purpose of employing a theoretic model of consciousness to clarify the meaning of selfhood only to find that selfhood cannot be
understood as a determination of the other? Once Ricoeur attempts to formulate his understanding of true self-constitution, the model of consciousness
characterized by domination does not hold anymore and runs counter to the
very goal of mutual self-affirmation. If mutual selfhood is to remain a task in
front of consciousness, then such a task should not hearken back to a necessary
third term construed as a principle of (dis)unity or (dis)proportion that can
account in advance for the possibilities of self-affirmation. The work of imagination must be redefined as a hermeneutic project in which the determination
of meaning is exchanged for a response to the call of the other, that is, an
understanding of the linguistic imagination where "I exchange the *me, master*
of itself, for the *self, disciple* of the text" (PH 144). If Ricoeur wishes to pass
through the cultural reservoir of meaning by means of the power of imagination, then the model employed to understand this creative act of humanity
should bear greater similarity to the task of becoming oneself with another.

CHAPTER THREE

METAPHORICAL REFORMULATION

Toward Mutual Selfhood

The juxtaposition of the two conceptual models of consciousness presented in *Fallible Man* is a puzzling development. For Ricoeur true selfhood is found through the affirmation of worth of the other who affirms my worth. Here the other is not secondary to the process of self-constitution, but essential and inseparable from my own self-esteem; "in the extreme case, this other is myself" (FM 124). Yet the approach toward the other, toward knowing and identifying the other as such, assumes that the meaning and value of otherness is known through passive receptivity in conjunction with the determinative activity of voluntary consciousness. Methodologically Ricoeur does not seem able to lay claim to true self-affirmation, but instead can only offer a form of "attestation" (OA 21–23), or testimony that this is what selfhood ought to be—a task that tries to overcome the domination of the other by aiming at mutual self-esteem by means the power of imagination. Ricoeur therefore links both transcendental consciousness and true self-constitution through this linguistically qualified power of the imagination that can analogically see oneself as another and another as oneself.

The preeminence Ricoeur gives to this work of imagination requires further reflection. As I have explained, Ricoeur's quest to purge subjectivity from its idealistic interpretations involves a reflexive implication of selfhood through textual reference. Since the self is decentered and is a "consciousness of something" other than self "before consciousness is for itself" (PH 115), explanation of the sense of the text is necessary for understanding the textual reference to this other world of possible selfhood. To say self is to mediate, by means of the dynamic process of imaginative interpretation, between the explanation and understanding of that which is other than self. The work of imagination is supposed to enlarge the self by seeing the other as similar without reducing the other to the same. What is ultimately at stake for Ricoeur is the quest for mutual selfhood divested of a self-grounding ego and oriented toward the diversity of otherness as constitutive of one's own existence. The imagination not only makes a connection between textual sense and reference, and between self and other than self; it also makes a connection between meaning and existence, thereby revealing the interpretive path that Ricoeur takes in order to engage in speculation concerning the being of self and the other than self, that is, selfhood.[1]

Contrary to the mutuality of the "mediating role of imagination [which] is forever at work in lived reality" (*Dialogues* 24), Ricoeur's early publications present us with a view of imagination that mediates disproportionately. Ricoeur's work begins with a description of the reciprocity between the voluntary and involuntary and between the voluntary self and involuntary otherness. At this early stage the singularity of the central function of the "I will" gives involuntary otherness its meaning. Although Ricoeur inserts the imagination at the heart of volition by giving it a mediating function, the dialectic remains a description from "the top down and not from the bottom up" (FN 5). Imagination does not mediate between equals but between a center of command and the diversity of affective otherness. Even though Ricoeur opens the *cogito* to affective otherness and thereby begins to decenter the ego (which he equates with the self), this anthropological description runs counter to the constitutive mutuality testified to at the end of *Fallible Man*, and once again taken up in Ricoeur's most recent publications. If one were to put Ricoeur's publications on a continuum between the centered and decentered self, *Freedom and Nature* and *Oneself as Another*, while not at opposite extremes, would nevertheless have considerable distance between them.

This contrast between the disproportionate nature of consciousness and the relation of self to the other-than-self receives its most intensified description in *Fallible Man*. While Ricoeur utilizes a model of disproportionate and determinate consciousness for initiating an inquiry into the true nature of self-consciousness, the outcome of his reflection is an understanding of selfhood that seeks a mutual connection with, rather than a domination of, the other. Ricoeur uses two different and incompatible conceptual models to develop his philosophical anthropology. While it might be possible to maintain a separation between these two different orders, Ricoeur's hermeneutical phenomenology, narrative anthropology, and tensive ontology exhibit such a high degree of conceptual similarity that any sort of radical difference between them would be unlikely. Therefore, either the intended outcome of self-constitution must be reformulated in such a manner as to maintain epistemological and ontological consistency, or the model of transcendental linguistic determination must give way to a model more suitable to that of mutual self-affirmation. Ricoeur chooses the latter alternative but engages in a reconstruction rather than the complete rejection of his model of determinative consciousness; hence, Ricoeur never seems to completely escape the priority of the voluntary will over the passive other.[2]

The philosophical call, so characteristic of Ricoeur's later works, to exchange the ego for a self discipled by the text is given initial philosophical shape through a reformulation of the transcendental determinative model of language. Rather than abandoning the linguistic mixture and medium that unfolds mutual self-constitution, Ricoeur builds on this rudimentary hermeneutic in such a manner as to allow the call for mutuality to recast his analysis of the creation of meaning in language. No longer focused on the determination of otherness by means of noun and verb, Ricoeur finds within the imaginative creation of metaphor a production of meaning that results from the "shock" of "predicative assimilation" or *rapprochement* between divergent semantic fields (IDA 7; FFSR 131). The rudimentary explanation, in *Fallible Man*, of the disproportionate mediating work of imagination is transposed from a primary act of denomination to that of predication within a metaphorical utterance. Since "metaphor has to do with semantics of the sentence before it concerns the semantics of a word" (IT 49), and as such is "the result of the tension between two terms in a metaphorical utterance" (IT 50), Ricoeur gives metaphor the weight of opening a textual world of mutual self-constitution through a "new predicative pertinence" produced by an *interactive* combination of signifiers rather than domination of a single meaning or noun over a perceptual field. Ricoeur's reformulation of the mediating work of the imagination is so fundamental that the "[t]ie between imagination and semantic innovation . . . [becomes] the core of our entire analysis" (IDA 3). Imagination and semantic creativity form an intricate relation of *vision and text* that opens the ego to possibilities of existing in the mode of selfhood.

The centering of the creative imagination in metaphorical discourse appears at first to be a contradiction in terms. The history of philosophical reflection on the nature of the imagination can be characterized, according to Ricoeur, as a "range of variation . . . [that] can be measured along two different axes: with regard to the object, the axis of presence and absence; with regard to the subject, the axis of fascinated consciousness and critical consciousness" (IDA 5). Along both axes theories of imagination appear as "knot of contradictions which . . . [characterizes] the shambles of the theory of the imagination today" (IDA 6). Ricoeur develops a conception of imagination more rudimentary than that founded on perception which unties this knot of contradictions without glossing over the tension within each of the poles of imaginativity. What Ricoeur proposes is a conception of imagination that is fundamentally a language-constructing activity from which visual images are derived.

To say that our images are spoken before they are seen is to abandon what we initially—but mistakenly—take for granted, namely, that the image is first and foremost a "scene" being played out on the stage of a mental "theater" for the benefit of an internal "spectator"; but this also means giving up a second point we also mistakenly assume, namely, that this mental entity is the stuff out of which we construct our abstract ideas, our concepts, the basic ingredient in some sort of mental alchemy. (IDA 6)

By giving up the notion of a prior presence of the "ingredients" of conceptual thought, Ricoeur transforms the very idea of the creation of meaning. Imaginative constructs are not meanings created behind one's back, so to speak, but up front through the vast polysemy of language. Rather than rooting meaning in a metaphysic of prior presence, the creation of meaning is found within the tension between imaginative presence and absence,[3] which simultaneously generates the consciousness of belonging to, and critical distance from, the polysemic being of metaphorical meaning. Imagination, Ricoeur explains, "lives in the conflict of 'proximity' and 'distance'" (FFSR 131) through a textual world of absence and presence.

Metaphorical reference allows Ricoeur to move from language to selfhood. The function of "predicative impertinence" provides a new model for the interpretive procedures required for understanding textual worlds and their intended meaning of selfhood. Ricoeur values metaphorical language for its ability to produce similarities or resemblances on the level of the statement: "resemblance itself must be understood as a tension between identity and difference in the predicative operation set in motion by semantic innovation" (RM 6). Through the tension between identity and difference, metaphor provides a model for textual reference, which paves the way for understanding narrative selfhood as an identity in difference, or as metaphorical transference between self and other than self. By reformulating in this manner the original model of determinative transcendental consciousness, Ricoeur finds a type of hermeneutics more reflective of the call to selfhood.

This unique ability of metaphorical utterance to open up a world of "second-order reference" results from the redescriptive power found in the "copula of the verb to be" (RM 7; OA 298). Metaphor says something about reality by redescribing it "as if it is like this or that," but the "metaphorical 'is' at once signifies both 'is not' and 'is like'" (RM 7). Metaphorical truth about reality is tensive, expressing reality in terms of identity and difference. In order to understand how human reality can be expressed this way, Ricoeur's metaphorical theory needs to be explained in greater detail, specifically, how metaphor constructs resemblances and how such resemblances refer to a redescribed reality that implies selfhood.

3.1   From Semantics of Discourse to the Work of Resemblance

The reformulation of determined meaning into an interactive creation of meaning through metaphorical utterance is the key to understanding Ricoeur's redevelopment of his philosophical anthropology and ontology. While Ricoeur does change his focus from the determined word to the metaphorical statement, this does not "obliterate . . . nominal definition in terms of word or name, because the word remains the locus of the effect of metaphorical meaning. It is the word that is said to take a metaphorical meaning" (RM 66). Ricoeur's change of focus is more than a simple shift from words to sentences; rather, Ricoeur's preoccupation with metaphorical statements involves a fundamental realignment of his methodology. The interaction of signifiers within metaphorical statements supplies Ricoeur with a hermeneutical model proportionate to his quest for mutual self-constitution.

Following Emile Benveniste's distinction between semiotics and semantics, or "the distinction between the fundamental units of language and of discourse: the signs and the sentence respectively" (RM 67), Ricoeur argues that the emergence of linguistic meaning takes place on the semantic level of discourse, that is, at the level of the sentence taken as a whole irreducible to its semiotic elements. Since "the meaning inherent in this whole is distributed over the ensemble of the constituents" (RM 67), linguistic meaning is the product of a sentence and not of individual words isolated from their contextual use. The signifiers that constitute the sentence provide an occasion for the *production* of linguistic meaning through an *interactive* process, rather than the *determination* of meaning by a *univocal* signifier. Ricoeur places the burden of the meaning of language on the interaction within a unit of discourse which, unlike the determinative model of language, has the possibility of being a "creation of limitless variety," and which captures "the very life of human speech in action" (RM 68).

In order to demonstrate this interactive capacity of metaphorical discourse to communicate or mean something, Ricoeur uses three traits of the structure of discourse. First of all, "discourse always occurs as an event, but is understood as meaning" (RM 70). Living language, while it is the actualization of a virtual semiotic code, takes place in time through an imaginative work of understanding that labors to identify the meaning of what is said and to communicate meaning through various forms of discourse. Discourse becomes a reality through the act that creates and re-creates meaning from the combination of semiotic signifiers. While discourse is always "an instant" of meaning and signs, and therefore "fleeting and transitory, it can be identified and reidentified as 'the same'; thus, meaning is introduced, in its broadest sense, at the same time as the possibility of identifying a given unit of discourse. There is meaning because there is sameness of meaning" (RM 70). In other words, the combination of signifiers used in the event of discourse offers the repeatability of meaning. However, the meaning that can be identified as the "same" does not reside in a semiotic substrate; it results from an act of understanding that must construct the meaning time and time again. "This is why this trait can be mistaken for an element of language; but what we have here is the repeatability of an event, not of an element of a system" (RM 70). While it is possible, for example, to read a text over and over again, the "sameness" of meaning has to do with the very possibility of reading, with an act of imagination that repeats, according to Ricoeur, the event of discourse. The sameness of meaning in this context has little to do with a single meaning rooted in signifiers; it has to do, Ricoeur contends, with the sameness of the event in which meaning occurs, thereby capturing the "event" in the semantics of discourse.

The importance of this distinction is paramount for Ricoeur. If the association is made between a single univocal meaning and the event of meaning, then the designation of sameness leaves no room for the category of the other or for the diversity of meanings. Reading would thus imply the reactualization of a predetermined meaning where interpretation would be nothing other than the activity in which we attempt to get the meaning right. For Ricoeur, meaning as event always implies both identity and difference, the same and the other. Sameness of meaning in the context of the dialectic of meaning and event simply shows that the discourse to be identified as such must generate meaning: meaning always occurs for discourse to be named as discourse. The dialectic of event and meaning does not mark a distinction between semantic and semiotic orders, but a distinction internal to the semantic order itself.

The discursive dialectic of event and meaning encompasses the ability of discourse to refer to a "reality" other than itself. This is the second trait of discourse Ricoeur emphasizes. The event of meaning, while dependent on, but not reducible to, a semiotic order, extends itself beyond language. Discourse exhibits an additional dialectic of semiotic sense and extralinguistic reference. On a semiotic level, "there is no problem" of reference; "signs refer to other signs *within* the same system. In the phenomenon of the sentence, language passes outside itself; reference is the mark of the self-transcendence of language. . . . This trait . . . marks the fundamental difference between semantics and semiotics" (RM 74). Semantic meaning is by definition that aspect of discourse which connects language use to "reality." And because discursive reference performs a "mediatory function between man and man, between man and world, and so integrating man into society and assuring the correspondence between language and the world" (RM 74), discourse is the foundational means for understanding these relationships. For Ricoeur the referential extension of language to "reality" simultaneously refers to and implicates selfhood.

Herein lies the third trait of discourse. The referential function of all forms of discourse has a dual reference. "To the extent that discourse refers to a situation, to an experience, to reality, to the world, in sum to the extra-linguistic, it also refers to its own speaker by means of procedures that belong essentially to discourse and not to language" (RM 75). The act of understanding the meaning of discourse involves the appropriation of a dual reference: a world and a self that could exist in that world. This, in a nutshell, is Ricoeur's herme-neutic of selfhood. The appropriation of possibilities for being oneself results from a hermeneutical method that is rooted in these three traits of discourse: discourse is by definition a meaningful event, and that meaning requires a dual method of explanation of semiotic sense and understanding of semantic refer-ence, the result of which is both the appropriation of world and an understand-ing of a self that could inhabit that world.

Using these three traits of discourse, Ricoeur draws from the disciplines of rhetoric, logical grammar, and literary criticism, key ideas that facilitate the construction of his own model of metaphorical production of meaning. Since discourse is a meaning event, metaphorical meaning must be seen as the result of an activity on the part of the reader. Foregoing the traditional formulation of the transference of meaning between different words, Ricoeur, borrowing from I. A. Richards, likens this activity to "a commerce between thoughts, that is, a transaction between contexts" (RM 80). The thought or meaning context asso-ciated with particular words within a metaphorical sentence is transformed by the reader into a relationship of exchange that produces new meaning. The words themselves do not contain this new meaning but provide the possibility for a reader to make a new association between them. Through the interaction of subject and predicate, or "focus and frame" (RM 85), metaphorical utterance allows for something new to be said. Metaphorical statements are not decora-tive devices in which one simply substitutes one lexical meaning for another; they are genuine creations of meaning that have not yet been added to the virtual system of semiotic signifiers. The production of metaphorical meaning through semantic interaction is irreducible to the dictionary meaning of its semiotic elements. Interactive metaphor "cannot be translated without 'loss of cognitive content.' Being untranslatable, it carries new information; briefly, it tells us something" that is not present in the original meaning context of its individual words (RM 87).

What distinguishes metaphorical utterance from other forms of discourse is the peculiar interaction of its subject and predicate. Citing Monroe Beardsley, Ricoeur explains that metaphor is a form of "self-contradictory attribution" (RM 94). Metaphor creates a contextual conflict between subject and predicate that can only be resolved through a recontextualizing act on the part of the reader. Metaphorical attribution presents "a conflict between designations at the pri-mary level of meaning, which forces the reader to extract from the complete context of connotations the secondary meanings capable of making a 'meaning-ful self-contradictory attribution' from a self-contradictory statement" (RM 95).

Ricoeur takes from Beardsley's work the foundational structure of his own concept of metaphorical meaning. The transition from primary self-contradictory
designations to secondary meaningful connotations is performed by a reader
who makes contradiction meaningful through a "power . . . to push the frontier
of non-sense further back" (RM 95). The reader constructs second-order meaning from first-order semantic contradictions. Metaphorical meaning results from
a reader-activated event that dialectically connects a logically incongruous subject and predicate. This is the poetic power of the imagination at work: "the
sudden insight of a new predicative pertinence, specifically a pertinence within
impertinence" (FFSR 131), the ability to see similarities among lexically discordant definitions.

        Ricoeur therefore explains that "there are probably no words so incompat-
ible that some poet could not build a bridge between them; the power to create
new contextual meanings seems to be truly limitless. Attribution that appears to
be non 'sensical' can make sense in some unexpected context. No speaker ever
completely exhausts the connotative possibilities of his words" (RM 95). Metaphorical statements make a transition between two levels of meaning: conven-
tional or "proper meaning," which "reflects only the catalogued lexical meanings
of words," and "figurative" or new " 'emergent meaning' that exists here and
now" (RM 96). New meaning is metaphorical meaning. Metaphor is more than
just an instance of discourse among others; it reveals itself to be the quintessen-
tial expression of living speech. This is why "the dictionary contains no metaphors; they exist only in discourse. For this reason, metaphorical attribution is
superior to every other use of language in showing what 'living speech' really
is; it is an 'instance of discourse' *par excellence*" (RM 97). And because metaphor is a genuine moment of creation and a true "semantic innovation without
status in . . . language" (RM 98), it can be used as model for the creation of
meaning in all other forms of discourse.

        The extension of the interactive structure of metaphor to other forms of
discourse serves as the basis for Ricoeur's hermeneutical methodology. Ricoeur
draws on Beardsley's insight that "the literary work is not only a linguistic entity
homogeneous to the sentence, differing from it just with respect to length . . .
[but] a whole organized at a level proper to the drawing of distinctions between
several classes of works" (RM 91) and which creates meaning through the
interaction of its semiotic elements. The process of creating new meaning on
the level of metaphorical discourse is duplicated on the level of the literary text,
although it is a duplication of increased sophistication. Metaphor "serve[s] as a
test-case . . . of the method of explication that is to be applied to the work itself,
taken as a whole. To put it in another way, the metaphor is taken as a *poem in
miniature*. The proposed working hypothesis is that if a satisfactory account can
be given of what is implied in this kernel of poetic meaning, it must be possible
equally to extend the same explication to larger entities, such as the entire

poem" (RM 94). Metaphor is significant for Ricoeur not only as a model of discourse par excellence; it also provides the "kernel" or the new "melodic germ" for the interpretative procedures that need to be employed for understanding all cultural works.

3.2 The Work of Resemblance

The metaphorical kernel of Ricoeur's hermeneutic, while foundational to his anthropology and ontology, remains rather undefined. Although Ricoeur attributes the emergence of new meaning to "a pertinence within impertinence" (FFSR 131), or the result of making sense from nonsensical predication, the details of this interaction need to be explored further.

In emphasizing the creative response of the reader to the literal self-contradictory attribution of metaphorical utterance, Ricoeur is working toward an explanation of the *creative power* to produce figurative meaning. By reaching beyond literal contradiction, the act of metaphorical meaning has the ability to see resemblances on a secondary, and ultimately deeper, imaginative level. While metaphor making is an activity of interaction, it is primarily an act of connection, a transition from a contradictory or conflictual level to a figurative level that combines the conflicting meaning contexts into a relational unity of resemblance. Metaphor "is the 'clash' on the literal level that leads one to seek out a meaning beyond the lexical meaning. . . . Metaphor is not quite the clash itself, but rather its resolution. One must decide, on the basis of various 'clues' provided by the context, which terms can be taken figuratively and which cannot. One must therefore 'work out' the parallelism between situations that will guide the iconic transposition of one to the other" (RM 190–191). Metaphor making can be explained as the production of a "kind of semantic 'proximity' established between the [contradictory] terms despite their 'distance' apart. Things that until that moment were 'far apart' suddenly appear as 'closely related'" (RM 194).

It is this paradox of attribution that brings us to the heart of Ricoeur's explanation of metaphor. Diversity of meaning and the unity of sudden insight belong together. In fact, Ricoeur insists that the "tension, contradiction, and controversion are nothing but the opposite side of the reconciliation in which metaphor 'makes sense'" (RM 195). Both are essential to the imaginative act of resemblance making. While literal resemblance results in logical contradictions, metaphorical resemblance results from a work of poetic resolution of these unusual predications. Contradiction and resolution are not separate processes; they result from the unified act of imagining. The creative production of meaning simultaneously incorporates "the protest [of] what remains from the former marriage, the literal assignation, destroyed by contradiction, [and] the yielding . . . to the new rapprochement" (RM 196). Metaphorical meaning combines contradiction or difference with the similar without reducing one to the other. Metaphorical unity does not overcome difference, it holds difference and identity together while it "opposes" them. "In the metaphorical statement," Ricoeur explains,

> "the similar" is perceived *despite* difference, *in spite of contradiction*. Resemblance, therefore, is the logical category corresponding to the predicative operation in which "approximation" (bringing close) meets the resistance of "being distant." In other words, metaphor displays the work of resemblance because the literal contradiction preserves difference within the metaphorical statement; "same" and "different" are not just mixed together, they also remain opposed. Through this specific trait, enigma lives on in the heart of meta- phor. In metaphor, "the same" operates *in spite of* "the different." (RM 196)

Metaphorical resemblance, one could say, brings about a "fusion of differences *into* identity" without destroying the semantic differences that adhere to seman- tic "fields" and "networks of significance" that are associated with the subject and predicate of literal contradiction (RM 198).

The unifying function of metaphorical resemblance is, for Ricoeur, what accounts for the emergence of new meaning in language. It is a process of *schematization* performed by the *imagination* in which "predicative assimilation enables the imagination to work . . . 'to see' . . . 'to see similarity' " (FFSR 131). Metaphor includes an iconic moment or an "image" that acts as "a gathering- point . . . of emerging meanings" (RM 199). Appropriating Kant's distinction between the productive and reproductive imagination, Ricoeur explains that

> in the same way, therefore, that the schema is the matrix of the category, the icon is the matrix of the new semantic pertinence that is born out of the dismantling of semantic networks caused by the shock of contradiction. . . . Metaphor is established as the schematism in which the metaphorical attribution is produced. This schematism turns imagination into the place where figurative meaning emerges in the interplay of identity and difference. And metaphor is that place in discourse where this schematism is visible, because the identity and the difference do not melt together but confront each other. (RM 199)

The imagination does not simply *reproduce* images from a linguistic medium and mixture; it *produces* images through the very same imaginative act that constructs figurative meanings. The emergence of meaning is a single process of productive schematization of metaphorical meaning-images.

The ability to image an emerging meaning is accounted for by the "phenomenon of reverberation" (RM 215; IDA 8; FFSR 129–130). Ricoeur borrows this curious phrase from Gaston Bachelard, who utilizes it to indicate a noncausal link between the moment of creation, whereby the "poet speaks on the threshold of being" (PS xii), and the being that reverberates through the sonorous poetic image. For Bachelard, the ability of being to reverberate through a poetic image reveals a connection that goes

> *immediately* beyond all psychology or psychoanalysis, [where] we feel a poetic power rising naively within us. After the original reverberation, we are able to experience resonances, sentimental repercussions, reminders of our past. But the image has touched the depths, before it stirs the surface, and this is also true of a simple experience of reading. The image offered us by reading the poem now becomes really our own. It takes root in the impression that we could have created it, that we should have created it. It becomes a new being in our language, expressing us by making us what it expresses; in other words, it is at once a becoming expression, and a becoming of our being. Here expression creates being. (PS xix)

The iconization of linguistic meaning that allows us to see being as. . . . (something), results from a deep ontological connection among image, language, and being. However, Ricoeur is careful with the appropriation of the notion of reverberation. Although he uses Bachelard's view of the poetic image, stipulating that such imagery parallels the symbolization of experience, he has no interest in Bachelard's quest for a "direct ontology" that attempts, through phenomenological description of the "pure imagination," to lay bare the original consciousness of creativity.[4] The birth of the image-symbol is not rooted in a metaphysic of original consciousness, or in a prior presence or meaning that language merely expresses.[5] For Ricoeur, meaning is an event of discourse, a work of the imagination, and therefore it happens "up front" in language.

The reverberative power of the creative imagination not only produces images (FTA 172), it also "radiates out in all directions, reanimating earlier experience, awakening dormant memories, spreading to adjacent sensorial fields" (IDA 8). The imagination organizes discordant experiences and ideas by making image connections between them. The vast diversity of possible imaginata can therefore be gathered together and organized into cultural works. This movement outward, or "the effect of reverberation, resonance, or echo, is not a secondary phenomenon" (IDA 8); it is a connecting act that joins speech and sight together to envision reality as something other than what has been received.

Imagination receives its most complete definition by this play of possibilities. Ricoeur explains that "the ultimate role of the image is not only to spread meaning over diverse sensorial fields but to hold meaning suspended in this neutralized atmosphere, in the element of fiction . . . .But it already seems that the imagination is really what we all mean by this term: a free play of possibilities in a state of uninvolvement with respect to the world of perception or action. It is in this state of uninvolvement that we try out new ideas, new values, new ways of being in the world" (IDA 8–9). More than a simple state of suspended disbelief, the iconization of meaning configures and reconfigures reality. By generating images rooted in linguistic meanings, the imagination suspends one kind of referential order for another. The imagination provides a distance, or even absence, from the everyday reality of sedimented or prefigured meaning, in order that a *presence* can be opened in front of the text.[6] The imagination provides a transition between reality as it is received, and a possible reality to be accomplished or reconfigured. What Ricoeur in essence is arguing for is a phenomenological reduction, or putting out of action, of one kind of being of the world, in order that the world of being opened up by metaphorical utterance may speak. For Ricoeur,

> the neutralizing function of the imagination with respect to the "thesis of the world" is only the negative condition required to free a second-order referential force. An analysis of the affirmative force deployed by poetic language shows that it is not just the sense which is split in the metaphorical process but the reference as well. What is eliminated is the ordinary language reference applied to objects which correspond to one of our interests, our primary interest in controlling and manipulating. By holding in abeyance this interest and the sphere of meaning it governs, poetic discourse allows our deep-seated insertion in the life-world to emerge; it allows the ontological tie uniting our being to other beings and to Being to be articulated. What is articulated in this way is what I call second-order reference and which in reality is the primordial reference. (IDA 9)

The iconicity of metaphorical attribution carries great significance for Ricoeur. The ability to see reality differently than the way it has been received is rooted in the power of imagination to construct images *from* diverse semantic fields. Semantic meaning provides the soil for imaginative images to blossom. But "images evoked or aroused in this way are not the 'free' images that a simple association of ideas would join to meaning. . . . They are 'tied' images, that is, connected to poetic diction. In contrast to mere association, iconicity involves meaning controlling imagery" (RM 211). Metaphorical utterance, by opening language to an imaginative world of images, provides a semantic ground and foundation for the possibilities of seeing reality as other and different than received. In this way, the emergence of meaning moves beyond language and becomes "fused" with "non-verbal" experience, with the fullness of imagery, without losing its dynamic power of maintaining identity in difference (RM 213).

The connection among language, imagination, and reality is fundamental. Imaginative "seeing as" can mediate between meaning and existence because it is both "an experience and an act at one and the same time" (RM 213), a reception of linguistic resemblance through the construction of new images. "Seeing as" is both the involuntary reception of images where "there is no rule to be learned for 'having images,'" and an act that "orders the flux and governs iconic deployment" (RM 213). Because "the same imagery which *occurs* also *means*" (RM 213), it has the ability to mediate between discourse and nonverbal reality. In other words, the work of the imagination is the "*fusion* of sense and the imaginary ... [which] is the necessary counterpart of a theory of interaction" (RM 214). Since the creation of meaning takes place in time, in the event of hearing or reading, it involves seeing reality in a particular manner. For Ricoeur meaning always has an extrinsic linguistic referent.

3.3   Reference and Reality

Using the Fregean distinction between sense and reference, Ricoeur explores the manner in which discourse transcends itself through its redescription of reality set in motion by the imaginative work of resemblance. Discourse calls for an interpretation to "display the world to which it refers by virtue of its 'arrangement,' its 'genre,' and its 'style'" (RM 220). While Ricoeur spends a great deal of time in numerous publications seeking to justify the "right to pass from [textual] structure ... to the world of the [poetic] work" (RM 220), I will accept this postulate of semantic reference as an implicit characteristic of discourse. My concern, instead, lies with the referential connection between discourse and reality, that is, the creation of a "second-level reference" (RM 221) that analogically redescribes reality by constructing linguistic models.

The ability of discourse to make a connection with reality is readily taken for granted in the field of science. However, scientific language describes reality through the construction of an imaginary model that is said to represent that reality. Ricoeur points out that the abstraction of a linguistic model that is seen as standing for reality is in fact an analogue of the original. "The model and the original resemble each other in their structures and not through sensible features" (RM 241). Scientific models "isomorphically" resemble reality in an imaginary mode that allows for a deeper understanding and further explanation of the original. Models offer the scientific mind a power of description that brings to light essential structures and relationships that might not be discovered through ordinary description. This is not a

deflection of reason, distraction by images, but the essentially verbal power of trying out new relationships on a "described model." This

imagination mingles with reason by virtue of the rules of correlation
governing the translation of statements concerning the secondary
domain into statements applicable to the original domain. . . . It is
the isomorphism of relationships that grounds the translatability of
one idiom into another and, in so doing, provides the "rationale" of
the imagination. But the isomorphism does not hold now between
the original domain and something constructed, but between that
domain and something "described." Scientific imagination consists
in seeing new connections via the detour of this thing that is "described." (RM 241–242)

While the parallel between models of scientific description and metaphorical
"seeing as" is quite obvious, models reveal something new about reality that was
"not discovered in the foregoing analysis" (RM 243). Since a model "consists in
a complex network of statements" (RM 243), a direct comparison with metaphorical statements is disproportionate. Ricoeur explains that the model's "exact
analogue would be the extended metaphor—tale, allegory . . . a metaphoric
network and not an isolated metaphor" (RM 243). The "poem in miniature,"
while providing the simplest example of the creation of meaning in language,
when extended to narrative configurations not only sees reality as . . . , but can
describe and redescribe reality through its expanded "metaphorical network
rather than by an isolated metaphorical statement" (RM 244).

Extended metaphors or fictions redescriptively refer *to* reality by providing
heuristic *models of and for reality.* The reference of an extended metaphor is of
a fundamentally different order than that of ordinary reference. Fictions, by
creating imaginative distance from reality, provide a means for not only rein-
venting or seeing reality otherwise than it has been previously described through
ordinary direct (determinative) description; it provides the imaginative space
within which "reality" is clarified, revealed, and understood.[7] Using Aristotle's
example of the tragic drama, Ricoeur explains that the metaphoricity of a narrative plot "consists in describing a less known domain—human reality—in the
light of relationships within a fictitious but better known domain—the tragic
tale—utilizing all the strengths of 'systematic deployability' contained in that
tale" (RM 244). By extending the power of metaphorical utterance to literary
works, Ricoeur utilizes the phenomenological procedure of the *epochè* to suspend the meaning of ordinary immediate experience to create a reference in
which "invention and discovery cease being opposed and where creation and
revelation coincide" (RM 246).

What appears as the cancellation of a primary world of meaning in favor
of a secondary imaginative world is for Ricoeur an opening onto a more fundamental level of reality where meaning is a simultaneous process of creation
and discovery. To see reality as this or that through the construction of imagi-

native fictions is to discover more about reality than is possible through direct reference language. Ricoeur argues that while seeing as . . . takes place through semantic innovation it is a simultaneous ontological process of speaking about being and hearing the speech of being. The work of imagination is the dynamic in which Being speaks through being spoken. Through the *muthos* or connecting voice of fiction the gift of imagination is connected to a *call*. Seeing reality as . . . is also "feeling [reality] as . . . the lack of distinction between interior and exterior" (RM 246), that is, feeling oneself as a fundamental unity of identity and difference. With poetic reference "the 'poetic textures' of the world . . . and the 'poetic schemata' of interior life . . . mirroring one another, proclaim the reciprocity of the inner and the outer" (RM 246). Thus, for Ricoeur the world of a poetic work not only provides a model of and for reality; it simultaneously provides a semantic model for selfhood through the fundamental connection between the inner self and outer world.

Here we see the deep connection Ricoeur has constructed among language, selfhood, and Being. By reformulating his original linguistic model of determinative consciousness into that of a metaphorical unity of identity and difference, Ricoeur provides himself with a hermeneutic that is extended beyond the creation of meaning in language to an extralinguistic reference that speaks in truth of selfhood and being. But as Ricoeur points out, this claim brings into question the understanding of their reality. Since second-order reference of metaphor and fiction redescribes reality through the suspension of ordinary determinative reference, does this mean that the referential world of the text is indeterminate and thereby ultimately lacking the ability to create the clearing for ontological speech? Not at all, because the dynamic of metaphorical utterance exposes an ontology that lives in the interplay of identity and difference.

Language only concerned with a determinative reference is a language of dead metaphor, a language that is intent on eliminating ambiguity and plurality through the control of meaning. However, language that demands only difference, only flux, is never in need of interpretation, for any reading is as good as another. Rather, Ricoeur insists that the dialectical tension first observed "between tenor and vehicle" must be maintained between "literal interpretation . . . and metaphorical interpretation," between "identity and difference in the interplay of resemblance," and between the interpretation of selfhood and Being. "In the most radical terms possible, tension must be introduced into metaphorically affirmed being" (RM 247). The conceptual pattern for the emergence of meaning as a "unity of identity in difference" becomes the new "melodic germ" for understanding language, discourse, reference, and reality. The original notion of mutual selfhood and being that Ricoeur pursued through the third quest for self-affirmation in *Fallible Man* is now given an additional tensive qualification. Ricoeur's ontology and corresponding philosophical anthropology are still expressed in terms of mutual affirmation through identity and difference, but this unity is understood as a tension between necessary counterparts. The meaning of the unifying term *selfhood* expresses a connection between self and other-than-self, and does so through a dialectical tension that is supposed to prevent the reduction of one to another. Likewise, Ricoeur's ontology consists in a combination of *"ontological commitment"* and critique of *"ontological naïveté,"* whereby the unifying term *to be* is understood as both "the critical incision of the (literal) 'is not' within the ontological vehemence of the (metaphorical) 'is' " (RM 255). Ricoeur believes that metaphorical utterance provides a model of interconnection that overcomes the disproportion of *Fallible Man* between determinative linguistic consciousness and the mutuality of selfhood and being.

Yet the question remains: Has Ricoeur really overcome the disproportion in *Fallible Man* between epistemology and ontology? After all, the movement from literal reference to metaphorical reference does resemble the movement of determinate consciousness to true self-consciousness. Further, is not disproportion by definition a kind of relational tension between elements? And therefore, could metaphorical utterance be viewed as a form of incongruity between literal domination and figurative liberation? Could one not also conclude that the determination of perceptual otherness by noun and verb is similar to the construction of the semantic resemblance that results from a clash of "unusual predicates"?

While these structural similarities do suggest Ricoeur's lack of conceptual progress, and account for our earlier comments regarding his reconstruction rather than the wholesale rejection of his model of determinative consciousness, such a reading fails to take into account that the tensive connection between identity and difference is the organizing principle of not just true self-consciousness but is constitutive of language itself. The disproportion between methodological determination and mutual self-affirmation has apparently vanished within the semantic structure of metaphorical utterance. Epistemology, philosophical anthropology, and ontology are all understood through the same conceptual pattern. But does identity now take precedence over difference on all three of these levels of discourse instead of only on the transcendental or epistemological level? While Ricoeur vigorously tries to maintain a mutual relation between identity and difference without reducing one to the other, and does make significant strides toward the development of a hermeneutic more suitable to the mutual structure of self-constitution or selfhood, does this uniformity of analysis among language, selfhood, and Being create new problems of its own?

CHAPTER FOUR

Narrative Imagination and Personal Identity

With the deployment of his model of semantic or metaphoric innovation, Ricoeur manages to bridge many of the fault lines that have separated the determinative model of transcendental or epistemological consciousness from the model of self-consciousness understood as the mutual affirmation of the self and the other. Building on the tension within the metaphorical statement, Ricoeur has made significant strides toward epistemological, anthropological, and ontological uniformity. Yet this resolution of methodological disproportion by way of the power of imagination to see similarity in difference takes us only partway on the journey toward the recovery and discovery of selfhood. Metaphor proclaims new meaning that corresponds with feeling oneself as a fundamental unity of identity and difference. The power of metaphor to see reality configured in a particular manner gives testimony to the vast breadth of human emotion. Imagination, however, is more than just feeling. Poetic expression takes place in time through action by individuals in community with others. Metaphor shows how one feels or sees the temporal character of one's own being in relation to other temporal beings and the temporality of Being. This requires an extended metaphor or narrative capable of giving testimony of the agent responsible for action. The journey of self-discovery must pass through linguistic configurations of human action, which give not only analogous *possibilities for* agency but also testimony *of* both individual and common deeds carried out and suffered. Identifying the agent responsible for such an act requires that the work of imagination expand the practical field of human experience by means of a narrative mode of discourse.

In the three-volume work *Time and Narrative* (1984–1988), Ricoeur launches a complex and highly detailed analysis of this interconnection between narrative and human experience. Forming a pair with *The Rule of Metaphor*, *Time and Narrative* continues to explore the significance of the work of

91

imagination for understanding experience. This "one vast poetic sphere that includes metaphorical utterance and narrative discourse" (TN 1:xi) brings to light "the change of distance in logical space that is the work of the productive imagination" (TN 1:x). Although no longer concerned primarily with "seeing reality as . . . ," narrative discourse nevertheless brings difference and identity together into a unifying structure. "The plot of a narrative is comparable to this predicative assimilation. It 'grasps together' and integrates into one whole and complete story multiple and scattered events, thereby schematizing the intelligible signification attached to the narrative taken as a whole" (TN 1:x). By grasping together into a complete structure the narrative function places the diversity of human temporal experience under the unifying operation of the plot. Ricoeur argues that the narrative function is "the privileged means by which we re-configure our confused, unformed, and at the limit mute temporal experience" (TN 1:xi). Narrative brings to language the diversity of human action by submitting it to the unifying and intelligible order of the story. In this manner, the narrative function repeats the conceptual pattern Ricoeur developed in *The Rule of Metaphor*: the production of a linguistic innovation that unifies identity and difference.

In spite of Ricoeur's introductory remarks concerning the purpose of *Time and Narrative*, his "common core presupposition [that] time becomes human to the extent that it is organized after the manner of a narrative," and conversely that narrative "is meaningful to the extent that it portrays the features of temporal experience" (TN 1:3), remains secondary to the somewhat hidden point of the entire work. It is only at the end of the third volume of *Time and Narrative* that the primary purpose of the whole work is revealed: "Here is the core of our whole investigation, for it is only within this search . . . by individuals and by the communities to which they belong, for their respective narrative identities . . . that the aporetics of time and the poetics of narrative correspond to each other in a sufficient way" (TN 3:274). This revelation is quite remarkable if one considers that the three volumes of *Time and Narrative* are more than eight hundred pages long and that the only thematic treatment of the concept of narrative identity in *Time and Narrative* spans a mere four pages and seems to be an afterthought in response to lingering problems that Ricoeur's investigations on narrative have been unable to resolve.[1]

Astonishing as this may seem, the search for identity should come as no surprise if set within Ricoeur's work as a whole. As I have shown, the initial search in *Fallible Man* for mutual self-affirmation takes place in and among the works of culture, and this quest for mutuality remains constant throughout Ricoeur's later hermeneutical investigations. In this regard, his investigation of the relationship between human temporality and the poetics of narrative reemploys the strategy of imaginative mediation as the key to anthropological and ontological truth. Just as metaphor proposes a world of possible axiological values, the proposals of narrative discourse require an agent responsible for the truth of history and fiction. Narrative refers to a world inhabited by identifiable agents capable of responding to the questions: "Who is speaking? Who is acting? Who is recounting about himself or herself? Who is the moral subject of imputation?" (OA 16). In other words, who is identified with and responsible for the world unfolded through the imaginative act of narration?

Ricoeur's understanding of metaphor sets the stage for the interpretation of multiple forms of discourse, each corresponding to different intentionalities of human experience. By asserting that the central dialectic of imagination is inherently innovative and semantic in structure, Ricoeur can offer a more complete interpretation of existence through other linguistic forms of human creativity. In particular, the extended metaphor or narrative has the capacity to bring to light the temporal process of identity formation. Narrative, like all creative discourse, is supposed to bring experience to language, but the particular experience that corresponds to the narrative form is the world of human temporality and action, that is, the world that subjects agents to change and is subjected to change by agents in search of their identity.

The events of my personal and our collective stories form a vast diversity from which I try to weave a meaningful narrative account of who I am in relation to who you are. The difference and otherness of my received past is taken up through the imaginative process of emplotment and given order and meaning in relation to my quest for sameness and identity. To search for one's identity is to accept responsibility for one's own past in relation to one's present "space of experience" and "horizon of expectation" (TN 3:208); it is an attempt to form a narrative whole from the diversity of events that I as an agent both carry out and suffer. For Ricoeur, "this narrative interpretation implies that a life story proceeds from untold and repressed stories in the direction of actual stories the subject can take up and hold as constitutive of his personal identity. It is the quest for this personal identity that assures the continuity between the potential or inchoate story and the actual story we assume responsibility for" (TN 1:74).

The search for identity is tied to the received past, but requires the past to be given a configuration marked with a stamp of ownership. Our fragmented storied past must be given a configuration that will have the power to refigure our experience in the construction of my personal and our collective identities. It is an interpretive process that begins with what Ricoeur calls "prefigured experience" and ends with the "refiguration" of our experience. The narrative function is a work of imagination that constructs a unifying plot that gives linguistic form to the mediation that takes place between the lived diversity of temporal experience and the unifying moment of action.[2] By organizing historical events into a narrative unity, communities and individuals can offer testimony of who they are and how they wish to mark their existence in the world.

This process of emplotment that moves from prefiguration through configuration to the refiguration of experience offers practical proposals for living. This narrative "arc" (TN 1:52) offers prescriptions *for* identity that are taken up and become constitutive *of* one's own identity through the deliberation of decision, the commitment of choice, and the initiative of action. What narratives offer are imaginary linguistic models or configurations for living that become identifiable with who we are through the reconnection of art and life, that is, the reconnection of the world of the text to the world of the reader.

While crucial with regard to his argument, Ricoeur readily admits to the difficulty posed by the intersection and reconnection of art and life, and it is a problem that is not lost to his critics.[3] Ricoeur argues that the connection between narrative and temporal experience is not accidental but "presents a transcultural form of necessity" (TN 1:52). Narrative and time are linked by the operative power of the "mimetic arc" of interpretation (TN 1:52). Ricoeur explains that "time becomes human to the extent that it is articulated through a narrative mode, and narrative attains its full meaning when it becomes a condition of temporal existence" (TN 1:52). The interpretation of the temporal world of human experience takes place through narrative configurations that are shaped by prenarrative structures and are completed by their return to life. This is the significance of the process of narrativization. Narrative mediates between the sedimentation and innovation of the practical field of human experience. Ricoeur writes: "My thesis is that the very meaning of the configurating operation constitutive of emplotment is a result of its intermediary position between the two operations I am calling mimesis1 and mimesis3" (TN 1:53).

By choosing the term *emplotment* Ricoeur hopes to capture the dynamic character of the relationship between temporal experience and narrative. The construction of narrative discourse is but one moment of the "arc of operations by which practical experience" is understood (TN 1:53). The configuring act of narration begins with (mimesis1) "a preunderstanding of the world of action, its meaningful structures, its symbolic resources, and its temporal character" (TN 1:54); it finds fulfillment in the "application" (mimesis3) of the referential intention in the life of the reader or listener. "It is the task of hermeneutics . . . to reconstruct the set of operations by which a work lifts itself above the opaque depths of living, acting, and suffering, to be given by an author to readers who receive it and thereby change their acting" (TN 1:53). The term *emplotment* signifies an intimate and necessary connection between the stories we tell about ourselves and the structure of human experience from which narratives arise and to which they return.

Narrative discourse is for Ricoeur a reflective way station, or critical moment of distanciation, which, while ontologically rooted in the practical world of experience, allows for the imaginative variation of what is received in order that narratives may refigure or reorganize experience into more meaningful patterns. For Ricoeur the ultimate significance of the connection between narrative and life is found in the analogous transferability of the identity of the text to that of persons and communities. Since Ricoeur takes the formation of personal and communal identity as the core of his entire investigation, the intelligibility of this mimetic arc is paramount for understanding the meaning of narrative identity. While there is obvious continuity between the creation of meaning in metaphor and narrative discourse, what must be explored in greater detail is the power of emplotment to create an identity that leads from narrative to the active moment of initiative where actual existing individuals assume a narrative configuration as their own. In other words, I want to carefully explain how Ricoeur understands the cycle of distanciation and application of the referential world of narrative to life.

To accomplish this task, and to help orient myself within the vast amount of material covered in the three volumes of *Time and Narrative*, I will reverse Ricoeur's order of presentation and examine some of his conclusions concerning narrative and personal identity before I unfold the process of narrative configuration.[4]

4.1 Narrative Identity

Exposing a "fracture" that exists between cosmological (objective) and phenomenological (subjective) time, Ricoeur situates the production of a "third time." Narrative time mediates and "bridges" this gap by "interweaving" the "respective ontological intentions of history and fiction" (TN 3:245). However, as Ricoeur readily admits, this mediation might very well be a "sign of the inadequacy of our poetics to our aporetics, if there were not born from this mutual fruitfulness an 'offshoot' . . . that testifies to a certain unification of the various meaning effects of narrative" (TN 3:246). The construction of narrative identity provides a unity of sameness and difference that bridges the gap between history and fiction, and in turn that between phenomenological and cosmological time.

Unlike the construction of metaphorical meaning, Ricoeur's concept of narrative identity is a quasi-semantic entity. Although narrative configurations offer models for identity, the choice one makes in the appropriation and application of such narrative proposals transfers a semantic textual identity from the imaginary mode to the practical dimension of human experience. "Here 'identity' is taken in the sense of a practical category" (TN 3:246). It is a poetic reply that is fulfilled in the initiative of action by an identifiable agent that can "answer the question, 'Who did this?' 'Who is the agent, the author?'" (TN 3:246). The response to this question unifies and brings about a certain degree of closure to the occultation of the aporetics of cosmic and phenomenological time. And the interweaving of historical and fictional intentionalities comes to rest with a reflective response to the question "Who?"

In spite of Ricoeur's designation of narrative identity as a unifying practical category, his elaboration of its meaning calls into question its function. Narrative identity is supposed to give a unifying response to the ambivalence of the philosophies of time. Further, the narrative formulation of identity is supposed to move beyond the debate of the substantialist *cogito* and the *anticogito* to provide a solution that can offer unity of self without the dismissal of diversity and otherness. Ricoeur explains that

> without the recourse to narration, the problem of personal identity would in fact be condemned to an antinomy with no solution. Either we must posit a subject identical with itself through the diversity of its different states, or, following Hume and Nietzsche, we must hold that this identical subject is nothing more than a substantialist illusion, whose elimination merely brings to light a pure manifold of cognitions, emotions, and volitions. This dilemma disappears if we substitute for identity understood in the sense of being the same (*idem*), identity understood in the sense of oneself as self-same [*soi-même*] (*ipse*). The difference between *idem* and *ipse* is nothing more than the difference between a substantial or formal identity and a narrative identity. Self-sameness, "self-constancy," can escape the dilemma of the Same and the Other to the extent that its identity rests on a temporal structure that conforms to the model of dynamic identity arising from the poetic composition of a narrative text. (TN 3:246)

According to this formulation, narrative identity gives unity to the self by allowing for a transference of narrative unity from the story of our life to actual experience. Narrative models for identity "become a provocation to be and to act differently. However this impetus is transformed into action only through a decision whereby a person says: Here I stand! So narration is not equivalent to true self-constancy except through this decisive moment, which makes ethical responsibility the highest factor in self-constancy" (TN 3:249). Just as narrative discourse places the diversity of events, characters, and reversals of fortune under the unity of the plot, so too does *ipse* identity place temporal diversity under its rule. Although these two processes are interlinked by the "mimetic arc," the transfer from literary textual identity to personal identity is actually more fundamental for self-constitution than the prefigurative features from which narrative takes distance. Careful note must be taken of this correlation between self-constancy and narrative identity. Ricoeur makes it quite clear that the problems of personal identity can have a meaningful solution if the solution rests on a temporal structure that in turn conforms to the dynamic identity of a text that is produced by the creative act of emplotment or narrative composition. Although the phenomenology of temporal experience and the production of narrative configurations are hermeneutically interlinked, the ultimate solution to the problem of identity lies within a creative act of imagination. Ricoeur gives priority to the narrative function over phenomenological description.[5]

Ricoeur readily admits the difficulty. Although narrative identity is proposed as a poetic resolution to the problems of the dialectic of narrative and temporal experience, "narrative identity is not a stable and seamless identity" (TN 3:248). The "application" of the narrative unity of a text to personal identity is far from a simple act. There is no single text; yet, there is an agent who must appropriate narrative meanings to form his or her identity.

The selection of significant meanings that are to become representative of who I am involves a highly complex procedure spread out over the course of my life. Compounding this difficulty is Ricoeur's assertion that life can never offer "total mediation" (TN 3:207). Narrative identity is "an open-ended, incomplete, imperfect mediation, namely, the network of interweaving perspectives of the expectation of the future, the reception of the past, and the experience of the present, with no *Aufhebung* into a totality where reason in history and in reality would coincide" (TN 3:207). There is no meta-narrative that can totalize my experience. Narrative identity is an identity of various stories. "Just as it is possible to compose several plots on the subject of the same incidents . . . so it is always possible to weave different, even opposed, plots about our lives" (TN 3:248). Ricoeur is convinced that within his concept of identity lies a diversity that no amount of narration can paper over and place under a unifying rule. "Narrative identity thus becomes the name of a problem at least as much as it is that of a solution" (TN 3:249). Therefore, the process of narrativization that gives configuration to the space of experience needs to be examined. Once this is completed, Ricoeur's concept of narrative identity and some of the critical difficulties that it implies can be addressed with greater precision and clarity.

4.2   The Mimetic Arc

Ricoeur's understanding of the concept of narrative identity is set within a "mimetic arc" of narrative representation that passes from the practical field of experience to a semantic level of linguistic meaning and back again to the practical world of human action. It is a three-step spiral process (TN 1:53, 71–72) that advances the understanding of personal and interpersonal identity through narrative representation of human action. Narrative takes distance from the practical world of action by giving it a literary or imaginative configuration with regard to identity formation. Ricoeur explains that "what certain fictions redescribe is, precisely, human action itself. Or, to say the same thing the other way around, the first way human beings attempt to understand and to master the 'manifold' of the practical field is to give themselves a fictive representation of it" (FTA 176).

Ricoeur's narrative arc repeats the central thesis of his hermeneutical phenomenology: linguistic distance coupled with the proximity of belonging. Although providing distance from the practical field, narrative texts belong to individuals and communities. The exchange of distanciation and appropriation adds a third step to the process of understanding. In order for narratives to be incorporated into identity formation, they must be rooted in the fundamental structures of practical experience—in Ricoeur's terminology, narratives must have prenarrative "features" (TN 1:54). Narrative emplotment gives configuration to features descriptive of our "preunderstanding of the world of action," specifically "its meaningful structures, its symbolic resources, and its temporal character" (TN 1:54). Through the power of emplotment, structural, symbolic, and temporal features of the world of practical experience are given a configuration in which the practical field is represented at a higher level. By providing mimetic models of the world of action, narratives offer literary alternatives for initiating action in the present. Although rooted in the prenarrative features of action, it is only through linguistic narrative configurations that this "mute" world (TN 1:xi) can be appropriated by the acting subject.

The description, narration, and appropriation of the practical field of action are distinct phases of a single "set of operations by which a work lifts itself above the opaque depths of living, acting, and suffering, to be given by an author to readers who receive it and thereby change their acting" (TN 1:53). Ricoeur presents the image of an arc: narration begins with the discordant and opaque character of human experience and ends with its refiguration. Rather than turning back on itself and simply returning to the same, the narrative arc should be seen as a snapshot of a lifelong process, or as a spiral that continually moves forward in time and understanding. "This circle is not however a vicious circle, because there is nevertheless an extension of meaning, progressive meaning, from the inchoate to the fully determined" (OPR 183). Once experience has been refigured during the moment of initiative, it becomes a sedimented element and part of a cultural repertoire available for narrative configuration. Reading calls for rereading. The three phases of the narrative arc are continually repeated as the arc spirals forward. Ricoeur explains that it is the "task of hermeneutics to reconstruct . . . the concrete process by which the textual configuration *mediates* between the prefiguration of the practical field and its refiguration through the reception of the work" (TN 1:53). Narrative configuration is the apex of an arc of operations that has significance only in relation to that which precedes and follows it. Similar to other operations of the imagination, narrative emplotment is a work of mediation.

4.2.1 *Prefiguration*

Mastering the "manifold" of practical experience through narrative imitation of action "requires . . . the capacity for identifying action in general by
means of its structural features" (TN 1:54). Ricoeur explains that each of these
features finds its place within a network of "intersignification." To identify a
specific action is—by implication—to identify "goals . . . motives . . . [and] agents
[who] can be held responsible for certain consequences of their actions . . . agents
[who] act and suffer in circumstances they did not make" (TN 1:55). The
preunderstanding of the practical field implies that "to act is always to act 'with'
others . . . [in] the form of cooperation or competition or struggle" (TN 1:55).
While not exhausting all the possible terms, Ricoeur intends to show how the
entire network of intersignification is mapped by "linking [each] term to every
other term of the same set" (TN 1:55). The network as a whole is constitutive
of the structure of human action.

The conceptual network of action forms a "paradigmatic order" (TN 1:56)
for narrative composition, and as such, this "semantics of action" (TN 1:54, 56)
is set within a meaning context. Employing Ernst Cassirer's formulation of
symbolic forms as "cultural processes that articulate experience," Ricoeur explains that action and experience are "always already articulated by signs, rules
and norms" (TN 1:57). Action always has significance, a meaning is always
"incorporated into action and decipherable from it by other actors in the social
interplay" (TN 1:57). Situated within "public . . . systems of interacting symbols" action acquires "an initial readability," a "texture" of "interpretants" that
makes the transition from practical to narrative understanding possible (TN
1:58). The symbolic mediation of action legitimizes Ricoeur's mimetic hermeneutic by providing a prenarrative tableau for narrative configuration. Action
can be read as "a quasi-text . . . insofar as the symbols, understood as interpretants,
provide the rules of meaning as a function of which this or that behavior can
be interpreted" (TN 1:58). Likewise narrative texts, because they give a
configuration to this vast array of prenarrative features, can be said to linguistically represent or stand for the practical field of experience.

By placing action within a symbolically mediated meaning context, Ricoeur
can subsume individual actions under socially regulated "cultural codes" that
function as "norms" or " 'programs' for behavior; they give form, order, and
direction to life" (TN 1:58). Actions are always "rule-governed behaviors" (TN
1:58). While one can offer a description of prenarrative symbolic meanings
through classification of individual actions under broader cultural categories,
such codes also function as "prescriptive norms" (TN 1:58). Practical understanding includes moral and ethical evaluations. Ricoeur writes: "As a function
of the norms immanent in a culture, actions can be estimated or evaluated, that
is, judged according to a scale of moral preferences. They thereby receive a

relative value, which says that this action is more valuable than that one. These degrees of value, first attributed to actions, can be extended to the agents themselves, who are held to be good or bad, better or worse" (TN 1:58). Since the implicit meaning of the conceptual network of action includes ethical evaluation, narrative configurations of action "can never be ethically neutral" (TN 1:59). To represent the practical manifold is to assume an ethical position in relation to the actions carried out or suffered by an agent or agents. Giving a narrative configuration or constructing an identifiable synthesis from heterogeneous elements of practical experience involves the construction of prescriptive representations. By drawing on the prenarrative features of practical experience, narrative configurations transform mere descriptive representation *of* experience into a prescriptive model *for* experience.

Description of the structure of action and its symbolic mediation is predicated on a third and more fundamental prenarrative feature. The temporal character of experience is "implicit in" action (TN 1:60). Action takes time to be accomplished, and it is the time of action that "calls for narration" (TN 1:59). While narrative emplotment uses various features described through a semantics and symbolism of action, such organization takes place *within* a temporal framework. The temporal structure of experience provides connectors between the practical field as a whole and the imaginative act of narrative configuration. To initiate action is to do so in the present; but the present is distended by the past and the future. The time of action has a before and after, a time of preparation and consequences that organizes the practical field around the moment of initiative (TN 3:230–233). Ricoeur explains that this structure of "everyday praxis orders the present of the future, the present of the past, and the present of the present in terms of one another. For it is this practical articulation that constitutes the most elementary inductor of narrative" (TN 1:60). The temporal organization of the practical field provides a ground for the temporal organization of narrative.

4.2.2 *Configuration*

Although the temporal organization of action is foundational for narrative configuration, like the other prenarrative features of the practical field, its relationship to narrative configuration is one of "presupposition and of transformation" (TN 1:55). Temporal, symbolic, and structural features constitute the first phase of a mimetic arc. Narrative configuration presupposes a basic understanding of the practical field, but also instills a transformation and break with the practical field through the introduction of imaginative distanciation initiated by the act of emplotment. Literature is not life, but a representation of life. "Yet despite the break it institutes, literature would be incomprehensible if it did not give a configuration to what was already a figure in human action" (TN 1:64). Narrative representation of the practical field initiates a new level of intelligibility in continuity with practical understanding but takes distance from life through the imaginative power to understand one's world "as if" it were different from that which has been received.

Ricoeur treats the configurative phase of the narrative arc as a unified act covering the entire narrative field. Although narration falls into the two great classifications of historical and fictional narrative, Ricoeur subjects both narrative forms to the rule of the "kingdom of the *as if*" (TN 1:64). Performing a narrative *epochè* that temporarily suspends the question of literary and historical reference, Ricoeur focuses on the configurative power of emplotment to organize events and characters into a narrative whole regardless of its reference to the "reality of the past" or the "unreality of fiction" (TN 3:157). For the purpose of this investigation I will accept Ricoeur's unification of the narrative field as justified. Since my interest lies in the correlation between the text and the self, the bifurcation of narrative literature into historical and fiction genres, while extremely important in the formation of different aspects of personal and communal identity,[6] is secondary to the fundamental act of existing in the mode of selfhood which is predicated on the power of narration to construct a "synthesis from the heterogeneous" (TN 1:66).

The mediating function of emplotment is "derivative from the dynamic character of the configuring operation" (TN 1:65). To configure experience is to mediate between what has been received and what is to come through various narrative forms of discourse. The sweeping scope of such practical mediation can be seen on a smaller scale "within [the story's] own textual field" (TN 1:65). Ricoeur explains that the operation of emplotment mediates by "drawing a configuration out of a simple succession" that brings "together heterogeneous factors" and constructs a temporal "synthesis of the heterogeneous" (TN 1:65–66). By connecting the diversity of heterogeneous narrative events in temporal succession with the central "thought" of an "intelligible whole," the operation of emplotment creates a narrative unity of identity and diversity or a "concordant discordance" (TN 1:66). This is the key feature of the narrative arc. The poetic narrativization of experience combines an "episodic" temporal dimension with a configuring act that "draws from this manifold of events the unity of one temporal whole" (TN 1, 66). Similar to the construction of metaphor, it is a work of imagination that places "an intuitive manifold under the rule of a concept" (TN 1:66). According to Ricoeur this affiliation between metaphor and narrative stems from their "kinship" with the Kantian "operation of judging," which Ricoeur has repeatedly employed as the paradigmatic function of the imagination (TN 1:66).

While narrative imagination "extracts a configuration from a succession," the unity of the temporal whole that constitutes the story is a poetic resolution of the inherent tension between the diversity of events and the identifying theme or central thought that holds the narrative together. This narrative "paradox" between the singularity of the central thought and the diversity of events is "resolved" according to Ricoeur by "the poetic act itself."[7] Constructing a story does not overcome the difference of "distention and intention" (TN 1:67), but makes this difference productive. The act of emplotment places a diversity of events into a temporal configuration that provides a "point of view from which the story can be perceived as forming a whole" (TN 1:67). This is what provides the "story's capacity to be followed. . . . To understand the story is to understand how and why the successive episodes led to this conclusion, which, far from being foreseeable, must finally be acceptable, as congruent with the episodes brought together by the story" (TN 1:66–67). The act of emplotment allows the reader to live into the temporality of the world unfolded by the configuration of events and "converts the paradox into a living dialectic" (TN 1:67). The text itself is only an encoded work of emplotment that needs to be brought to life through the work of readers and listeners. In other words, the poetic act of emplotment is repeated every time the story is read or told in order to bring the story to life.

The connection between the poetic act of narrative composition and that of reading signifies the transition, within the narrative arc, from narrative configuration to refiguration. While configuration takes imaginative distance from life, the act of reading reconnects language to life. It is here that textual identity is applied to the identity of persons and communities. With reading, narrative meaning is appropriated from the virtual world of the text and incorporated into the actual world of the reader "wherein real action occurs and unfolds its specific temporality" (TN 1:71). This is the point of intersection that offers Ricoeur the promised path toward the interpretation of selfhood; but it is also a point to which some of Ricoeur's critics take great exception.

4.2.3 *Refiguration*

Ricoeur refers to the transfer[8] between narrative texts and persons as the refiguration of experience. Texts do provide models for temporal experience and action, but such a repertoire of possibilities is more than a smorgasbord of possible identities; it is intended as discipleship toward selfhood (TN 1:78). For Ricoeur the world of the text is ultimately an ethical world instructing the subject toward intersubjective action that requires stability of purpose and faithfulness toward others through a "decision whereby a person says: Here I stand" (TN 3:249). The text's "provocation to be and to act differently" requires ethical action, and "so narrative identity is not equivalent to true self-constancy except through this decisive moment, which makes ethical responsibility the highest factor of self-constancy" (TN 3:249). Personal identity is connected to narrative identity by way of appropriation of models for existence, but narrative identity is a linguistic construction, whereas personal identity is practical. The two forms of identity are intimately linked, but it "still belongs to the reader, now an agent, an initiator of action, to choose among the multiple proposals of ethical justice brought forth by reading. It is at this point that the notion of narrative identity encounters its limit and has to link up with the nonnarrative components in the formation of an acting subject" (TN 3:249). The difference between language and life, narrative identity and self-constancy, imaginative possibility and decisive choice, needs to be kept in mind as we examine Ricoeur's concept of the refiguration of experience.

The key to understanding the character of the analogical transfer from texts to persons lies in the similarity between the imaginative act of configuration and the act of reading. Ricoeur explains that "to follow a story is to actualize it by reading it" (TN 1:76). The refiguration of experience is initiated and brought to temporary closure through the reception of a narrative work by a reader. Just as emplotment is an imaginative act that grasps together a diversity of events into a temporal whole, so too is reading an imaginative act that forms a synthetic unity from the narrative arrangement of events and characters. In this sense, "if emplotment can be described as an act of judgment and of the productive imagination, it is so insofar as this act is the joint work of the text and reader, just as Aristotle said that sensation is the common work of sensing and what is sensed" (TN 1:76). The act of reading engages the virtual world of the text from within the reader's actual world of experience. Not content to simply repeat experience, the imagination links narrative composition and receptive reading to produce a unity of identity and difference within the text and within the experience of the reader. Narrative configuration is completed through an act of reading that produces a possibility for experience which, when taken up through decision and action, refigures experience and therein personal identity. Each time a text is read the narrative arc is repeated; this repetition takes place from the new vantage point of personal identity that the previous reading produced.

Like the act of emplotment, refiguration is fundamentally productive in nature. Reading produces a connection between the text and the reader that allows Ricoeur to understand the world of the text *as if* it were the actual world of the reader. The world of the text must become "unreal" to refigure the "real" (TN 3:157). Even though Ricoeur develops his concept of the narrative arc by placing brackets around the great division of the narrative field into historical and fictional narrative, the privilege accorded to fictional narrative is clear. Historical narrative is primarily a reproductive act of imagination that assumes the "reality" of the past as its referent (TN 3:142–156), whereas the referent of fictional narrative is supposedly "unreal" (TN 3:157–179). To affect the reader and refigure his or her experience, the reproductive work of historical narrative must be placed under the rule of the productive work of fiction. For, as Ricoeur argues, only the "unreal" or imaginative world of fiction is "undividedly reveal-ing and transforming. Revealing, in the sense that it brings features to light that were concealed and yet already sketched out at the heart of experience, our praxis. Transforming in the sense that a life examined in this way is a changed life, another life" (TN 3:158). Only then can a transformation take place be-tween the narrative power to see the temporal world of human action *as if* it could be inhabited by a responsible agent, and the actual *being* of the agent in search of his or her identity.

The priority Ricoeur gives to the productive power of imagination to refigure experience requires that "refiguration must free itself, once and for all, from the vocabulary of reference" (TN 3:158). If both historical and fictional narratives can be understood through "productive reference," then both narrative forms will have the capacity to produce an innovation within the world of the reader. Read-ing is a synthetic activity that constructs an analogy between the world of the text and the reader. If the narrative form, regardless of its division into fictional and historical narratives, can produce such an application, then both literary forms must be understood in the productive mode of the "as-if."

4.2.4 *Reproductive Imagination*

Ricoeur explains that historical narratives are supposed to "stand for" what happened in the past. "Unlike novels, historians' constructions do aim at being *re*constructions of the past. . . . They owe a debt to the past, a debt of recognition to the dead, that makes them insolvent debtors" (TN 3:142–143). To give "intellectual articulation" to the "feeling expressed through this sense of debt" to represent the past as it really was, Ricoeur employs the categories of "the Same, the Other, and the Analogous" (TN 3:143).

Although historians must assume that their narrative reconstructions cor-respond to previous events, this reenactment of the past in the mind of the historian can never be completely subsumed under the concept of the "Same." The goal of this type of historical knowledge is to overcome the temporal distance between past events and the act of reconstruction. Yet the question remains: "How can we call an act that abolishes its own difference in relation to some original act of creation, re-creation? In a multitude of ways, the 're' in the term reenactment resists the operation that seeks to wipe out temporal distance" (TN 3:147).

Narrative reconstructions of the past are qualified by a temporal differ-ence and distance that frustrates the universal application of the category of the "Same." However, the inverse category of the "Other" is inadequate on its own to account for the temporal difference between the present and the past. According to Ricoeur, the efficacy of the past in the present precludes a negative ontology of difference. "In the last analysis, the notion of difference does not do justice to what seems to be positive in the persistence of the past in the present" (TN 3:151). The difference between the past and the present is not radical. What Ricoeur wants to develop is a historical epistemology—and an ontology of being as . . .—that can combine the categories of the "Same" and of the "Other" by way of the "Analogous." "When we want to indicate the difference between fiction and history, we inevitably refer to the idea of a certain correspondence between our narrative and what really happened. At the same time, we are well aware that this reconstruction is a different construction of the course of events narrated" (TN 3:151–152). The desire of the historian to "render [the past] its due" must, therefore, take into account both the reproductive correspondence between the narrative and past events, and the temporal distance separating these events from the narrative (TN 3:152).

As an extended metaphor, narrative discourse is analogical discourse that sees the world of acting and suffering *as* configured in a particular manner. In this regard the historian must display a "double allegiance: on the one hand, to the constraints attached to the privileged plot type; on the other hand, to the past itself, by way of the documentary information available at a given moment. The work of the historian consists in making narrative structure into a 'model,' an 'icon' of the past, capable of 'representing' it" (TN 3:152). Although Ricoeur is quick to point out that a narrative model of the past must not be "confused . . . with a model, in the sense of a scale model, such as a map, for there is no original with which to compare this model," its "iconic value" can be maintained if it is understood not as "a relation of reproduction, reduplication, or equivalence but [as] a metaphorical relation . . . [that is,] things must have happened *as* they are told in a narrative such as this one" (TN 3:153–154). The historical past must assume the analogous structure of a metaphorical narrative. The past must be seen *as if* it happened the way the narrative plot arranges past events; in other words, historical events come under the rule of the productive imagination.

Joining his previous analysis, in *The Rule of Metaphor*, of the ontological significance of the as-if structure of analogy, Ricoeur once again makes the power to "see" the past *as* configured in a particular way correlative with "being-as." The analogous vision of the past goes beyond historical epistemology. Historical narrative brings "the being-as of the past event . . . to language" (TN 3:154). Although this ontological foundation remains relatively undeveloped in *Time and Narrative*, Ricoeur nevertheless predicates this productive analogy on an analogical ontology. Asking how historical narrative can refer to the past through the act of narrative emplotment or the extended metaphor, Ricoeur points out that

the key to the problem lies in the functioning, which is not merely
rhetorical but also ontological, of the "as," as I analyzed it in the
seventh and eighth studies of my *Rule of Metaphor*. What gives
metaphor a referential import, I said, itself has an ontological
claim, and this is the intending of a "being-as . . ." correlative to the
"seeing-as . . ." in which the work of metaphor on the plane of language may be summed up. In other words, being itself has to be
metaphorized in terms of the kinds of being-as, if we are to be able
to attribute to metaphor an ontological function that does not con-
tradict the vivid character of metaphor on the linguistic plane; that
is, its power of augmenting the initial polysemy of our words. The
correspondence between seeing-as and being-as satisfies this require-
ment. (TN 3:155)

The power of imagination to construct a narrative configuration that stands for
past events *as if* they happened that way, implies an analogical ontology where
"being-as is both to be and not to be" (RM 255). In other words, historical
narrative represents the past through the analogous unity of "identity and otherness" (TN 3:155).

Ricoeur's recourse to this enigmatic ontology of "being-as" is not only the
connecting foundation between the historical narrative and the being of the
past; it also performs an even larger task of legitimizing the connection between
the act of emplotment proper and human experience. Historical narrative is but
one type of narrative literature that finds its place within Ricoeur's arc of narrative configuration. As in the case of Ricoeur's ontological reflections in *The
Rule of Metaphor*, the development of an ontology of being-as takes place
within his investigation of the work of imagination, and is secondary to, or
derivative of, the literary unity of identity and difference. Questions can be
raised, however, whether the requirements for an ontology of identity and difference are fully provided for from within the productive act of metaphor construction; and subsequently whether the problem of personal identity can be
adequately addressed from within the concerns of identity and difference that
are central to narrative discourse. These questions are significant and will require a thoughtful response at the end of my investigation of Ricoeur's concept
of selfhood.

4.2.5 *Refiguration Through Receptive Reading*

The analogous relationship that historical narrative establishes with the
past refigures experience by instilling a sense of debt through receptive reading.
Narrative transforms the past imaginatively by making it productive in the

moment of reception, that is, "undividedly revealing and transforming" (TN 3:158). The productive work of imagination, interwoven into the reproductive historical intention, is thereby opening historical narrative to affect the process of refiguration. In this way, "all forms of writing, including historiography, take their place within an extended theory of reading. As a result, the operation of mutually encompassing one another . . . is rooted in reading . . . [and] belongs to an extended theory of reception, within which the act of reading is considered as the phenomenological moment" (TN 3:180–181). Reading is a work of application. "It is only in reading that the dynamism of configuration completes its course. And it is beyond reading, in effective action, instructed by the works handed down, that configuration of the text is transformed into refiguration" (TN 3:158–159). While reading marks the path of narrative application for the initiation of meaningful action, it also marks the "intersection" that gives the "work of fiction . . . [its] significance" (TN 3:159). The relation between the "fictive world of the text and the real world of the reader" requires "the phenomenon of reading . . . [as] the necessary mediator of refiguration" (TN 3:159). One must be able to "imagine that" (TN 3:181) the temporal world of the reader can be "seen as" the world of a narrative text in order to innovatively refigure experience. Both historical and fictional narratives refigure experience under this rule of analogy, that is, under the rule of emplotment governed by the logic of metaphor that reconnects art to life through the transformation of "seeing as" into "being as."

This task of narrative refiguration requires an act of the productive imagination that interactively constructs the meaning of the text. While the rhetorical force of the text *affects* the reader, the interaction between the world of the text and the world of the reader calls for an *active* response on the part of the reader. As Ricoeur explains, "this being-affected has the noteworthy quality of combining in an experience of a particular type passivity and activity, which allows us to consider as the 'reception' of a text the very 'action' of reading it" (TN 3:167). The effect of the rhetoric of persuasion on the reader is passive; the meaning of its world of otherness (TN 1:78) results from the productive activity of reading.

Ricoeur accounts for this duality within the act of responsive reading through dialogue with Wolfgang Iser and Roman Ingarden.[9] In particular, Ricoeur focuses on Iser's appropriation of Ingarden's concept of the incomplete nature of literary texts—incomplete with regard to "image-building concretization," and with regard to the world of the text (TN 3:167). Since the text requires a reader to activate the literary intention of the "sequence of sentences," thereby changing the fulfillment of the literary intention each time the story is read, Iser proposes that the text must have a "wandering viewpoint" (TN 3:168). This concept "expresses the twofold fact that the whole of the text can never be perceived at once and that, placing ourselves within the literary text, we travel with it as our reading progresses" (TN 3:168). The indeterminate nature of the viewpoint reveals a dynamic relationship comparable to the act of emplotment. Reading is "a drama of discordant concordance" in which the attempt to "concretize" the "image of the work" fluctuates between the extremes of a complete "lack of determinacy [and] . . . an excess of meaning" (TN 3:169). In "this search for coherence" the reader oscillates between the "illusion" of complete familiarity and "the negation resulting from the work's surplus of meaning, its polysemanticism, which negates all the reader's attempts to adhere to the text and to its instructions. . . . The right distance from the work is the one from which the illusion is, by turns, irresistible and untenable. As for a balance between these two impulses, it is never achieved" (TN 3:169). Reading is a "vital experience" (TN 3:169) that calls for readers to concretize the image of the text through the refiguration of their own experience. Never static, every act of reading enters into a dynamic exchange between the configured structure of the text and the imaginative world of meaning, either to fall prey to its persuasive force and succumb to the illusion of familiarity, or to appropriate some portion of its polysemanticism in order to "transform" experience. The act of reading lives within this dialectic of "freedom and constraint" (TN 3:177), that is, within the space of imagination that Ricoeur continually describes as the interplay of activity and passivity.

According to Ricoeur, the act of receptive reading must also be understood in conjunction with the "public reception of a work" (TN 3:171). Although every act of reading is an individual response, the meaning of the text is always understood by individuals in community with other readers and the traditions within which they read. Each generation responds to a text through its own "logic of question and answer" (TN 3:172), hoping to find a "solution for which they themselves must find the appropriate questions, those that constitute the aesthetic and moral problem posed by a work" (TN 3:173). This is properly the *Wirkungsgeschichte* of the text, to use here Hans-Georg Gadamer's term. In this way, the relationship between an individual and a community of readers opens subjectivity to another dimension of otherness. To understand a text is to gain "knowledge" of another world of reference in conjunction with other readers.

The goal of reading in community with others is to effect a response that produces not only an intelligible configuration of the text, but more significantly, the refiguration of experience by way of intersubjective knowledge. To truly understand a text is to bring it to completion in life; therefore, "application orients the entire process teleologically" (TN 3:174). Rather than leaving the reader with an abstract "recognition of the text's otherness" (TN 3:175), Ricoeur argues that the process of narrativization must overcome this difference by constructing a sameness or identity between text and reader. Using Hans Robert Jauss's triadic distinction among "*poiesis, aisthesis, catharsis*," Ricoeur explains that the aesthetic pleasure received from the actualization of the world of the text, if it is to return to the living world of the reader, must move beyond aesthetic experience to a cathartic effect "that is more moral than aesthetic: new evaluations, hitherto unheard of norms, are proposed by the work, confronting or shaking current customs" (TN 3:176). The cathartic effect releases the reader from the imaginative world of meaning to clarify experience by means of the moral instruction that reading has produced.

This is the key to Ricoeur's concept of refiguration. "Thanks to the clarification it brings about, catharsis sets in motion a process of transposition, one that is not only affective but cognitive as well, something like *allégorèse*, whose history can be traced back to Christian and pagan exegesis" (TN 3:176). To refigure experience is to draw an *analogy* between the work of mimesis2 and mimesis3. Reading does not merely extract moral content from the configuration of the text, but attempts to forge a conjunction of identity between text and reader. This transposition of new evaluations and norms requires that the reader actualize them in the intersubjective world of agents and patients. The reader must identify with, and take responsibility for, the cathartic effect that impacts on the moment of initiative and action, the moment that defines who we are. In other words, the narrative arc is completed with an allegorizing application of the world of the text in the immediate world of the reader. But since the narrative arc forms the necessary means for understanding experience, to understand the text is to make one's own subjectivity identical with that proposed by the text. This is not only an identity with regard to the content of the text, for the very structure of the text becomes identical with the reader through cathartic application. *Seeing oneself as* that proposed by the text becomes, by means of choice and action, *being oneself as* that proposed by the text. Refiguration transforms more than moral evaluations, the very subjectivity of the one who accepts responsibility for his or her actions configured by the world of the text becomes transformed by the possibilities the world of the text proposes.

This solution creates many problems. Ricoeur recognizes the paradoxical nature of his formulation of refiguration and points out several "dialectical tensions" that need to be taken into consideration if his proposal for narrative identity is to be made productive (TN 3:177–179).

First of all, the work of imagination allows the reader to take distance from the "narrator's vision of the world," but the reader is nevertheless constrained by the "force of conviction" or "strategy of persuasion" the author employs to communicate his or her worldview. Although this "dialectic between freedom and constraint, internal to the creative process," requires a "struggle" toward a "fusion of horizons of the expectation of the text with those of the reader," the tension itself is not resolved and both poles of the dialectic stand over and against each in "precarious peace" (TN 3:177–178).

Second, this cessation of hostility follows only if the seduction of the narrative voice is juxtaposed to the imaginative distance demanded by the reader

to avoid the "terror" of the text. Even though Ricoeur explains that "this oscillation between Same and Other is overcome only in the operation characterized by Gadamer and Jauss as the fusion of horizons . . . [which is] an analogizing
relation," it is only "held to be an ideal type of reading" (TN 3:178). In fact, the
tension between text and reader, or the Same and the Other, is never completely overcome; rather, the analogizing relation is an "imperfect mediation"
in which the Same and the Other continually struggle not necessarily for domi-
nance over each other, but for the creative formation of an "open-ended, incomplete" analogous relationship between them (TN 3:207).

Third, this conflict for the "issue" of the text is placed more squarely on
the shoulders of the reader than on "the world the work projects." The dialectic
between the world of the text and "sheer subjectivity of the act of reading" (TN
3:179) gives primary responsibility for the construction of meaning to the reader
in community with others. This, according to Ricoeur, gives the reception of
the work a "historical dimension" and calls for a "chain of readings" to address
the question: "What historical horizon has conditioned the genesis and the
effect of the work and limits, in turn, the interpretation of the present reader?"
(TN 3:175). But the connection between the historical community and the
individual reader is secondary and "remains under the control of the properly
hermeneutical question—what does the text say to me and what do I say to the
text?" (TN 3:175). Therefore, the hermeneutical issue of the text, in spite of the
conflict between the Same and the Other, and freedom and constraint, is focused on the response to the text of an individual reader ruled by the productive
imagination.

These paradoxical features are characteristic not only of the act of
refiguration, but also of its productive solution, namely, narrative identity. Reading allows for the analogical transfer of the configured lesson of the text to the
reader. Through the distance the imagination takes from experience, the human world of action is transformed under the refigurative power of reading
itself. As Ricoeur explains, "reading appears by turns as an interruption in the
course of action and as a new impetus to action" (TN 3:179). It is both a "stasis
and an impetus" to take distance from, and to act in the actual world of human
action and suffering. Reading opens an imaginative space within experience to
affect experience. In this space of experience an analogous connection is made
between the identity of texts and that of persons, a space within which the
imagination is reconnected with life in order to initiate action.

The narrative refiguration of experience completes its trajectory with the
initiation of action. Through choice and action narrative possibilities become
representative of the acting subject and become part of the production of one's
narrative identity. Yet, this "practical" solution of identity has problems of its
own. In particular, Ricoeur's explanation of the means for the analogical transfer of identity pushes the question of agency to the forefront but does not seem

able to give an account of who this agent is. In fact, Ricoeur takes what appears to be a step backward from a decentered narrative retrieval of selfhood, and calls for the phenomenological recovery of the "I will," the "I can," and the "I do," present in the analysis of action.

Employing Reinhart Koselleck's distinction between the "'space of experience' and 'horizon of expectation'" (TN 3:208), Ricoeur unfolds a hermeneutic of historical consciousness that interprets the immediacy of the analogous transfer as "present initiative" distended by the expectation of the future and the effect of the past. This is the space of experience in which the Other and the Same, identity and difference, are brought together under the unifying rule of the analogous. The distance of the Other is brought close to the Same through a "beginning" of action in the intersubjective world of actual experience. Ricoeur's "proposal" is "to connect the two ideas of making-present and initiative. The present is then no longer a category of seeing but one of acting and suffering. One verb expresses this better than all the substantive forms, including that of presence: 'to begin.' To begin is to give a new course to things, starting from an initiative that announces a continuation and hence opens something ongoing. To begin is to begin to continue—a work has to follow" (TN 3:230). The beginning of action initiates the transition from a world of possibility to the actual work of identity formation by an agent who must assume responsibility for what is done. In the present the "provocation to be and act differently . . . is transformed into action only through a decision whereby a person says: Here I stand!" (TN 3:249), this is who I am, and this is what I have done! I am the one who is willing to accept responsibility for this action!

The space of experience is the dynamic of decision or the moment of innovation in relation to our history of sedimented choice. Here identity is formed through the application or analogical transfer of texts to persons. But if the present space of experience is the place where personal and communal identity is formed, the place where I exchange my ego for a self discipled by the other, who is this "I" that takes a stand? Who is this "I" that wills to be constant in relation to another? For Ricoeur, in *Time and Narrative*, the "Who?" is answered through "the phases traversed by a general analysis of initiative. Through the 'I can,' initiative indicates my power; through the 'I do,' it becomes my act, through interference in intervention, it inscribes my act in the course of things, thereby making the lived present coincide with the particular instant; through the kept promise, it gives the present the force of preserving, in short, of enduring" (TN 3:233). While such description might uncover meanings of agency, what remains unclear is why Ricoeur could not develop such an analysis of action without recourse to the concept of narrative identity. But more important, what does such description really say about who this "I" is? Is this "I" myself, the self, oneself, my ego, my subjectivity, my identity, or "oneself as self-same [*soi-même*] (*ipse*)" (TN 3:246), that is "self-constancy" (TN 3:247)? Ricoeur uses these terms interchangeably; their meaning is ambiguous. However, with the publication of *Oneself as Another*, Ricoeur exerts a tremendous effort to clarify such confusion.

4.3   Narrative Identity Between Art and Life

Ricoeur's proposal for the analogous application of the lesson of the text to the actual world of the reader is convincing in its simplicity and power to reshape the world of human action. While Ricoeur points to the formation of narrative identity as the productive resolution to the tension between art and life, he fails to provide the reader of *Time and Narrative* with a more explicit explanation of what he means by identity. Even though this concept of identity is presumed from the beginning of the first volume of *Time and Narrative*, Ricoeur offers us little more than scant reference to the term without further elaboration. Yet the clarification of this concept is crucial not only for explaining the process of the narrativization of experience, but also for understanding Ricoeur's formulation of selfhood as developed in *Oneself as Another*. Therefore, further exploration of Ricoeur's concept of narrative identity is warranted.

In an article entitled "The Text as Dynamic Identity" (1985), Ricoeur outlines the central features of the type of identity that arise from the poetic composition of a text. The problem of the identity of the text is for Ricoeur one among many other philosophical problems tied to the question of identity in general. It is Ricoeur's hope that the investigation of the "dynamic identity" of narrative texts, "in spite of the deliberate narrowness of my starting-point, . . . will release some broader vista from which to survey the act of poetic composition that Aristotle called *poiesis* and will also give us access to those features of *poiesis* which support procedures of identification compatible with its various modes of historicity" (TDI 175–176). Although specific to the narrative text Ricoeur's proposal for a point of orientation within the broader philosophical question of identity will become the paradigmatic solution for the question itself.

One of the key difficulties of the question of identity is its division into mutually exclusive alternatives of either identity as *sameness* or identity as *difference*. While neither alternative provides an adequate solution in isolation from the other, Ricoeur attempts to combine both concepts into a productive mediation that steers clear of two "pitfalls: that of taking identity in the too narrow sense of *logical* identity, or of indulging in the delights of the game of sameness and difference" (TDI 175). By setting up the problem of identity as a path to be navigated between these two extremes, Ricoeur offers a concept of identity that is a *dynamic* unity of sameness and difference.[10]

Building on his model of the linguistic creation of meaning, Ricoeur develops four "propositions" essential to his concept of dynamic identity. First of all, this concept of identity must be able to gather diversity into a unified whole. Narrative emplotment as a "synthesis of the heterogeneous" is paradigmatic of this function. Emplotment combines "events or incidents . . . circumstances, agents, interactions, ends, means, and unintended results, [into] an intelligible whole which always allows one to ask about the 'theme' of the story" (TDI 176). Narration combines a vast diversity of "features" into a single organizing theme Ricoeur refers to as "a concordant-discordant whole." Narrating a series of events is to "mediate" between the singularity of the "serial order" of the whole story and the diversity of features necessary for the story to be told (TDI 176). Further, it is a temporal mediation between the "story's incidents which constitute the episodic side of the story," and the "configurational act of narrating" that brings about "integration, culmination, and closure" (TDI 177). The synthesis constructed by the act of emplotment sets the temporal whole or the organizing serial order of the story's theme in relation to the heterogeneous diversity of temporal events and features. Ricoeur likens the temporal mediation of emplotment to a mediation "between time as passage and time as duration" (TDI 177). The synthetic activity of emplotment constructs an enduring temporal theme or concordant whole from the diversity of events and prenarrative features that are subject to "the pure, discrete, and interminable succession" of the passage of time. Therefore, the identity of a text is linked not only with the central theme of the story, but with "what is enduring in the midst of what is passing away" (TDI 177) within the temporality of the story told.

The ability to construct a synthetic unity from heterogeneous narrative features is a form of imaginative intelligibility. This is Ricoeur's second proposition. Emplotment "grasps together" an array of various events and features and places them under the rule of narrative. It is like the Kantian concept of judging that places "some intuitive manifold under a rule. This is precisely the kind of *subsumption* that emplotment executes by putting events under the rule of a story, one and complete" (TDI 178). The imagination generates narrative rules for subsumption of intuitive diversity. Just as the creation of new meaning "connects the level of understanding and that of intuition by generating a new synthesis, both intellectual and intuitive, . . . emplotment generates a mixed intelligibility between what can be called the *thought*—the theme, or the topic of the story—and the intuitive presentation of circumstances, characters, episodes, changes of fortune, etc." (TDI 178). Narrative intelligence grasps the whole through its constitutive elements, but the intelligible rule or thought that governs the meaning of events is of a practical rather than theoretical nature. The central narrative "thought" universalizes the diversity of narrative features by providing a pedagogical model of human experience. As Ricoeur points out, poetry has the "capacity to 'teach' " (TDI 177), to organize features of human experience into a particular pattern or configuration that represents and imitates the practical world of action. The narrative function, just as the metaphorical function of the imagination, creates new meaning but at a level that provides a *model for* action by providing a narrative *model of* action.

The universalizing or paradigmatic function of the narrative imagination is not static. Identifying a particular narrative schematism means to set it within a narrative tradition that has developed around a plot typology. This is Ricoeur's third proposition concerning the dynamic identity of the text. To identify a text is to place it within a living tradition that "relies upon the interplay between innovation and sedimentation" of narrative models (TDI 181). Such a tradition has specific narrative forms, genres, and types from which "we get a hierarchy of paradigms which are born from the work of the productive imagination at these several levels" (TDI 181). While the reception of sedimented narrative models provides rules for the initiation of new narrative works, the matrix of imaginative activity that generates narrative schemata does not live in the virtual world of narratological structure, but exists through the creation of "a singular work, *this* work" (TDI 182). The narrative imagination functions in the exchange of received rules for the creation of narrative meaning, and the innovative creation of new narrative meaning that may augment or change entirely the rules for modeling human action. Ricoeur explains that "each work is an original production, a new existent in the realm of discourse. But the reverse is no less true: innovation remains a rule-governed behavior. The work of imagination does not start from scratch. It is connected in one way or another to the paradigms of a tradition" (TDI 182). The act of narrative emplotment is a form of rule-governed deviation, where poetic creation lives in a dynamic spiral of sedimentation and innovation. To identify a text is to find its "point of equilibrium between the process of sedimentation and the process of innovation, and implies a twofold identification, that of the paradigms that it exemplifies and that of the deviance that measures its novelty" (TDI 183).

The identity of a text and the question of identity as a whole finds its formal conceptualization in this dual or dialectical concept of identity. A narrative is a productive work that combines the unifying function of emplotment with the diversity of narrative features; it provides universal teaching models *for* action by constructing narrative models *of* action; its production marks a point on a line between the sedimentation and innovation of such pedagogical paradigms. The dialectic tension central to each of these narrative propositions gives the concept of identity its dynamism. Identity does indeed provide unity, but it is a provisional unity that continually travels between sameness and difference, a practical unity that offers instruction *for* life by being instructed *by* life. Since emplotment is the activity of imaginative configuration, every effort of telling, writing, or reading a story takes a different position on the line between sedimentation and innovation. In this sense, every act of emplotment is different, yet every act still remains a synthetic union of the heterogeneous, a model for action, and an instantiation on the continuum between received rules and new narrative structures. The dialectical tension that this concept of identity exhibits makes the process of identification a truly dynamic undertaking.

Ricoeur combines these three features of identity with regard to texts into a larger dialectic that allows for the transference of this dynamic concept of identity to the reader. Ricoeur explains that it is only within the dynamic of meaning and existence that identity comes to life. This is the fourth and final proposition: "as a dynamic identity, it emerges at the intersection between the world of the text and the world of the reader. It is in the act of reading that the capacity of the plot to transfigure experience is actualized" (TDI 183). As we have seen in the chapter dealing with Ricoeur's hermeneutical phenomenology (see 1.4), the productive imagination spirals forward, moving between the poles of distanciation and belonging. By following the ascending movement created by linguistic works, a world of possibility is opened in front of consciousness which can become a new mode of belonging. The world proposed by the text becomes the critical counterpart of the immediate world to which the reader belongs. The interpretive relationship between text and reader is the "intersection" at which the possibility of the world of the text is actualized in its application to life. It is the point at which the "inside world" of the text and the "outside world" of the reader are intertwined to such an extent that the interpretation of the dynamic identity of the text becomes the interpretation and "*disclosure*" of a possibility to be actualized by the reader (TDI 183). The narrative world with its unifying plot and diversity of characters and events is transferred through reading to the reader, who also inhabits a world or "*horizon* of the circumstances and the interactions which constitute the proximate web of relationships for each agent" (TDI 183).

Ricoeur's four propositions concerning the dynamic identity of the text give articulate shape to the matrix of activity that defines the process of refiguration. The interactive dynamic of text and reader is crucial for the formation of identity. Narration or emplotment is the activity of giving shape to the world of meaning, but it also implies a passive reception of the sedimentation of tradition. This is equally true for the identity of the reader, who configures the meaning of the text by being configured by the text. Ricoeur explains that "to follow a story is to *enact* or *re-enact* it by reading. If, therefore, emplotment may be described as an act of judgment at the level of the productive imagination, this is so to the extent that emplotment is the joint work of the text and its reader, in the same way that Aristotle called sensation the common work of the 'sensed' and the 'sensing' " (TDI 184). To form one's own identity the agent must synthesize the heterogeneous, the different, the other. The agent must gather together into a unified whole the diversity of his or her experience and must be able to universalize his or her action as a living model for others to read. For Ricoeur, the formation of our identity requires the subsumption of difference under the unifying rule of our choice, initiative, and action; but does such voluntary unification place diversity and difference under the rule of the same? Does the formation of personal identity require the reduction of difference to the singularity of the voluntary "I will"? Is Ricoeur reaffirming, albeit in narrative form, that "the will is the one which brings order to many of the involuntary" (FN 5)?

The significance of this problem should not be underestimated. At stake is Ricoeur's assertion that narrative not only can refigure experience but that it has the capacity to refigure and transform the identity of the reader, that is, the claim that art can and should transform life. If, however, Ricoeur's model of refigurative transformation simply repeats the phenomenological insight (*Wesensschau*) of voluntary singularity (the "I will") over and against involuntary otherness, then Ricoeur's ontological speculations regarding selfhood, and the process of narrative discipleship, may be simply nothing more than a sophisticated version of what has already been worked out in *Freedom and Nature*. So how does Ricoeur's understanding of narrative refiguration advance his understanding of selfhood without, on the one hand, simply recovering a preexistent model of the voluntary *cogito* within the semantic structure of narrative discourse, and on the other hand, not advocate a radical discontinuity between the prenarrative phenomenological features of consciousness and the reader's refigured identity?

Although Ricoeur's narrative arc is precisely intended to circumvent such mutually exclusive alternatives of either the artistic determination of life or the reduction of art to mere representation of some form of original experience, he nevertheless is deeply concerned that the "very thorny problem to reconnect literature to life by means of reading" (OA 159) will expose a fissure that may exist between them.[11] Hence, Ricoeur's attempt to "attack" and overcome "the paradox we are considering here: stories are recounted, life is lived," must also address the question of "an unbridgeable gap [that] seems to separate fiction and life" (LQN 25). This problem not only animates the production of narrative identity, but has initiated sharp debate among some of Ricoeur's critics as well.[12] This is particularly true of David Carr,[13] who takes Ricoeur to task for adopting a position that comes close to the "standard view," which assumes that the narrative "form is 'imposed upon' reality . . . [and that] it distorts life. At best it constitutes an escape, a consolation, at worst an opiate, either as self-delusion or . . . imposed from without by some authoritative narrative voice in the interest of manipulation and power. In either case it is an act of violence, a betrayal, an imposition on reality or life and on ourselves"[14] Although Carr hesitates to offer a definitive judgment, stating that "I am not sure where the author [Ricoeur] stands on this issue," he nevertheless shows little appreciation for Ricoeur's formulation of the relationship between narrative and life.

Carr argues that Ricoeur has in fact reversed the proper order and should have placed the priority on the phenomenology of temporality, which should provide the dynamic structure for the narrativization of experience. According

NARRATIVE IMAGINATION AND PERSONAL IDENTITY

to Carr, narratives should conform to the descriptive features of temporality and not the reverse. Carr argues that art should be the *reproduction* and discovery of experience "mirroring the sort of activity of which life consists"(OPR 172), not its creative *production*. Critiquing Ricoeur's dialectic of narrative concord and temporal discord Carr writes: "If lived temporality is essentially (if not completely) discordant, and if art—narration in particular—brings concord, then art cannot be the simple imitation of life, in the sense of mirroring or representing it. Narrative mimesis for Ricoeur is not reproduction but production, invention. It may borrow from life but it transforms it" (OPR 170). Fearing that such production implies that temporal experience lacks any structure of its own, and therefore that Ricoeur needs to "describe a world *as if* it were what apparently . . . it in fact is not" (OPR 171), Carr asks if Ricoeur does not end up equating the difference between art and life with "the difference between the chaotic and the formed, the confused and the orderly." If this is true, then it "would seem to amount to the assertion that life cannot be lived without literature" (OPR 173).

To justify such a critique of Ricoeur's position Carr would have to demonstrate that the temporal structure of existence is in fact within the realm of description apart from narration, and this Ricoeur believes to be impossible.[15] Through careful examination of the best examples of the phenomenology of time Ricoeur demonstrates how they create some of the very problems that it seeks to resolve (TN 3:12–96). According to Ricoeur, without the mediation of narrated time and the production of narrative identity, temporal experience remains without a voice. "A life is no more than a biological phenomenon as long as it has not been interpreted" (LQN 27–28). To predicate, as Carr does, personal or communal identity on a pure phenomenology or ontology of temporality sets aside the necessity of the mimetic relationship between narrative art and life, which calls for choice and action that can transform the "space of experience," and not simply duplicate it.

Gary Madison, however, argues the contrary. Quoting Ricoeur, he explains that existence "cannot be separated from the account we can give of ourselves. It is in telling our own stories that we give ourselves an identity. We recognize ourselves in the stories we tell about ourselves. It makes little difference whether these stories are true or false, fiction as well as verifiable history provides us with an identity" (HP 95). Madison goes on to explain that "when we seek to understand human events, which is to say, action, to *account* for them, the giving of an account invariably assumes the form of telling a story. To understand an experience or an event is to make sense of it in the form of a story. . . . Text and action are quite simply inseparable" (HP 97–98). Although Madison appears to be simply restating Ricoeur's understanding of the relationship between narrative and life, he takes a position which, according to Carr's "standard model," would disconnect narrative even more from life.

Contrary to Carr's critique of the inadequacy of Ricoeur's concept of narrative invention, Madison faults Ricoeur for the narrative or metaphoric "discovery" of life or so-called reality. "Metaphorical discourse is indeed creative and inventive, and yet, this *creation* is a *discovery*. Ricoeur seems to be saying that there are in some sense or other, certain objective 'essences' which language articulates—although it may only be able to do so in certain cases when it is used creatively, innovatively" (HP 82–83). This reference to "objective essences," or one could also say to extralinguistic reality, Madison finds troubling. For Madison language does not refer to a "reality" outside language; rather "the world referred to by language is what it is only because of the way it is linguistically referred to. The world, in short, is a function of language. . . . Strictly speaking, there would no longer be any extralinguistic reality to which language could be said to refer; reality would be constituted differently in accordance with the different ways we use to speak about it, and, in the final analysis, there would be as many 'realities' as there are languages" (HP 83–84). Even though Madison admits that Ricoeur would "express reservation" about such *inter*linguistic reference to "reality," metaphorical invention is "the *only* means for talking about them [things] meaningfully and truthfully and in a direct and straightforward fashion" (HP 85). Reality is an invention of language and not its discovery. "Reality is nothing other than a metaphor which is taken literally and is *believed* in" (HP 85). For Madison the only relationship of consequence is the narrative refiguration of experience. It matters little that narratives mirror life; what matters more is that life is continually transformed by the power of metaphor and narrative. "[T]he real 'meaning' of a metaphor lies not in what it 'says' but in what it 'shows' . . . what it does, the perlocutionary effect it has on us. . . . I am *not* saying that metaphors have no meaning. I am saying that their meaning *is* their power to effect a change of attitudes, direction, and, ultimately, understanding of the part of the listener or reader" (HP 150). Since "reality" is the product of a dead metaphor that had a profound perlocutionary effect on the part of a "believer," Carr's complaint that the "standard view" imposes narrative on life makes little sense to Madison outside some sort of rational essentialism.

Both Carr and Madison raise important issues with regard to Ricoeur's understanding of the relationship between art and life; but these alternatives of "sheer change and absolute identity" (LQN 33) seem to undo their own critical positions and point to a solution that Ricoeur's unique formulation of the narrative arc has already taken into consideration. In wishing to move beyond Ricoeur's dialectic of creation and discovery of extralinguistic reality, Madison appears to be supporting a view of language that is only creative, cut off from any underlying temporal structure. Yet Madison makes a connection between art and life much in the same way as Ricoeur does between metaphor/narrative and the prenarrative features of temporal experience. Madison writes that "reality in the ordinary sense, the so-called extralinguistic referent of language, is thoroughly relative to language itself and is its 'product,' but reality in the deeper sense (what we might call 'being') is not determinate (has no essence) and is not the product of language but is its creative source. And this source is to be located in the lived experience which all humans share in, in one form or another" (HP 86–87). Although Madison qualifies this deeper meaning of "being" by explaining that "as its creative source, it can be said to be what is *analogically* common to all the creative or metaphorical, i.e., 'analogical,' uses of language" (HP 87), he nevertheless concludes that creative language grows out of experience before it forms experience. Isn't this precisely Ricoeur's point, that narrative configuration is preceded by prenarrative features that provide the resources for narrative creation? And isn't the narrative and metaphorical creation of reality also a discovery of the source that gives it life?

David Carr's rejection of the narrative refiguration of experience suggests that narrative meaning can only be a discovery of a more fundamental temporal experience. Yet even a reproductive view of narrative cannot dismiss its power to transform experience through action. If experience can be told, surely the purpose of such a story is not just to catalogue experience, but to inform readers of the meaning of experience and add something to the reader's self-understanding. Wouldn't this type of expanded self-understanding be a transformation of experience, a call to be and act in a manner that is different or other than the way one had previously acted? In other words, doesn't Carr, due to his preoccupation with the fear of fictional violence, miss Ricoeur's point about the narrative function of refiguration?

Brushing aside Carr's accusation that he is an advocate of the "standard view," not to mention his ridiculous claim that "perhaps the proponents of the standard view just read too many stories and lead very dull or cluttered lives" (OPR 166), Ricoeur argues that the alternative of either the narrative "distortion of life, or its representation" (OPR 180) is too restrictive. Ricoeur goes on to explain that "the concept that I proposed of a refiguration which would be at once 'revelatory' and 'transformative' seems to me to introduce a concept of representation which does not imply a mirror relation . . . [but] escapes the dilemma according to which either history falsifies life, does it violence, or reflects it. I wonder if a standard model exists under which one may group every author mentioned and which constrains each to a yes or no answer" (OPR 180). Narrative representation is for Ricoeur always a productive reproduction, a creative innovation in connection with a discovered sedimentation, a dynamic process in which he "believes that it is possible to avoid the alternative proposed by David [Carr] and instead embrace both horns of the dilemma: a *life* in search of its own *history*" (OPR 181).

This is the central point of *Time and Narrative*: individuals and communities are in search of their narrative identity. Life looks for narratives that will give a meaningful configuration to events both carried out and suffered. Narrative identity is both an innovation that adds something new to the "space of experience" and a discovery of our inchoate story. It gives a configuration to life in order that it can become a configuration for life, that is, a prescriptive innovation that transforms experience. Discovery and innovation are not conflicting alternatives that cancel each other out; rather, they form the core dynamic of Ricoeur's proposal for identity and selfhood.

> Our life, when then embraced in a single glance, appears to us as the field of a constructive activity, borrowed from narrative understanding, by which we attempt to discover and not simply to impose from the outside the *narrative identity which constitutes us*. I am stressing the expression "narrative identity" for what we call subjectivity is neither an incoherent series of events nor an immutable substantiality, impervious to evolution. This is precisely the sort of identity which narrative composition alone can create through its dynamism. (LQN 32)

For Ricoeur this *discovery* of one's narrative identity mitigates the violence of a literary artifice. And the construction of one's narrative identity plays with possibilities for subjectivity through the *"narrative voices* which constitute the symphony of great works such as epics, tragedies, dramas and novels" (LQN 32). One's narrative identity is a composition of a musical score fashioned from the cacophony and lack of determinacy of our temporal experience. It is both a disconnection and reflection of life that can dismiss the opposing accusations of sheer change or absolute sameness by proposing a dynamic concept of identity that is a unity of sameness and difference.

Therefore, in response to the question concerning the relation between narrative art and life, Ricoeur writes that

> an unbridgeable difference does remain, but this difference is partially abolished by our power of applying to ourselves the plots that we have received from our culture and of trying on the different roles assumed by the favorite characters of the stories most dear to us. It is therefore by means of the imaginative variations of our own ego that we attempt to obtain a narrative understanding of ourselves, the only kind that escapes the apparent choice between sheer change and absolute identity. Between the two lies narrative identity. (LQN 33)

Rather than enclosing oneself within the text, or limiting the text to reflect a phenomenological description of temporality, Ricoeur's narrative arc is both the discovery and innovation of identity; it is both life as art and art as life.

As the bridge between art and life, Ricoeur's formulation of narrative identity poses, however, a significant problem. Is Ricoeur suggesting that narrative identity straddles a difference between two different selves: a narrative self and an ontological self? Is there for Ricoeur a self that is objectively identified and structured through narrative discourse, and a deeper, more mysterious self correlative with such objectifications? If so, is Ricoeur redeploying a variation of Husserl's phenomenological correlation between some sort of transcendental subjectivity and the objectification of the acts of consciousness? Is Ricoeur's proposal for narrative identity ultimately guilty of reasserting the presence of a voluntary *cogito* over and against the polysemic flux of symbol, myth, and discourse? And does self-identification require a heroic effort of consent to all that is other, different, and involuntary? While a claim of radical Husserlian dualism is perhaps too strong, given Ricoeur's refutation of transcendental idealism, it nevertheless points to a significant problem that requires further careful reflection.

CHAPTER FIVE

IDENTITY AND SELFHOOD

With the completion of the previous chapter, which illustrates the expansion of the configural function from metaphor to narrative, I have shown how, according to Ricoeur, the dynamic identity of narrative texts solves the problem of personal identity. The narrative arc finds completion in the moment of initiative by refiguring experience. By providing a temporal mediation between the past and the future, the narrative imagination inaugurates a process that incorporates openness into the moment of narrative closure. Narrative configuration brings together the diversity of experience: narrative emplotment constructs a dialectical (or analogical) relation between unity and diversity, between the same and the different. It is Ricoeur's contention that such narrative openness and diversity prevents narrative closure and unity from encircling the problem of identity within the category of the same. Not only is this true for the dynamic identity of the text, it is equally true for personal and communal identity. Since the search for one's narrative identity is Ricoeur's ultimate point of orientation for the narrativization of experience, personal and communal identity emulate the dynamic structure of the identity of narrative texts. Identity is a dialectic of unity and difference, of closure and openness. For Ricoeur the problem of textual and personal identity is formulated and resolved through this dialectical relation of the "same" and the "other."

With the publication of *Oneself as Another* (1992) Ricoeur expands this formulation of identity to include the problem of selfhood. Although never absent from his discussions on method and language, the discipleship of the self by way of the other has been a constant, albeit delayed, theme in his work. By reserving the question "What is a human?" for the "end of a series of prior questions such as: What can I know? What must I do? What am I allowed to hope?" (NP 89), the problem of selfhood has remained in the shadow of these monumental questions of method put in this very order by Kant himself. Ricoeur's "detour by way of objectification" (OA 313) has been an indirect path toward

123

the self, favoring a mediated rather than an immediate reflection on selfhood; but this has come at a price, the detour is so long that it can be mistaken for the destination. Yet, from the outset, Ricoeur's hermeneutical inquiries have been in service of a project of self-recovery and self-discovery. Hermeneutics, let us recall, is for Ricoeur a form of reflective philosophy that "considers the most radical philosophical problems as those that concern the possibility of *self-understanding* as the subject of the operations of knowing, willing, evaluating, and so on" (OI 12). Explaining and understanding the multiple operations that give testimony of selfhood are of fundamental concern to Ricoeur. However, while linguistic reference to the self is the implicit goal of Ricoeur's hermeneutical inquiries, explicit treatment of the question of selfhood has been astonishingly minimal.

In *Oneself as Another*, the anthropological quest for self-affirmation becomes thematic once again. Ricoeur's thirty-year detour through the complexities of interpretive mediation returns to the question of selfhood that dominated his earlier work. Has Ricoeur's hermeneutical meandering accomplished his intended goal of exchanging the ego for a self discipled by the otherness of the text? Has the thirty-year hiatus between *Fallible Man* and *Oneself as Another* been able to move Ricoeur beyond the dialectic impasse of determination and mutuality? If the hermeneutical reorganization of the question of selfhood is not a vicious circle simply returning back to its presumed starting point, but a progressive spiral that advances his understanding of the meaning of selfhood, then, as Ricoeur insists, the question of selfhood must "supersede . . . the quarrel over the cogito" (OA 4). It must move beyond the philosophies of the *cogito* and *anticogito*, and in that sense move beyond the anthropological position adopted in *Freedom and Nature* and *Fallible Man*. Therefore, I want to explore Ricoeur's response to the question of selfhood developed in *Oneself as Another* and test this hermeneutical reformulation to see if it is indeed a philosophy of selfhood, and if it offers an advance over his early philosophical concept of a *cogito* in search of its other.

Ricoeur's hermeneutic of selfhood employs two different but interrelated strategies of investigation: an analysis of selfhood that reflects itself in its objectivities, and an ontology of selfhood that grounds such objectifications. This difference, which Ricoeur also refers to as first- and second-order discourse (OA 298), approaches the question of selfhood from two different directions: from the outside inward by means of phenomenological and analytical description, and from the inside outward through the ontological "metacategory of being as act and as power" (OA 303). In each case the subject of investigation is supposed to be the same: selfhood. On the one hand Ricoeur examines the objectivities of selfhood, namely, "(discursive, practical, narrative, and prescriptive predicates) in the reflective [*réflexif*] process of the self";[1] on the other hand, not wanting to reduce selfhood to reflection and its objective structures, Ricoeur turns to an ontological investigation that asks the question, "What mode of being, then, belongs to the self, what sort of being or entity is it?" (OA 297). This duality of approach is meant to suggest not that there are two selves (one objectively describable and the other only available through ontological discourse) but that the self is structured so that ontological testimony, or attestation of selfhood (OA 299–302), is needed to complete a hermeneutic of selfhood.

This methodological duality is necessitated by Ricoeur's proclamation that "to say *self* is not to say *I*. The *I* is posited—or deposed. The *self* is implied reflexively [*à titre réfléchi*] in the operations, the analysis of which precedes the return towards this self."[2] The immediate recovery of this reflexive self, or "self in relation,"[3] is blocked by the mediating objectivities in which the operations or activities of the self are reflected. The interpretation of selfhood is predicated on the analysis of these objectifications in which the self reflects itself and is thereby available for interpretation.[4] Therefore, the work of interpretation is at once a "fragmentary" effort to catch sight of multiple self-reflections in the objectivities of the self, and a work of unification that designates the self as "*conatus*," the productive power responsible for this diversity of activities (OA 315).

This duality of approach repeats the dialectic of unity and difference central to Ricoeur's concept of metaphor, narrative, and identity; thus it should not be surprising that Ricoeur's hermeneutic is conducted from within a semantic analysis of selfhood. "[T]he three major features of the hermeneutics of the self, namely, the detour of reflection by way of analysis, the dialectic of selfhood and sameness, and finally the dialectic of selfhood and otherness ... [are] progressively uncovered ... introducing by means of the question 'who?' all the assertions relating to the problematic of the self, and in this way giving the same scope to the question 'who?' and to the answer—*the self*" (OA 16). The "objectivities" in which the self is reflected are subjected to an interrogative form of analysis. To each objectification—linguistic, practical, narrative, and ethical—the question "who?" is addressed, and in each case Ricoeur asserts that "the self" is the only appropriate response. "Who is speaking? Who is acting? Who is recounting about himself or herself? Who is the moral subject of imputation?" (OA 16). These questions are all answered with "the self!" that "take[s] refuge in the inexpugnable retreat of the question 'who?'" (OA 302). Yet, as Ricoeur remarks, this interrogative approach is "fragmentary." The question "who?" does not find a unity of response. Each reply does not say "The Self," but identifies the subject who is now speaking, now acting, now narrating, and so on. Each field of inquiry finds an answer appropriate to its own requirements, and in each case Ricoeur believes to uncover a different dimension or modality of selfhood. But as Ricoeur readily admits, this fragmentation of meaning is compounded by the fact that "in introducing the problematic of the self by the question 'who?,' we have in the same

stroke opened the way for the genuine polysemy inherent in this question itself"
(OA 19), that is, a polysemy inherent within the dialogue of question and answer.
Therefore, to whom does this fragmentation of meaning refer? To a linguistic,
practical, narrative, or ethical subject identified within the language game of each
objectivity? Is there a fundamental unity that can hold this polysemy of question
and answer together?

        For Ricoeur "this fragmentation . . . has a thematic unity that keeps it
from the dissemination that would lead the discourse back to silence. In a sense,
one could say that these studies together have as their thematic unity *human
action* and that the notion of action acquires, over the course of the studies, an
ever-increasing extension and concreteness" (OA 19). The cumulative effect of
the analysis of each of the objectivities underscores not so much a foundational
subjectivity or a first-person *cogito* but a productive power that makes these
activities possible. The unity that Ricoeur has in mind is a "merely analogical
unity"[5] and not that of an ultimate foundation that characterizes the "*philosophies of the subject*" that are "formulated in the first person—*ego cogito*" (OA
4). Ricoeur assures his readers that his hermeneutic of selfhood has "superseded . . . the quarrel over the cogito" (OA 4) and that he is not interested in
the development of a "first philosophy" predicated on a self-founding ego.
Characterizing his philosophy of selfhood as "practical" or "second philosophy"
(OA 19), Ricoeur believes he can move beyond the identification of self with
an "ultimate foundation" (OA 19) by deriving an ontology of selfhood from an
analogical identification of "the multiple uses of the term 'acting,' which, as we
have just mentioned, receives its polysemy from the variety and contingency of
the questions that activate the analyses leading back to the reflection on the
self" (OA 19–20). It is not that Ricoeur is uninterested in the development of
a unifying ontology, but the foundation of such discourse is inherently polysemic
and therefore can only give testimony of selfhood within a hermeneutical context that oscillates between sedimentation and innovation of meaning.

        While Ricoeur designates his hermeneutic of selfhood as "second phi-
losophy" in contrast to "first philosophy," it is questionable whether its secondary standing with regard to the certainty of an ultimate foundation warrants the
further designation of "practical philosophy." Ricoeur formulates the thematic
unity of his studies around the analogical "uses to the term 'acting,' " but this
use is fragmented by an "analytic-reflective structure" (OA 19) that looks for
testimony of selfhood within the interaction of question and answer peculiar to
various objectifications of meaning. Since these objectivities are further frac-
tured by the infinite variation of meaning that almost allows both question
(who?) and answer (the self!) to slip away and escape hermeneutic understanding, Ricoeur's description of this fragmentation, and conversely that of unity, is
more a semantic analysis of multiple meanings of action than the development
of a practical philosophy. Although Ricoeur attempts to lay claim to the "ana-

logical unity of human action" (OA 20), there appears to be a kind of short circuit that jumps from the construction of an analogy among multiple identifications of the semantic meaning of the term *action*, to the claim that this analogous relation is indicative of the ontological unity of selfhood. Yet, if these are identifications of the linguistic, practical, narrative, and ethico-moral self, can Ricoeur offer anything more than a description of the unity of action from within these objectivities? In other words, does Ricoeur, for all his discussion about selfhood, place himself in a methodological position that collapses his philosophy of selfhood into a philosophy of identity?

This correlation between the question "who?" and the response "the self" must be understood in two different ways: (1) through the objectivities of self, which are interpreted by Ricoeur as texts,[6] an analogy can be drawn between the semantic similarities that identify the self as the appropriate response to the question "who?"; and (2) through an ontology of selfhood predicated on the attestation provided by this analogical unity.

This difference between first- and second-order discourse is intended to circumvent the debate between the "modern" *cogito* and a "postmodern" *anticogito*.[7] But what remains unclear is how recourse to analogical unity accomplishes this task. After all, action is performed by someone, it is never general. Agents are responsible for their actions. Self-reference by way of analogy still has a common referent: the subject of the action performed. Even though Ricoeur dismisses a singular action that posits the *cogito* as the self-grounded-ground of subjectivity, reference of the analogical unity of action to a "metacategory of being as act and power" (OA 303) still implies a *cogito*-subject to which these actions can be predicated.

The indirect implication of a ego-subject does not escape Ricoeur's attention. The concluding chapter of *Oneself as Another* is an investigation of the ontological substrate of the analogical unity of selfhood. Reappropriating the skeletal framework of Aristotle's metaphysics, Ricoeur asks "whether the great polysemy of the term 'being,' according to Aristotle, can permit us to give new value to the meaning of being as act and potentiality, securing in this way the analogical unity of action on a stable ontological meaning" (OA 20). This is a puzzling question. Until now Ricoeur's hermeneutical inquiries have rejected the idea of stable ontological meaning. Language is under the rule of metaphor. Change and development of language define Ricoeur's understanding of the interpretive act. Therefore, to search for a stable ontological meaning to support a hermeneutic of selfhood seems to run counter to the hermeneutical spiral of change and development. After all, what precludes giving definition to the self in the form of a single stable substance or function if that stability is derived from the stability of ontological meaning?[8]

In this sense, Ricoeur poses a difficult problem. Is it possible to move beyond the multiple identifications of self that a hermeneutic of continual

configuration and reconfiguration have brought to light? Can a stable ontological meaning be given to selfhood when the understanding of human experience has been predicated on the polysemy of meaning? Does Ricoeur simply
pose a rhetorical question to draw attention to the complexity of ontological
reflection in the light of the hermeneutical disavowal of ultimate foundations?
At first this appears to be the case. Ricoeur's affirmation of the polysemy of
meaning also applies to any and all ontological formulations that lend support
to a hermeneutic of selfhood. For Ricoeur,

> this reevaluation of a meaning of being, too often sacrificed to being-
> as-substance, can take place only against the backdrop of a plurality
> more radical than any other, namely that of the meanings of being.
> Moreover, it will quickly become apparent that the ontology of act
> and of potentiality will in turn open up variations of meaning difficult
> to specify because of their multiple historical expressions. Finally,
> and most especially, the dialectic of the same and the other, read-
> justed to the dimensions of our hermeneutic of the self and its
> other, will prevent an ontology of act and potentiality from becom-
> ing enclosed within a tautology. The polysemy of otherness . . . will
> imprint upon the entire ontology of acting the seal of the diversity
> of sense that foils the ambition of arriving at an ultimate foundation,
> characteristic of cogito philosophies. (OA 20–21)

While this diversity of meaning may preclude resting a hermeneutic of selfhood
on a stable ontological meaning, we are still faced with the same problem.
Ricoeur assumes that the semantic analogy drawn from these variations of
meaning makes reference to the extralinguistic being of selfhood. Language,
according to Ricoeur, refers to reality, in this case the reality of selfhood. But
constructing an identifying analogy from polysemic speech is still speech, albeit
of a different kind, which Ricoeur takes as attestation of the actual unity of
selfhood. Hence, Ricoeur's analysis of the objectivities of the reflective process
of selfhood does not give testimony of the intimacy of selfhood; rather, the
linguistic, practical, narrative, and ethico-moral objectivities give testimony of
an analogical semantic unity of identity.

Therefore, it remains unclear what Ricoeur has in mind with the first-
order polysemic identifications of selfhood and the second-order ontological
unity behind the semantic unity of identity. Neither *cogito* nor *anticogito*, this
ontological self nevertheless appears to have a quasi-metaphysical unity that has
not escaped the "great oscillation that causes the 'I' of the 'I think' to appear,
by turns, to be elevated inordinately to the heights of a first truth and then cast
down to the depths of a vast illusion" (OA 4–5). Ricoeur's intention to recover
an understanding of selfhood beyond this debate is perhaps an overly optimistic
ambition. On the one hand, Ricoeur seems to affirm postmodern *différance*, the

impossibility of retrieving original meaning, and the significance of the question "Who comes after the subject?";[9] and on the other hand, he wants to affirm the being of a self (via Aristotle, Spinoza, and Heidegger) that can halt this "dissemination that would lead the discourse back to silence" (OA 19). Ricoeur, despite his assertion to the contrary, seems to be describing the meaning of selfhood somewhere between the metaphysical singularity of a first-person *cogito* and the radicality of the shattered *cogito*,[10] not unlike his description in *Freedom and Nature* of the wounded *cogito* understood as the voluntary one over and against involuntary otherness.

Ricoeur's disavowal of both the *cogito* and *anticogito* is therefore not a disavowal of subjectivity, let alone of self and selfhood. The conclusion "that the 'I' of the philosophies of the subject is *atopos*" (OA 21), is not a rejection of ontological inquiry. However, second-order ontological discourse must, according to Ricoeur, reflect the analogous unity of first-order discourse which is the semantic source for the reflexive (ontological) structure of selfhood that Ricoeur differentiates from "sameness" and dialectically connects with "otherness" (OA 297).

It is remarkable that this formulation of analogous unity uses the correlation between the self and the other-than-self as constitutive of selfhood. If selfhood is understood by means of the identification of the agent of action, and action is in turn understood through a semantic network of intersignification, then the other-than-self must first be identified and named as an opposing term within the same network before it can be recognized as the other in its own right. If this is indeed the case, then Ricoeur has not developed a philosophy of selfhood in which otherness is constitutive of intimate self-reflexivity; rather, what Ricoeur has developed is a philosophy of identity in which the self and the other are encircled by self-sameness.[11] Alterity and selfhood fall under the unifying rule of linguistic identity formation, which finds its fullest expression in narrative discourse ruled by the work of emplotment, which is in turn under the rule of metaphor.

For Ricoeur, otherness and selfhood are dialectically united by language, by a common network of intersignification; but, who constructs this unity? Who is responsible for this dimension of sense that unites the other to the self? Is it not, according to Ricoeur, the self who engages in "a transfer of *sense* . . . [where] the sense of ego is transferred to another body, which, as flesh, also contains the sense of ego" (OA 334). Is this what Ricoeur means by "the movement from ego toward the alter ego, [which] maintains a priority in the gnoseological dimension" over the "movement coming from the other towards me" in the "ethical dimension" (OA 335, 340–341, 315)? If this is true, then Ricoeur is simply repeating, albeit in a more sophisticated and nuanced form, the priority of the voluntary (*ipse*) self over involuntary (*idem*) otherness.

To proceed with this investigation of Ricoeur's philosophy of selfhood I will outline its development as presented in *Oneself as Another*, and argue that

Ricoeur collapses the problem of selfhood into that of identity. The organizational structure of *Oneself as Another* can be understood in two different ways: the order of presentation, and the order of analysis concerning the structure of selfhood. On two occasions Ricoeur insists that the order of presentation of the various "studies" has no real systematic cohesion. Since self-reflection is fragmented and its analogical unity is predicated on the resemblance between responses to the question "who?" rather than on any methodological necessity, it "permit[s] the reader to enter into this inquiry at any point" (OA 19 n. 24). Even though Ricoeur uses a "three-step rhythm: describing, narrating, prescribing," to organize the studies, he argues that "this ordering . . . serves a merely didactic function, intended to guide the reader through the polysemy of action. Depending on the question asked, however, this threesome can be read in a different order. No approach is primary in every respect" (OA 20). While Ricoeur may be correct to insist on the circularity of the order of presentation, requiring the reader to enter the investigation with any one of the questions, there is a degree of linearity to this order that puts its variability in doubt. Like the mediating function performed by narrative configuration in *Time and Narrative*, the "three-step rhythm" employed here in *Oneself as Another* ascribes a similar position of mediation to narrative identity. The "two extremes" (OA 120 n. 5) of mediation are those of *idem* identity and *ipse* identity, that is, self-sameness and self-constancy. The order of presentation in *Oneself as Another* duplicates the narrative arc: just as narrative configuration is preceded by prefiguration and followed by refiguration, the development of the analogical unity of selfhood begins with the descriptive features of self-sameness and then ends with a prescription for selfhood that is intended to refigure self-sameness by way of self-constancy. So the reader may very well enter the circle at any point, but the order of presentation unfolds a model of identity formulated on the basis of a linear structure of argumentation. Therefore, contrary to Ricoeur's claim, this linearity of mediation precludes any arbitrariness of the order of presentation.

5.1 Identity and Language

Ricoeur begins his interpretation of selfhood with an investigation of semantic self-reference in contrast to what he believes to be a pragmatics of reflexive self-designation in the act of utterance. Semantic self-reference and pragmatic self-designation are combined to form the first level of self-identification. This cross-pollination between semantics and pragmatics opens a vast array of problems. While many of these problems put in doubt Ricoeur's claim that he is truly working within, and further developing, a pragmatics of language, this debate will for the most part be set aside as it falls outside the scope of this study. For me the central concern is how Ricoeur understands the objectifications of self to give testimony of actual selfhood. On numerous occasions Ricoeur's utilization of a dialectical impasse as a productive advance of his position brings together concepts and ideas that one could take substantial issue with. Yet, more often than not, Ricoeur's interest is with the act of mediation that produces a working dialectic rather than the adherence to a strict orthodoxy of the representative traditions that stand behind these concepts. After all, the most fundamental dialectic for Ricoeur is that of innovation and sedimentation, the transformation of traditions in the imaginative moment of mediation.

Since the world of the text has been the locus of Ricoeur's hermeneutical inquiries it is not surprising to see his project of self-identification begin with language. Texts refer to worlds that present places for self-habitation. In this sense, texts have a dual reference: to the self and to the world that makes that mode of existing in selfhood possible. For Ricoeur the interpretation of "the world of the text" is at the same time an interpretation of the self. Therefore, the most basic level of self-interpretation has to follow the "path of identifying reference [where] we encounter the person for the first time" (OA 27). Language, through the employment of "individualization operators," can "designate one and only one individual" in distinction from all others (OA 28). To individualize is to "aim at one and only one specimen, to the exclusion of all the others of the same class" (OA 30). According to Ricoeur, this only has meaning in relation to an "utterance, understood as an event in the world" (OA 30). Thus, language makes reference to individuals in relation to two types of "others": the individual in distinction from "all others," and the individual in distinction from the immediate other present in the event of utterance. In this way, Ricoeur begins to show how he will place in juxtaposition a semantically generalized reference to individual persons and a pragmatical reference to the self involving for its own constitution a reference to an individualized other.

However, the individualizing intention of language lacks the specificity needed to identity persons as "divisible without alteration" (OA 28). Therefore, Ricoeur appropriates Strawson's concept of "basic particulars" and explains that

> this strategy consists in isolating, among all the particulars to which we may refer in order to identify them (in the sense of individualizing given above), privileged particulars belonging to a certain type, which the author calls "basic particulars." Physical bodies and the persons we ourselves are constitute . . . such basic particulars in the sense that nothing at all can be identified unless it ultimately refers to one or the other of these two kinds of particulars. In this way, the concept of person, just as that of physical body, is held to be a primitive concept, to the extent that there is no way to go beyond it, without presupposing it in the argument that would claim to derive it from something else. (OA 31)

The advantage of Ricoeur's adoption of this position also points to its weakness. The person included within the category of basic particulars "remains on the side of the thing about which we speak rather than on the side of the speakers themselves who designated themselves in speaking" (OA 32). Semantic self-reference can identify an individual person, but "what matters for unambiguous identification is that the interlocutors designate the same thing. Identity is described as sameness (*mêmeté*) and not as selfhood (*ipséité*)" (OA 32). Strawson gives priority to "what" the person is, thereby placing the question of selfhood within a semantics of personal identity; but Ricoeur, with his preference for the question "who?," assumes that he can move beyond the semantics of identity to a pragmatics of the "speaking subject" (OA 40). While the strength of Strawson's concept of basic particulars allows for the identification and reidentification of persons in a public or objective manner, Ricoeur points out that this exclusion of selfhood simply describes the person as unique and recurrent among other basic particulars that are also unique and recurrent, and thereby fails to distinguish self-designation from reference in general.

The individualizing intention of language must specify with greater precision that which is individualized. Again taking the lead from Strawson, Ricoeur argues that basic particulars can be designated as "bodies, since these best satisfy the criteria of localization in the single spatiotemporal schema" (OA 33). Identifying reference can therefore be said to apply either to things or persons as "primitive" particulars that are subject to predication. In the case of persons we have "a single referent possessing two series of predicates: physical predicates and mental predicates" (OA 33). The advantage of this singularity of personhood is that it allows the term *person* to embrace the totality of possible predicates without equating a single predicate with the person as such.

This advantage is, however, only partial. While the identifying reference of language points to persons as primitive particulars, for Ricoeur, speech about persons must also be speech that designates who the speaker is; but this "poses a problem . . . [of] understanding how the self can be at one and the same time a person of whom we speak and a subject who designates herself in the first person while addressing a second person" (OA 34–35). According to Ricoeur, semantic reference calls for an examination of the pragmatical person who designates herself in the act of speaking. This is not to say that the person identified as a basic particular is of no relevance in a hermeneutic of selfhood, but only that identification of this type of sameness of persons is not enough for the full identification of who the self is.

Semantic self-reference is and remains essential to Ricoeur's hermeneutic of selfhood. Although the attribution of predicates to persons "carries with it no specific character to distinguish it from the common process of attribution" (OA 35), such self-reference has the benefit of being applicable to anyone and everyone. Since the person is determined by means of predicates that are attrib-

uted to "one" person, they are also attributable to "each one" (OA 36). Semantic self-reference designates a universal self that is the *same* for all other persons.
In doing so, semantic self-reference points out that selfhood must be more than
semantic universality. At the end of the "first study" Ricoeur writes:

> I wish to state, one last time, the importance that must be attached
> to this thesis. First . . . this double ascription to "someone" and to
> "anyone else" is what allows us to form the concept of mind. . . .
> Mental states are, to be sure, always those *of* someone, but this
> someone can be me, you, him, anyone. . . . The correlation "some-
> one"—"anyone else" . . . imposes a constraint from the start. . . .
> There is no pure consciousness at the start. We shall now add: there
> is no self alone at the start; the ascription to others is just as primi-
> tive as the ascription to oneself. I cannot speak meaningfully of my
> thoughts unless I am able at the same time to ascribe them poten-
> tially to someone else. (OA 38)

Ricoeur's hermeneutic of self establishes from the outset and at its most basic
level of semantic analysis the primordiality of the correlation between self-
identity and that of the other. However, since this simultaneity of reference
designates "each one" and "everyone," it lacks the referential adequacy to designate anything more than universal self-sameness or *idem* identity. For Ricoeur,
sameness of self is essential to the question of selfhood, but fails to take into
account a "dissymmetry in ascription": "ascribing a state of consciousness to
oneself is *felt*; ascribing it to someone else is *observed*" (OA 38). Procedures of
identifying reference can only define selfhood in terms of a shared concept of
sameness, but they fail to take into account one's own feeling of *reflexive self-
designation* that stands over and against the particularity of the "otherness of the
other" (OA 39). Although Ricoeur concedes to the difficulty of "acquiring simultaneously the idea of reflexivity and the idea of otherness" (OA 39), he
nevertheless sets himself to the task of analyzing this simultaneity that is indicative of *ipse* or selfhood identity.

To move beyond this sui-referential character of the "objective" person,
Ricoeur turns to a pragmatical "investigation into the conditions that govern
language use in all those cases in which the reference attached to certain
expressions cannot be determined without knowledge of the context of their
use, in other words, the situation of interlocution" (OA 40). According to Ricoeur,
the mistake of semantic self-reference is to treat the person as a thing among
other things. Through a pragmatical analysis of the "act of speaking itself"
Ricoeur believes that he can uncover the identity of the self who is in fact the
subject of that act of speech. By turning away from the question "what?" to the
question "who?" in the dialogical interchange between "I" and "you," Ricoeur
makes the assumption that he is no longer engaged in semantic analysis. He

seems to confuse and reduce pragmatics to the question "who?" and does not
see that he himself treats the question "who?" in the same way as the question
"what?" How is extralinguistic reference to "what" a person is argumentatively
different from identifying "who" a person is? On the one hand Ricoeur assumes
that analysis of self-reference acquires information about the sameness of persons, and on the other hand he assumes that analysis of self-designation acquires information about the selfhood of persons.

This confusion becomes more obvious in Ricoeur's attempt to mediate
between self-reference and self-designation. Since each speech act is reflective
of the acting subject, the "predicative operation itself" also implicates the subject who performs the act of predication (OA 43). The significance of this
connection is paramount, for it allows the referential aim of identification to be
connected to the question "who?" Ricoeur explains that "*it is not statements
that refer to something but the speakers themselves who refer in this way*; nor do
statements have a sense or signify something, but rather it is the speakers who
mean to say this or that, who understand an expression in a particular sense. In
this way, the illocutionary act is joined to a more fundamental act—the
predicative act" (OA 43). This predicative act no longer merely refers to a
person, but places the person within a "first-person" reciprocal situation of
interlocution. "Facing the *speaker* in the first person is a *listener* in the second
person to whom the former addresses himself or herself. . . . The utterance that
is reflected in the sense of the statement is therefore straightaway a bipolar
phenomenon: it implies simultaneously an 'I' that speaks and a 'you' to whom
the former addresses itself" (OA 43).

For Ricoeur this type of pragmatics simply specifies selfhood with the
precision of the shifter "I" and thereby offers only a marginal advancement over
semantic self-reference. Analysis of the speech act shows that the use of the first-
person pronoun "indicates the one who designates himself or herself in every
utterance containing the word 'I' " (OA 45). Identity is tied to the one using the
pronoun "I," and this Ricoeur believes to be evidence of a form of selfhood that
cannot be applicable to anyone or everyone else. Pragmatic identification of self
fails "to pass the test of substitution" which "confirms the fact that the expression does not belong to the order of entities capable of being identified by the
path of reference" (OA 46). Rather, the self appears as "the *fixation* that results
from speaking . . . to a unique center of perspective on the world, [or] *anchor-
ing*" (OA 49). The self thus appears as "a *singular perspective*" and "world-limit"
in relation to an interlocutionary other (OA 51). Semantic reference and the
shifter "I" are therefore distinguished by their universality and singularity of
identification, which Ricoeur attributes to a difference between the questions
"what?" and "who?" However, what Ricoeur fails to clarify is how this description of the singularity of the self is any different from universality. While the
particularity of the situation of interlocution will indeed limit the terms of

identification to those participating, is not this type of description applicable to all situations of interlocution regardless of who is present? Has not Ricoeur simply switched from a semantic description of third-person identity to first-person identity without really investigating how the users of language are affected by the speech they use?

This reduction becomes even more evident when Ricoeur tries to mediate the divide between "the twin questions: *Of whom* does one speak in designating persons . . . and *who* speaks by designating himself or herself as 'locutor' (addressing an interlocutor)?" (OA 17). Through "mutual borrowings which allow each to accomplish its own design" (OA 52), self-reference and self-designation are brought together under the process of institutionalized naming.[12] Ricoeur explains that "the conjunction between the subject as the world-limit and the person as the object of identifying reference rests on a process of the same nature as inscription" (OA 53). One's birth certificate brings together both a universal reference to a person, and the reflexive self-designation that this particular person is an "I" who designates himself or herself in this universal manner. "In this way, 'I' and 'Paul Ricoeur' mean the same person" (OA 54). While it is true that a name shares the common inscription of a formal name with every other person and also identifies a particular individual person, a birth certificate is simply a text that gives information: I am a Canadian, born in Toronto, given a name by my parents which I use to identify myself to others. Such mediation is a semantic means for answering Ricoeur's questions of "what?" and "who?," that is, a semantic or textual means for combining a description of self-sameness and selfhood.

In spite of this reduction Ricoeur claims that this singularity of identification points to the inescapable structure of selfhood. Since speech is always a form of "interlocution," the one who speaks is bound up with the listening recipient of the act of speech. For Ricoeur this attestation of selfhood is understood in a relational context of agent and patient. Hence, "every advance made in the direction of the selfhood of the speaker or the agent has as its counterpart a comparable advance in the otherness of the partner" (OA 44). Although this type of dialogue conveys the idea of a friendly exchange between equal conversation partners or, as Ricoeur puts it, "an exchange of intentionalities, reciprocally aiming at one another" (OA 44), to choose polite conversation as a characterization of this relation of exchange is highly arbitrary and without apparent foundation. Situations of interlocution can range from angry argument in which combatants try to dominate each other, to tender words that encourage mutual pleasure between lovers. Therefore, while selfhood may indeed be inescapably linked to the other, what seems to be taken for granted is the reciprocal possibility of inverting the relationship between agent and patient, and patient and agent to guarantee such reciprocity.

While Ricoeur attempts to clarify the structure of this dialectical concept of selfhood, asking if it can be "founded on a more fundamental reality" (OA

54), he only gives a few clues as to how such an ontology of selfhood might disclose "the kind of being that can lend itself in this way to a twofold identification—as an objective person and as a reflecting subject" (OA 54). For Ricoeur the identification of the reflecting subject in mediation with his or her objective personhood is only partial attestation of the being of selfhood and needs to be expanded through further description of the other objectivities of selfhood. Ricoeur believes that his analysis of this reflecting subject puts him in touch with one of the activities of selfhood that forms its analogical unity. However, as I have shown, Ricoeur's description of the reflecting subject is only a more specific form of semantic analysis that identifies the first person in distinction from third-person identification. This type of analysis can only identify the reflective structure of selfhood as objectified in language after the fact, forming the basis of my critique that a short circuit takes place between the analogy constructed from multiple responses to the question "who?" and the ontological or actual unity of selfhood.

5.2   Identity and Sameness

Ricoeur's linguistic analysis of identity has significant consequences for his philosophy of selfhood. The continuity of the structure of argumentation between his analysis of the "what?" and "who?" of identity brings into doubt the discontinuity that "pure selfhood" is supposed to exhibit "in polar opposition" (OA 165) to the permanence of character and self-sameness. If the "what?" of selfhood is semantically expressed as sameness, how can the question "who?" give expression to a form of selfhood that is different from sameness when both questions are connected to each other through a common network of intersignification (OA 58, 94–96)? Simply shifting from a universal description of identity to a more specific individual description does not seem to warrant the conclusion that selfhood can have a purity all to its own in contrast to *idem* identity. Furthermore, since Ricoeur adopts throughout *Oneself as Another* a method of analysis that is predicated on the discursive distinction between the questions "what?" and "who?," the other "objectivities" of selfhood—"practical, narrative, and prescriptive" (OA 187 n. 22)—will also exhibit this collapse of *ipse* selfhood into a semantics of *idem* identity. Hence, the subject matter of *Oneself as Another* has more to do with variations of meaning with regard to identity than with the act of existing in the mode of selfhood or self-constitution.

This confusion between the questions "what?" and "who?" is particularly evident in Ricoeur's analysis of the acting self. Reiterating his distinction between the semantic "path of identifying reference" and the pragmatic "path of self-designation" (OA 57), Ricoeur encloses both of his leading questions within a common "organization" (OA 57, 95–96). Explaining that "the key notions of the network of action draw their meaning from the specific nature of the answers given to the specific questions which are themselves cross-signifying: who? what? why? how? where? when?" (OA 58), Ricoeur states that such answers are only known by "actually knowing how to use the entire network of intersignification" (OA 58, 95–96). This "network crisscrossing the semantics of action" (OA 95) includes both the questions "what?" and "who?" that Ricoeur had previously separated in order to designate selfhood in contrast to sameness.[13]

Within the semantic network of action all the terms have interrelated meaning. However, Ricoeur "privileges" the question "who?" with "access to the concept of agent . . . [as] someone . . . to which are attributed both mental and physical predicates" (OA 58). Although "the question 'Who did this?' can be answered by mentioning a proper name, by using a demonstrative pronoun (he, she, this one, that one), or by giving a definite description (so and so)" (OA 59), the specificity of identifying only one self-designating agent to which the action can be ascribed is done "by obtaining an answer to the chain of questions 'what?' 'why?' 'how?' and so on" (OA 95). On the one hand, Ricoeur's network of intersignification answers the question "who?" by referring to "replies render[ing] something in general a someone" (OA 59); on the other hand it is supposed to stop the endless "searching for the motives of an action" through "the designation of the agent, usually by citing his or her name: 'Who did that? So and so.'"[14] For Ricoeur the question "who?" has the remarkable ability to comply with the demand for a general identifying reference to a "someone" who acts, and with the self-designating agent of action who takes responsibility for his or her acts. However, since both these universal and individual responses to the question "who?" only have meaning within the "network crisscrossing the semantics of action," it is by means of the identification of what remains the same in action "that we understand the expression 'agent' " (OA 95).

The self-designating agent is so tightly interwoven into the semantic network of action that Ricoeur attempts to make a connection between the so-called pragmatic agent and the self by means of a "short circuit" (OA 92, 94). Since Ricoeur holds the agent accountable for the "what?" and "why?" of action, it must be within the agent's "power-to-do" (OA 95) in order that the action can be ascribed to it. This *arkhe* of action is for Ricoeur also an *autos*, so that both the originator of action and the self are understood from within the semantic network of action. Ricoeur redeploys his concept of the creation of metaphorical meaning to clarify this connection: "the tie between principle (*arkhe*) and self (*autos*) is itself profoundly metaphoric, in the sense of 'seeing-as,' which I discuss in *The Rule of Metaphor*? Does not ethics, in fact, demand that we 'see' the principle 'as' self and the self 'as' principle? In this sense the explicit metaphors of paternity and of mastery [OA 89–92] would be the only

way of putting into linguistic form the tie arising out of the short circuit between principle and self" (OA 93–94). It is from within the network of something in general, that is, within descriptions of sameness, that Ricoeur makes a
jump from agency to selfhood.[15]

Ricoeur adds to his confusion between the "what?" and "who?" by making the astonishing claim that these linguistic questions of identity must be
surpassed and need to be understood as "propaedeutic" in character (OA 113).
Correctly finding his own analysis of ascription in particular, and of linguistic
identity more generally, to be "partial and as yet [an] abstract determination of
what is meant by the ipseity (the selfhood) of the self " (OA 111), Ricoeur hopes
to advance his interpretation of selfhood through "a specific supersession of the
strictly linguistic viewpoint," and hence also the "supersession" of "the transition from semantics to pragmatics" (OA 111). Explaining that the only real
achievement of the analysis of language and action lies in "determining what
specifies the self, implied in the power-to-do, at the junction of acting and the
agent" (OA 113), Ricoeur believes he can conclude these investigations as if
they were a separate topic without consequence for his explorations of the
"entire problematic . . . of *personal identity*" (OA 114). Further, one would assume that the advance of Ricoeur's pragmatical analysis toward his understanding of the ipseity of the self would be carried forward and be expanded on in
subsequent reflection.

Ricoeur, however, complains that his own analysis of "the approach to the
self along the second line of the philosophy of language, that of utterance, has
also failed to give rise to any particular reflection concerning the changes that
affect a subject capable of designating itself in signifying the world" (OA 113).
While this complaint is indeed valid and indicates the direction needed to be
taken for the development of a philosophy of selfhood, the fault does not lie
with pragmatical analysis as such, but with Ricoeur's twofold assumption that
pragmatics can be equated with the investigation of a topic that has a practical
subject matter as its focus, and that the question "who?" offers a privileged point
of access to selfhood regardless of its inclusion within a semantic network of
intersignification that identifies the self in terms of *idem* identity or sameness.

If, as Ricoeur states, the meager results of his analysis of language and
action are to be taken as "propaedeutic" for the development of the philosophy
of selfhood, then it would appear that the preparatory ground that has been
cleared is not that of material content but the formal juxtaposition of the questions "what?" and "who?" correlative with the distinction between self-sameness
and the ipseity of the self. According to Ricoeur, such "abstract determination"
(OA 111) needs to be made concrete if it is to facilitate the development of a
hermeneutics of selfhood. This is accomplished for Ricoeur through the mediating structure of narrative identity. He writes: "I hope to show that it is within
the framework of narrative theory that the concrete dialectic of selfhood and

sameness—and not simply the nominal distinction between the two terms employed up until now—attains its fullest development" (OA 114). Yet, as I have explained, Ricoeur's formal distinction between the "who?" and "what?" of selfhood holds both questions within the semantics of sameness and thereby places the problematic of *ipse* identity "within the dimension of something in general" (OA 123). This is not only evident in Ricoeur's "nominal distinction" between *ipse* and *idem* identity; it is equally apparent in his "concrete" analysis of "personal identity" which "can be articulated only in the temporal dimension of human existence" (OA 114).

According to Ricoeur temporality opens the problem of identity to the "question of *permanence in time*" (OA 116) through its objectification in narrative discourse (OA 187 n. 22). As I have indicated in my analysis of *Time and Narrative*, Ricoeur claims that "time becomes human to the extent that it is articulated through a narrative mode, and narrative attains its full meaning when it becomes a condition of temporal existence" (TN 1:52). This is equally true for the temporal configurations of personal identity. Self-sameness is now given a form of permanence that can be articulated in the narrative mode as one's "character" in contrast to a more specific type of permanence, which he refers to as "the pure selfhood of self-constancy" (OA 165) "associated with the ethics of 'keeping one's word' " (OA 123). Asserting that this type of differentiation places *idem* and *ipse* identity at opposite ends of a narrative continuum (OA 118–124), Ricoeur once again tries to open a space "where selfhood frees itself from sameness" (OA 119). However, this narrative opposition of sameness and selfhood seems to be based on the assumption that the "relational invariant" of sameness (OA 118) is of a fundamentally different order than the "self in relation" (FS 262) that defines the constancy of the ethical structure of pure selfhood.

Even though Ricoeur maintains his claim that the "question 'who?' . . . is irreducible to any question of 'what?'," he is still inclined to describe "a form of permanence in time that is a reply to the question 'Who am I?' " (OA 118), which identifies the self in terms of the semantics of sameness. On the one hand, the narrativization of *idem* and *ipse* identity is defined by Ricoeur as two types of "permanence in time" (OA 118) that exhibit a relational structure of some sort of sameness which can be placed on the same narrative plane; on the other hand, *ipse* identity is supposed to be a form of "innovation" that can break free from all forms of "sedimentation" that are associated with *idem* identity (OA 121). But when we look at Ricoeur's own description of *idem* identity, this difference between *idem* and *ipse* appears to be more a difference of descriptive specificity between variations of sameness than the difference between sameness and selfhood as such.

Ricoeur points out that the type of permanence in time that is characteristic of *idem* identity centers on "a concept of relation and a relation of relations" (OA 116) that can be expressed as "*numerical* identity," as "*qualitative* identity," and as "the *uninterrupted continuity* between the first and the last stage in the development of what we consider to be the same individual" (OA 116–117). Accordingly, such a "structure" (OA 117), "relational invariant," or "determination of a substratum" (OA 118) identifies the permanence of selfhood associated with the "whatness" of self, whereas the "permanence of time that is a reply to the question 'Who am I?' " (OA 118) identifies a voluntary power to be self-same or self-constant (OA 123) that "marks the extreme gap between the permanence of the self and that of the same and so attests fully to the irreducibility of the two problematics one to the other" (OA 118). This contrast forms the basis of Ricoeur's claim that selfhood is not sameness. Yet the differentiation between sameness and self is quite puzzling: both are defined in terms of concepts of relation, both are variations of permanence, and both employ the same semantic network of intersignification, albeit a narrative network, to answer the "what?" and "who?" of selfhood.

To clarify this difference of meaning between these two concepts of permanence in time, Ricoeur connects them to the concepts of "*character* and *keeping one's word*" (OA 118). "By 'character,' " Ricoeur explains, "I understand the set of distinctive marks which permit the reidentification of a human individual as being the same" (OA 119). No longer described in terms of the "absolute involuntary" (OA 119 n. 4, 120), character becomes "emblematic" (OA 119) of a "pole in a fundamental, existential polarity" (OA 120) that includes such things as "lasting dispositions," "habits," "traits," and "acquired identifications" (OA 121). Character is for Ricoeur a pole of "stability" that "assures at once numerical identity, qualitative identity, uninterrupted continuity across change, and finally permanence in time which defines sameness" (OA 122). Ricoeur identifies persons by means of the sedimentations of traits that allow for reidentification of that which remains permanent in time.

This concept of character is confusing. Ricoeur's assertion that the "what" and the "who" of identity are irreducible to one another is contradicted by his own observation that "when we speak of ourselves, we in fact have available to us two models of permanence . . . *character* and *keeping one's word* " (OA 118). If the "what" of persons is not to be equated with the "who" of selfhood, how can character be used to "speak of ourselves" when Ricoeur has insisted that such self-designation is only found "within the orbit of the question 'who?' " (OA 169, 17, 45). Compounding this confusion, Ricoeur explains that character cannot be simply equated with sameness, for it "expresses the almost complete mutual overlapping of the problematic of *idem* and of *ipse*" (OA 118). However, this "adherence of the 'what?' to the 'who?' " (OA 122) must also be distinguished as *idem* identity in "polar" opposition to selfhood (OA 118, 120, 123, 124). How can such opposites be both identical and different? How can the "traits" that identify the invariant of sameness, be different from "those traits which tend to separate the identity of the self from the sameness of character"

(OA 123)? Even Ricoeur's language here is the same: traits are the marks of stability of one's character, yet here we see Ricoeur use this term to designate what supposedly cannot be understood by means of the concept of sameness. Further, if *ipse* identity is understood in opposition to the stability of character, what does Ricoeur mean when he refers to the permanence of selfhood? Is self-constancy unstable permanence, or perhaps discontinuous continuity?

For Ricoeur, the key to understanding this overlap and differentiation between character and self-constancy is found in the narrative operation of emplotment. Rather than placing selfhood and sameness in irreconcilable opposition to each other, their difference can be made "productive" through a mediation of narrative discourse which constructs a dynamic identity that "provide[s] a poetic reply" (OA 147) to the paradox of personal identity. In this context narrative is "a vast laboratory for thought experiments"[16] that "opens an *interval of sense* . . . [which is] filled in" (OA 124) by the narrative identity of the character in the story. Repeating his analysis of the operation of emplotment conducted in *Time and Narrative*, Ricoeur explains that the narrative arc produces a "dynamic identity which reconciles the same categories that Locke took as contraries: identity and diversity" (OA 143). The narrative plot unifies the diversity of events and actions into a narrative whole. By extending this unifying work to characters within the narrative, the "identity of the character is comprehensible through the transfer to the character of the operation of emplotment, first applied to the action recounted; characters, we will say, are themselves plots" (OA 143). Hence, "the character preserves throughout the story an identity correlative to that of the story itself" (OA 143); therefore, "it is the identity of the story that makes the identity of the character" (OA 148). Here the use of the term *character* unites on a narrative plane both the "who?" and the "what?" of identity.

According to Ricoeur, the character of the story presents a specific imaginative variation or mediation that fills in the "interval of sense" between his two concepts of identity. Narrative identity is therefore forever "oscillating between sameness and selfhood" (OA 124, 151), proposing any number of possible identities, provided that they fall within the dialectical alternatives of *idem* and *ipse* identity. Ricoeur explains that this "space of variation open to the relations between these two modalities of identity is vast. At one end, the character in the story has a definite character, which is identifiable and reidentifiable as the same" (OA 139, 148). Here selfhood and sameness "tend to overlap and to merge with one another" (OA 149, 165) as in the heroic figure (OA 149) and in "everyday experience" (OA 149, 118–119). At the other end of this narrative spectrum "we reach an extreme pole of variation where the character in the story ceases to have a definite character" (OA 148–149), where "we encounter limiting cases in which literary fiction lends itself to a confrontation with the puzzling cases of analytic philosophy" (OA 149, 139).

Narrative identity is always some sort of mixture between the alternatives of sameness and selfhood. However, selfhood is never without "the support of sameness" (OA 149, 124). In fact, when Ricoeur wants to take into account the "lesson . . . taught to perfection by contemporary plays and novels" concerning "the loss of identity" (OA 149), he notes that when "the narrative approaches the point of annihilation of the character, the novel also loses its own properly narrative qualities. . . . To the loss of the identity of the character thus corresponds the loss of the configuration of the narrative and, in particular, a crisis of closure of the narrative" (OA 149). Without the coherence and stability of sameness, selfhood identity is lost. And if selfhood is left without the support of sameness, the narrative text loses its productive power to offer a "poetic reply" to the dialectic opposition of *idem* and *ipse* identity. By playing on the difference between selfhood and sameness narrative emplotment may offer an exceeding wide variety of literary identities, but permanence "on the plane of selfhood . . . is found . . . only in character" (OA 267). Self-constancy without sameness is not an option within Ricoeur's understanding of narrative identity.

The problem with this narrative project is that selfhood is once again objectified in a manner that continues the collapse of selfhood into sameness. The "what?" of action, narrativized, is made "correlative" with the "who?" of the character. "[N]arrative structure joins together the two processes of emplotment, that of action and that of the character" (OA 146). Hence the narrativization of action extends the semantic network of intersignification from the "chain" of the questions "what?" "who?" "how?" and so on, to a "chain that is none other than the story chain. Telling a story is saying who did what and how, by spreading out in time the connection between these various viewpoints" (OA 146). Narration combines the "finite . . . attribution to someone" and the "infinite . . . search for motives . . . in the twofold process of identification, involving plot and character" (OA 146–147). Hence, Ricoeur's claim that narrative discourse resolves the problems of personal identity in actuality only makes the semantic network of intersignification "productive on another level of language" (OA 147).

The consequences of this narrative objectification of personal identity are such that Ricoeur is confronted once again with the difficult problem of "the gap . . . between fiction and life" (OA 159) central to his discussion of refiguration in *Time and Narrative*. Ricoeur reasserts his claim that "in my own treatment of the mimetic function of narrative, the break marked by the entry of narrative into the sphere of fiction is taken so seriously that it becomes a very thorny problem to reconnect literature to life by means of reading."[17] Ricoeur readily admits that "the very act of reading gives rise to obstacles on the return path from fiction back to life" (OA 159, 166). Only now, with regard to narrative identity, this path of application becomes the task of finding out "how . . . the thought experiments occasioned by fiction . . . contribute to self-examination in

real life" (OA 159). "*Appropriation*" (OA 162; HHS 190–193) or application of
the narrative identity of the text is, as Ricoeur has shown in great detail (TN
3:157–179; TDI 175–186), an interactive process between the world of the text
and that of the reader. Through reading the dynamic identity of the text is
transferred to the reader.[18] With the extension of the identity of the text to the
character within the narrative, Ricoeur's problem becomes that of the connection between the narrative character and the identity of the reader. Ricoeur
explains that "the possibility of applying literature to life rests, with respect to
the dialectic of the character, upon the problem of 'identification-with' " (OA
159 n.23). Narrative "returns to life along the multiple paths of appropriation"
(OA 163) by providing characters as "models of interaction . . . [and] intelligibility" (OA 162). The reader refigures his or her own experience through the
"identification-with" the character in the story. But as Ricoeur has repeatedly
emphasized, the narrative identity of the character always "overlaps" *idem* and
ipse identity. Reading is, therefore, the appropriation of a model of identity that
always has the support of sameness. While the objectification of selfhood in the
figure of the narrative character might very well be a model for living, it is not
a model of selfhood; rather, narrative identity offers a model of self-sameness
which the reader can identify-with.

5.3   Identity, Selfhood, and Ontology

In spite of the collapse of ipseity into the identity of the same, Ricoeur
insists that selfhood has a meaning beyond "its contrast with sameness" (OA
297). Faced with "the hypothesis of the . . . loss of identity, confronting this
Ichlosigkeit that was at once Musil's torment and the meaning effect unceas-
ingly cultivated by his work" (OA 166), the question "who?" becomes for Ricoeur
descriptive of a "self deprived of the help of sameness" (OA 166). According to
Ricoeur, the oscillation between *idem* and *ipse* identity puts into question the
narrative objectification of selfhood. Only an ethics of agency or the ethico-
moral identification of selfhood can answer the question: "Who am I, so incon-
stant, that *notwithstanding* you count on me?" (OA 168). To the threat of such
"extreme destitution" comes the ethico-moral response, "Here I am!" (OA 167).
The voluntary act of ethical and moral self-constancy that makes a person
available for another, is for Ricoeur the "most advanced stage of the growth of
selfhood" (OA 171). But this new level of analysis does not change the structure
of argumentation which places the question of selfhood within a semantic
network of intersignification. Ricoeur is once again attempting to identify the
self as the "subject of action" by means of an objectification in which the self
is supposed to reflect itself in and which takes place through "predicates such
as 'good' and 'obligatory' " (OA 169). Ricoeur writes: "The ethical and moral

determinations of action will be treated here as predicates of a new kind, and their relation to the subject of action as a new mediation along the return path toward the self" (OA 169). In fact, the "new" level of analysis is not so much the description of selfhood without the support of sameness as much as it is a description of "moral identity . . . based . . . upon . . . narrative identity" (OA 295), which is in turn unfolded within Ricoeur's philosophy of action or agency.

This is the key to understanding what Ricoeur means by selfhood with regard to "all objectivities (discursive, practical, narrative, and prescriptive predicates) in the [reflective] process of the self."[19] By identifying the subject of speech, action, and narration, Ricoeur unfolds multiple points of reference to a power of agency. According to Ricoeur, each study provides "further enrichment and greater preciseness" (OA 294) to his initial claim that the question "who?" and the response "the self" are correlative. This is equally true of his analysis of ethico-moral identity, where Ricoeur understands selfhood as the identification of the one who responds to "the nakedness of the question . . . 'Who am I?' . . . with the proud answer 'Here I am!' " (OA 167). The act of ethical constancy, predicated on his preceding analysis of the semantics of action, is taken by Ricoeur as the most precise meaning of selfhood. Therefore, to ask "Who is the moral subject of imputation?" (OA 169) is not an investigation of selfhood without sameness; rather, what Ricoeur explores is the "teleological aim and the deontological moment" (OA 171) involved in the interaction between agents described within the network of intersignification. In order to develop a model of agency that aims *at the 'good life' with and for others, in just institutions* (OA 172), Ricoeur is simply extending his network of intersignification to include a prescription for appropriate interaction between agents. Since Ricoeur is convinced that "We never leave the problem of selfhood as long as we remain within the orbit of the question 'who?' " (OA 169), the question of selfhood is always framed within a philosophy of action that revolves around the determination of "who?" is acting by means of key terms such as agency, power, activity and passivity (OA 17, 104, 302).

5.3.1 Objectifications of Power

Ricoeur's response to the question "who?" is a multilayered objectification of agency wherein speech acts are understood as the "exchange of intentionalities, reciprocally aiming at one another" (OA 44). Accordingly, the act itself can be taken as descriptive of "the selfhood of the speaker or the agent [which] has as its counterpart . . . the otherness of the partner" (OA 44). By identifying the agent of the speech act, Ricoeur believes he also simultaneously describes in part the central feature of ipseity or selfhood.

This initial identification of selfhood is expanded through Ricoeur's sub-sequent analysis of action. By looking for a correlation between "a principle that is a self, and a self that is a principle" (OA 91), Ricoeur concludes that this principle must be within the agent's "power to act. . . . To say that an action depends on its agent is to say in an equivalent fashion that it is in the agent's power" (OA 101). The analysis of agency shows that the self is understood as power, and that power is constitutive of selfhood. What Ricoeur has in mind is a specific form of power that is articulated through a discourse in which "the 'I can' will be able to be recognized as the very *origin* of the connection be-tween the two orders of causality" (OA 111), that is, between the order of freedom and nature (OA 104–105). To ascribe an action to an agent is to make the agent responsible for his or her intervention "in the course of the world, an intervention which effectively causes changes in the world" (OA 109). Dupli-cating his description in *Freedom and Nature*, where the deliberative process of decision and action forms the "nexus of the voluntary and the involuntary" dimensions of the *cogito* (FN 9–10), Ricoeur in *Oneself as Another* explains that "[a]scription consists precisely in this reappropriation by the agent of his or her own deliberation: making up one's mind is cutting short the debate by making one of the options contemplated one's own" (OA 95). The phenomenology of the "I can" ascribes a voluntary power of action to an agent and this, Ricoeur believes, gives "only a partial and as yet abstract determination of what is meant by the ipseity (the selfhood) of the self" (OA 111).

The similarity between Ricoeur's early description of voluntary conscious-ness in *Freedom and Nature* and the power-to-do of selfhood as described in *Oneself as Another* is striking. Yet, to simply equate Ricoeur's early voluntarism with his understanding of the ipseity of selfhood would be misleading. Ricoeur's pursuit of the identity of the agent within a semantic network of action frames his understanding of selfhood, and thus qualifies the meaning of the power-to-do. Action is always interaction with others and therefore the ipseity of the self can only be described in conjunction with other agents within the same net-work of intersignification, not on the basis of a phenomenology of individual consciousness. For Ricoeur, one either initiates action or is subjected to action. Hence, the power-to-do marks for Ricoeur an "original correlation between acting and suffering" (OA 320) that extends the analysis of agency to that of morality. Ricoeur writes: "For my part, I never forget to speak of humans as acting and suffering. The moral problem . . . is grafted onto the recognition of this essential dissymmetry between the one who acts and the one who under-goes, culminating in the violence of the powerful agent."[20]

This concept of the power-to-do attains its fullest meaning with ethical and moral constancy. For Ricoeur this voluntary power erupts in an affirmation of one's identity by affirming its accountability and responsibility to others as one who is steadfast in response to the "expectation of the other who is count-ing on me" (OA 268, 165). Just as decision is cut short in the moment of action, the claim of accountability through which the agent avows his or her constancy, cuts short the ethical-moral debate and asserts, "'Here I am!' by which the person recognizes himself or herself as the subject of imputation [and] marks a halt in the wandering that may well result from the self's confrontation with a multitude of models for action and life, some of which go so far as to paralyze the capacity for firm action. . . . 'I can try anything,' to be sure, but 'Here is where I stand!'" (OA 167). Ethico-moral identity reflects a particular orienta-tion that an agent assumes in relation to other agents. Thus, the power-to-do is also a "*power-in-common* . . . of the members of a historical community to exer-cise in an indivisible manner their desire to live together" (OA 220). While such relations of power can involve "a fragile balance in which giving and receiving are equal" (OA 188), more often than not the exercise of power is "the occasion of violence" found in "the *power* exerted *over* one will by another will" (OA 220). The "original correlation between acting and suffering" (OA 320) can degenerate into relations of "domination in which political violence re-sides" (OA 220), and thereby demands a moral reply to negate the violence of power-over through the steadfastness of identity or constancy that holds "the initial dissymmetry between agent and patient" in check (OA 222, 225).

The response of "the *no* of morality . . . to all the figures of evil" (OA 221) does not mean that Ricoeur says no to the fundamental dissymmetry between agents and patients. While Ricoeur details the "descending slope" of the horrors of violent interaction, the "occasion of violence, not to mention the turn toward violence, resides in the *power* exerted *over* one will by another will" (OA 220). On the one hand, Ricoeur seems to be saying that the relationship between agent and patient provides the opportunity for violence and evil, but since it is only its occasion, or point of least resistance for maleficence, it is not itself responsible for violence. Yet on the other hand, he states that "it is difficult to imagine situations of interaction in which one individual does not exert a power over another by the very fact of acting" (OA 220). The ambiguity reflected here in Ricoeur's analysis of moral identity parallels that between fault and fallibility found in *Fallible Man*.[21] Although Ricoeur declares the anthropological struc-ture of fallibility innocent, moral fault is made possible because of the dispro-portion between the infinite aim and the finite moment of the process of self-constitution.

5.3.2 *Selfhood or Identity?*

Ricoeur's analyses of linguistic, practical, narrative, and ethico-moral iden-tity all respond in the same way to the question "who?" Each analysis identifies a form of agency that progressively completes Ricoeur's understanding of selfhood. What remains in question is whether these forms of identity are objectifications of a more fundamental reflexive structure of selfhood or whether Ricoeur's understanding of selfhood simply repeats his analysis of the various meanings of identity and thereby restricts selfhood to sameness. After all, does not Ricoeur repeatedly state that the purist form of selfhood can be equated with *ipse* identity, that is, with a form of identity that he is unable to rescue from its collapse into self-sameness or *idem* identity?

Ricoeur addresses this problem by means of a contrast between the phenomenological analysis of identity and the ontological speculation regarding selfhood. While each identification of agency offers, according to Ricoeur, testimony of some aspect of the activity of the self, this attestation of selfhood as the power of initiative and the power to be self-constant must go beyond this "first-order discourse" to a "second-order discourse" (OA 298) that can address the question: "What mode of being, then, belongs to the self, what sort of being is it?" (OA 297). For Ricoeur the phenomenology of identity is linked to an "*analogical* unity of action" (OA 303), understood as the fundamental act of existing in the mode of selfhood. This is the "self" that Ricoeur correlates with the multiple responses to the question "who?" But does Ricoeur's analogical model of the unity of action have anything more to contribute to his understanding of selfhood than he has already said with regard to the multiple variations of the power of agency? Ricoeur himself puzzles over this difficulty when he begins his ontological reflection on selfhood: "the language of act and of power has never ceased to underlie our hermeneutical phenomenology of acting man. Do these anticipations justify our joining the simply analogical unity of human action to an ontology of act and of power?" (OA 303). Even though Ricoeur claims that this mediated response to the question "who?" is ontological attestation[22] of the intimate relation that the self has to its own existence, the fact that his ontology of selfhood more or less duplicates his description of the objectivities—be they of a discursive, practical, narrative, or prescriptive nature (OA 187 n. 22)—makes his question even more significant.

Ricoeur's ontological reflection is intended, in part, to reaffirm his contrast between selfhood and sameness (OA 297–298) not only on the level of first-order discourse, but also on the level of the "metacategory of being as act and as power" (OA 303). Here "the distinction between selfhood and sameness does not simply concern two constellations of meaning but involves two modes of being" (OA 309). This assertion is quite remarkable. If sameness is a mode of being in contrast to the being of selfhood, Ricoeur has duplicated a first-order distinction on what he refers to as the second-order level of discourse. As I have shown, Ricoeur contrasts sameness with selfhood throughout his investigations of identity. This is a contrast within the objectivities of the reflective process of the self. If, as Ricoeur confirms, this distinction is also the distinction between two modes of being, is this a differentiation of being made between first-order and second-order discourse, or a difference within second-order discourse itself? If it is an ontological difference, then Ricoeur's ontology simply duplicates the phenomenological difference between two forms of identity. However, since Ricoeur is making a differentiation between the "pure selfhood of self-constancy " (OA 165) and the mode of being that selfhood is, it would appear that Ricoeur's ontology of selfhood is a duplication of *ipse* identity.

This ontological duplication of *ipse* identity is clearly evident in Ricoeur's appropriation of Heidegger's concepts of *Dasein* and *Vorhandenheit*. Ricoeur explains that "the ontological status of selfhood is therefore solidly based upon the distinction between two modes of being, *Dasein* and *Vorhandenheit*. In this regard, the correlation between the category of sameness in my own analyses and the notion of *Vorhandenheit* in Heidegger is the same as that between selfhood and the mode of being of *Dasein*" (OA 309). This declaration contradicts Ricoeur's analyses of the objectivities of the reflective process of the self. By joining together the concept of sameness and "presence-at-hand" (OA 309), as distinguished from selfhood and *Dasein*, Ricoeur elevates self-constancy to the status of the being of selfhood. But Ricoeur's analyses of identity are predicated on the correlation between *idem* and *ipse* identity.[23] This dialectic pair is a phenomenological distinction that includes both forms of identity as part of the process of objectification: *idem* identity corresponds to a universal description of self-sameness, and *ipse* identity corresponds to a more specific individual description of self-constancy. Therefore, to move one of the terms of a common network of intersignification from the first-order phenomenology of agency to the second-order discourse of Being simply duplicates *ipse* identity on a higher level of discourse.

To add to this confusion, Ricoeur, hoping to find in Heidegger a companion notion comparable to the analogical unity of action, immediately returns to the semantic network of intersignification to make this connection. According to Ricoeur, what needs to be appropriated from Heidegger's analysis of *Dasein* is a primordial correlation between the self and the world. Ricoeur explains that "only a being that is a self is *in* the world; correlatively, the world in which this being is, is not the sum of beings composing the universe of subsisting things or things ready-to-hand. The being of the self presupposes the totality of a world that is the horizon of its thinking, acting, feeling—in short, of its *care*" (OA 310). When Ricoeur goes on to make a more precise term for term correlation between his own interpretation of the self and Heidegger's analysis of selfhood, he immediately reemploys his first-order discourse of the semantics of action for what he calls the second-order speculation concerning the being of selfhood. "Once the answer to the question 'who?' can be answered only through the detour of the question 'what?' and the question 'why?,' then the being of the world is the necessary correlate to the being of the self. There is no world without a self who finds itself in it and acts in it; there is no self without a world that is practicable in some fashion" (OA 310–311). The "what?" and "why?" of action are now equated with the being of the world and are included "within the orbit of the question 'who?'" (OA 169, 16). While these relations of intersignification have been maintained throughout Ricoeur's analysis of the various forms of identity, what is the point of this appropriation of Heidegger's analytic of *Dasein* if Ricoeur continues to express selfhood in terms of the semantics of agency and interaction? While Ricoeur does acknowledge that his ontology of selfhood has "elevated . . . action . . . to the level of a second-order concept in relation to the successive versions of action that we have presented in the preceding studies, or yet again, in relation to our threefold series, more epistemological than ontological: description, narration, prescription" (OA 312), this extension seems unable to say anything more than what has already been said with regard to the phenomenology of agency and power.

Ricoeur's ontology of selfhood is in essence an ontology of the power-to-do of agency. Now it is important to note that Ricoeur has four different meanings for the term power: *power-to-do and act* (OA 220, 113), *power over* (OA 220), *power-in-common* in distinction from domination (OA 220, 257), and *power as productivity* (OA 315). Although Ricoeur does seem to move beyond the simple enumeration of the multiple meanings of power, the being of selfhood is nevertheless expressed in terms of the unity of "act and power" (OA 303). In dialogue with Aristotle's *Metaphysics*, Ricoeur claims that the concept of *energeia-dunamis* can be reappropriated in the development of an ontology of selfhood if two features in particular are made significant: (1) this ontology must be "centered" in human action, and (2) it must be "decentered" with respect to "other fields of application" in that it "points toward a ground of being, at once potentiality and actuality against which human action stands out. . . . If an ontology of selfhood is possible—this is in conjunction with a ground starting from which the self can be said to be *acting*" (OA 308). Linking this interpretation of "Aristotelian *praxis* . . . to my own concept of the power-to-act" (OA 312) Ricoeur intends to provide the "idea of an analogical unity of acting" (OA 313) that can, on the one hand, be centered in the being of a self that "is essentially an opening onto the world" (OA 314), and on the other hand, be "rooted" in a *"ground at once actual and in potentiality . . .* against which selfhood stands out" (OA 315). Ricoeur further qualifies this meaning of power through a reference to "Spinoza's *conatus*" (OA 315). Declaring that the power of being must be understood as the "effort to persevere in being, which forms the unity of man as of every individual" (OA 316), Ricoeur is quick to point out that "power here does not mean potentiality but productivity, which is not to be opposed to act in the sense of actuality or realization" (OA 315). The unity of selfhood is construed as the power-to-do that is fundamentally creative in its action.

This is the extent of Ricoeur's development of the ontology of selfhood. How does this say anything more than what has already been described in his preceding studies? What Ricoeur appears to be offering is a further description of the power of agency. Adding that the power-to-do must also be essentially creative or productive seems to be stating the obvious: if an agent is to be held accountable for his or her action, agency must surely include the capacity to produce one's own actions. In fact, Ricoeur's objective identifications of power as initiative and ethico-moral self-constancy have a great deal more to say about the human project than this ontology of the productive power to persevere in being.

Perhaps Ricoeur's ontological reflections should be seen as an ontology of identity rather than of selfhood. How does Ricoeur distinguish the *being* of selfhood from that of sameness? On the basis of the correlation between the question "who?" and the questions "what?" and "why?" And how does Ricoeur distinguish the *meaning* of selfhood from that of sameness? On the basis of universal and individual descriptions of identity that collapse selfhood or *ipse* identity (Who?) into sameness or *idem* identity (What?).

CONCLUSION

My analysis of Ricoeur's understanding of selfhood has pointed to a rather abstract problem with regard to a difference between semantics and pragmatics, a difference hardly noticeable within the complex, problematic question of selfhood. So far my text has only brought forward this particular subplot, the significance of which, as it concerns the question of selfhood, has not been made entirely clear. What remains to be shown is how Ricoeur's collapse of the pragmatics of selfhood into the semantics of identity affects his understanding of selfhood. This is not to say that Ricoeur's philosophy of selfhood is without significant merit—quite the contrary. All I want to do is simply point to a few problems in Ricoeur's formulation of selfhood that render it less than productive in its reception of the other.

Ethical Reciprocity or Mutuality?

Central to Ricoeur's philosophy of selfhood are multiple descriptions of the correlation between the self and the other. Subjectivity is always understood as a form of polysemic linguistic intersubjectivity[1] that displaces the self as its own foundation. This is the great strength of Ricoeur's position. The self is not grounded within itself, but linked to otherness, others, and the unnamed Other,[2] in a manner that precludes totalization. However, what remains to be addressed is the nature of such intersubjectivity. It is one thing to claim that the self is a wounded ego-*cogito*, broken open in the passivity of involuntary otherness; however, it is another thing to describe the actual effect that this other has in relation to the voluntary self, and to describe the relationship that ought to be in place when one exists in the mode of selfhood. How does one formulate the structure of this relationship? Is it one of complementarity, reciprocity, mutuality, equality, inequality, submission, domination, subordination, symmetry, or asymmetry? While Ricoeur calls for the ego to be discipled into selfhood by way of the other, the question remains as to how this relation of the self to the other, and of the other to the self, is lived. This question is made all that more urgent given Ricoeur's collapse of the problem of selfhood into that of identity. Is the other under the rule of the same? Does Ricoeur's formulation of the ethics of selfhood place the other under the control of pure self-constancy, under the rule of voluntary consciousness that needs to exercise its freedom over and against that which is a threat to freedom? Is this why Ricoeur is preoccupied with the reciprocity between the self and other selves?

The answer to these difficult questions can be found in the manner in which Ricoeur grafts his analysis of friendship into his phenomenology of consciousness. Originally mapped out in *Freedom and Nature*, the reciprocity of the voluntary and involuntary is now, in *Oneself as Another*, used to classify agency into the dual categories of action carried out and action suffered. For Ricoeur the self is either acting or acted upon; and since pure self-constancy is brought to language most forcefully through the promise, whereby the self is defined entirely by its own action toward the other, the acting voluntary self needs to act in order to be a self. What begins to emerge from Ricoeur's "little ethics" (OA 290) is a model of selfhood that is restricted by this dual alternative of activity or passivity, a restriction that ultimately holds his philosophy of selfhood captive to the identity of the same.[3]

Coupling together the "ethical aim and the deontological moment" (OA 171) of action, Ricoeur hopes to find a reciprocal balance between the power-to-do of the agent and patient. Claiming a priority of the ethical "aim over the norm" of morality (OA 171), Ricoeur wants to affirm the reciprocity of human action as primordial in contrast to "the *no* of morality" (OA 221) which is needed to reject all "the figures of nonreciprocity in interaction" (OA 220). The ethical intention of action aims *"at the 'good life' with and for others in just institutions"* (OA 172), whereas morality replies to the violence of domination resulting from the "initial dissymmetry between agent and patient" (OA 222). This affirmation of the reciprocity between oneself and another, and the negation of the disfiguring power of nonreciprocity, is given a dialectical formulation that is supposed to produce "practical wisdom" (OA 241) for responsible action that meets the particular needs of self and other in the situation of interaction.

These three moments of action (ethical, moral, and practical) are predicated on Ricoeur's formulation of the reciprocal power between the self and the other. This is the primordial meaning of ethical action: mutual self-esteem where "each loves the other *as being the man he is*" (OA 183). Although borrowing from Aristotle, Ricoeur employs this model of friendship to develop an understanding of reciprocity that is "split into two by mutuality," a dual affirmation of the origin of self-esteem in the self and the other, rather than the singularity of "a genesis based on the Same, as in Husserl, or a genesis based on the Other, as in Lévinas" (OA 183, 331, 335). Ricoeur extracts from Aristotle's concept of friendship an "inclusive concept of solicitude, based principally on the exchange between *giving* and *receiving*" (OA 188). In this economy of reciprocity, friendship marks a "fragile balance in which giving and receiving are equal, hypothetically" (OA 188). The commerce of friendship is not only measured in terms of equality but takes place among equals, among friends that are able to act with equal capacity, able to give and receive without diminishing the power of each other. While power is reciprocal in friendship, mutual friendship is a balance of such power. Ricoeur explains that "this balance can be considered as the midpoint of a spectrum, in which the end points are marked by inverse disparities between giving and receiving, depending on whether the pole of the self or that of the other predominates in the initiative of exchange" (OA 188). Mutuality is thus for Ricoeur a lack of disparity in the reciprocal exchange of giving and receiving between friends, between selves of equal power.

But is this type of reciprocity really what mutuality is all about? To give and receive in mutual affirmation of oneself and another is something quite different from the reciprocal exchange of power, where one gives and receives out of need or lack. Does one give in order to receive, and receive in order to give? Is the reciprocity of acting with equal capacity an attestation of mutual selfhood or an attempt to keep the tally sheet balanced and remain out of debt? Reciprocity needs to be carefully distinguished from mutuality. Reciprocity is a gift of death,[4] which forces one to choose between "power-over (with its corollary of power-under), or power-held-in-abeyance (to avoid domination)."[5] For Ricoeur this is a choice between "the reduction, even the destruction, of the capacity for action, of being-able-to-act, experienced as a violation of self-integrity" (OA 190), or acting in the mode of voluntary self-constancy on behalf of the other. Mutuality, however, should be something beyond the calculation of activity and passivity. It is, as Ricoeur has pointed out, more than simply choosing between the self or the other (Husserl or Lévinas). There must be a form of simultaneity that includes voluntary giving and receiving as constitutive of selfhood. Such mutuality should not be understood in terms of an economy of power described through a phenomenology of the "I can,"[6] but in terms of "non-oppositional difference—an economy of love ... [where] the desire of each evokes the desire of the other: mutual recognition, mutual yielding/receiving, mutual delighting, mutual empowering."[7] The economy of love does not worry about a balance of power, but simply gives, and "[i]n giving to the other, I, paradoxically, in being received, am enlarged and enhanced—receiving, in the words of Lévinas, 'inspiration.' In receiving the other, I expand, and paradoxically through my receiving, give."[8]

Isn't this precisely Ricoeur's point, the central core of his hermeneutics of selfhood? Doesn't Ricoeur insist that the ethical aim rooted in friendship is the "most advanced ... growth of selfhood" (OA 171) and is intended to affirm both the self and the other? Yes! Ricoeur's position is a genuine advance beyond the alternatives of the exaltation of the self over the other, or the sacrifice of the self for the other. And yes, Ricoeur is arguing for a simultaneous genesis of the self and the other that has clearly shown the positing of the *cogito* to be the

great "transcendental pretence"[9] of modern philosophical thought. But is this
other, this friend who reciprocates power, a genuine other, or my fellow "man,"[10]
my like in whom I find like, my companion in whom I see myself, in whom
I recognize sameness and not alterity, whom I find to be identical without
difference, an interchangeable self?

Finding Lévinas's "absolute exteriority" of the other to "establish no relation at all" (OA 188), Ricoeur, in concert with the "admirable analyses of
Lévinas's *Totality and Infinity*, to say nothing here of his *Otherwise than Being*"
(OA 189), nevertheless struggles to find a suitable point of mediation that does
not succumb to reducing the other to a mirror of the self. Complaining that the
radical asymmetry of Lévinas's formulation of the "self 'summoned to responsibility' by the other" (OA 189) leaves the self without reciprocal capacity for
response, Ricoeur explains that "taken literally, a dissymmetry left uncompen-
sated would break off the exchange of giving and receiving and would exclude
any instruction by the face within the field of solicitude. But how could this sort
of instruction be inscribed within the dialectic of giving and receiving, if a
capacity for giving in return were not freed by the other's very initiative" (OA
189)? For Ricoeur there must be some way for the summons to be reciprocated
that is not forced to choose between the alternatives of radical dissymmetry
where the other "has to storm the defenses of a separate 'I' " (OA 190), or the
radical symmetry where the self is reduced to complete passivity by the injunction of the other.

At the heart of Ricoeur's formulation of dialectical selfhood is, as I have
already noted, a "spectrum" of reciprocity that balances the power between self
and other. What avoids the destructive imbalance of a monogenesis from the
self or the other is something called "benevolent spontaneity" (OA 188). Ricoeur
explains that

> on the basis of this benevolent spontaneity, receiving is on an equal
> footing with the summons to responsibility, in the guise of the self's
> recognition of the superiority of the authority enjoining it to act in
> accordance with justice. This equality, to be sure, is not that of
> friendship, in which giving and receiving are hypothetically bal-
> anced. Instead, it compensates for the initial dissymmetry resulting
> from the primacy of the other in the situation of instruction, through
> the reverse movement of recognition. (OA 190)

The recognition of the authority of the other to summon me to responsibility
does not reduce the self to a state of total passivity—quite the opposite. The
other summons me to act. In fact, the action performed by the self on behalf
of the other returns the imbalance of power to a state of equilibrium. It is here
that the problematic formulation of voluntary selfhood begins to emerge. In
order to offer hope of mediation between the self and the other, Ricoeur must

ensure that reciprocal power is rooted in the benevolent use of power. Disparity and lack of reciprocity between agents is held in check by a primordial spontaneity that has the genuine capacity to act on behalf of the other. While others summon me to act on their behalf due to their lack of power, it is the benevolent use of my power to act, and not my passivity, that brings this disproportion back into a state of mutual balance.

At the opposite end of this spectrum of reciprocity, where the initiative for action comes from the self, rather than from the call for justice coming from the other, Ricoeur places the other in a position of passivity for the reception of the self's benevolent action. This is a puzzling inversion. Whereas the other provokes spontaneous benevolent action within the self, this does not reduce the self to powerlessness. Yet, when Ricoeur considers "the reverse of injunction," where the power of the other is suffered as "the reduction, even the destruction, of the capacity for acting, of being-able-to-act, experienced as a violation of self-integrity" (OA 190), the other is relegated to a condition of pure passivity. "Here initiative, precisely in terms of being-able-to-act, seems to belong exclusively to the self who *gives* his sympathy, his compassion, these terms being taken in the strong sense of the wish to share someone else's pain. Confronting the charity, this benevolence, the other appears to be reduced to the sole condition of *receiving*" (OA 190). At one end of the spectrum of power we have a self enjoined to *act* benevolently, and at the other end a self who *acts* out of sympathy; the other either provokes me to *act* in a benevolent manner (that is, to act in the mode of ipseity), or is the occasion for the self to *act* in a sympathetic manner. The self always acts from a position of power, whereas the power of the other seems to be situated somewhere between calling me to action and being purely receptive to my action.

In some ways this position of strength that characterizes the self is not surprising. What else would one call a self defined by voluntary self-constancy? Yet, such a formulation seems to be in complete contrast not only with the spirit of Ricoeur's understanding of intersubjective selfhood, but also with his preoccupation with the evil and pain suffered by those who have been the recipients of disproportionate power.[11] As Ricoeur explains,

> in true sympathy, the self, whose power of action is at the start greater than that of its other, finds itself affected by all that the suffering other offers to it in return. For from the suffering other there comes a giving that is no longer drawn from the power of action and existing but precisely from weakness itself. This is perhaps the supreme test of solicitude, when unequal power finds compensation in an authentic reciprocity in exchange, which, in the hour of agony, finds refuge in the shared whisper of voices or the feeble embrace of clasped hands. . . . A self reminded of the

vulnerability of the condition of mortality can receive from the
friend's weakness more than he or she can give in return by drawing
from his or her own reserves of strength. (OA 191)

Ricoeur is at pains to open voluntary selfhood to the affect of loss and suffering
in the other. He wants to understand selfhood as "suffering-with" the other (OA
190), and to engage in "what Lévinas calls the 'suffering for the useless suffering
of the other person.' "[12] But why then is Ricoeur's formulation of selfhood expressed in terms of the variability of power of the other and not that of the self?
Receiving the injunction from the other does not put the self in a comparable
position of suffering as is the case with the suffering other, nor does the sympathetic self give an injunction to the receptive other. Ricoeur's understanding
of the self is that of either spontaneous benefactor or sympathetic agent; that is,
an acting self that responds in a different manner in differing circumstances.
The *dissymmetry* of power between the self and the other remains a constant
factor at either end of the spectrum without really changing the self's power or
capacity to act. While Ricoeur does indeed describe a reciprocity of giving and
receiving, why is there no mention of the self calling the other to act out of
benevolent spontaneity on behalf of the self, or the suffering self who can no
longer give but out of feeble weakness?

   It seems that ipseity or voluntary self-constancy always implies an active,
deciding, projecting self, in order to exist in the mode of selfhood, in the
innovative power (*conatus*) of selfhood. The ethical aim for the good life is
simply the extension of such innovative creativity, although now it is understood
as the innovation to act on behalf of the other. This is "who" the self is: a
fundamentally active, as opposed to passive, self. Who then are other persons?
My doubles who are powerful like me, or the passive recipients of my power?
If others are mirrors of myself, we are at war, exerting power-over each other;
hence, the need for willful benevolence, and the "No!" of morality (OA 220–
225). If others are reduced to passivity, they are no longer other; they have
become the utilitarian extension of my will, necessary for voluntary selfhood.

   While Ricoeur is rightfully insistent that selfhood is formed in relation to
the other, and that this relationship ought to be reciprocal and even mutual, the
other, whether in a position of giving or receiving, is designated as other by
virtue of its effect on the active self. Of course, on the phenomenological level
this makes sense: the other, while not entirely inside or outside myself,[13] affects
me (OA 191). For Ricoeur such affectivity can only be relegated to the involuntary, the passive, which at best becomes "incorporated into the course of
motivation on the level designated by Aristotle with the term 'disposition' " (OA
191), and at worst becomes the absolute involuntary that I encircle with my
power to consent.[14] Therefore, when Ricoeur concludes that "friendship appear[s]
as a midpoint where the self and the other share equally the same wish to live

together" (OA 192), the inequality at the extremes of the spectrum of reciprocity does not really seem to be equalized at all. Even though Ricoeur emphasizes that mutuality equalizes disparity, this is accomplished through self-duplication, that is, through the reversibility and simultaneity of roles: "when I say 'you' to someone else, that person understands 'I' for himself or herself. When another addresses me in the second person, I feel I am implicated in the first person; reversibility concerns simultaneously the roles of speaker and listener, as well as the capacity of self-designation presumed to be equal in the sender of the discourse and in its receiver. But these are simply roles that are reversible" (OA 192–193). Even though Ricoeur adds nonsubstitutability to this role reversal, who is this other that I cannot exchange positions with? The other must be like me, my duplicate needed to balance the dissymmetry of power of active selfhood and passive otherness. The other is just like me, the same as me, the other is me, or at least I must presume the other to be analogous to me.[15] How else can Ricoeur state that "all the ethical feelings mentioned above belong to this phenomenology of 'you too' and of 'as myself'[?] For they well express the paradox contained in this equivalence, the paradox of the exchange at the very place of the irreplaceable. Becoming in this way fundamentally equivalent are the esteem of the *other as a oneself [l'autre comme un soi-même] and the esteem of oneself as an other [soi-même comme un autre]*" (OA 193–194; SA 226).

The fundamental dissymmetry of power between agent and patient is a puzzling development in Ricoeur's understanding of selfhood. The ethical aim to live well with others is for Ricoeur an original affirmation of *ipse* identity. The economy of exchange that characterizes reciprocal selfhood "denote[s] the primordial relation of the self to the self's other on the ethical level" (OA 203), and therefore functions as a prescription for existing in the mode of selfhood. Although morality is the "enunciation of a norm of reciprocity" (OA 219) that stems the tide of "violence" occasioned by the "initial dissymmetry between what one does and what is done to another" (OA 220), Ricoeur makes it clear that negation, the "No!" to the disfiguring face of evil, is always secondary to the affirmation of reciprocal selfhood. Saying "Yes!" to the "mutual exchange of self-esteems, is affirmative through and through. This affirmation, which can well be termed original, is the hidden soul of the prohibition. It is what, ultimately, arms our indignation, that is, our rejection of *indignities* inflicted on others" (OA 221).

Herein lies the puzzle. Is Ricoeur's prescription for selfhood a corrective response to the violence occasioned by the dissymmetry between agent and patient, or is the prescription itself predicated on a primordial dissymmetry that has given priority to the agent of action over the patient, that is, to selfhood as *"homo capax,"*[16] as the "I can," as the power-to-do (albeit benevolent power-held-in-abeyance) over the recipient of my power? This alternative of primordial dissymmetry or corrective response is significant, and brings us to the heart of Ricoeur's problematic formulation of selfhood, a problem that has remained unresolved since its first formulation in *Fallible Man*.[17] Does Ricoeur need to affirm the primordiality of benevolent spontaneity in order to prevent the domination of one agent over the other? Or does his understanding of selfhood have room for mutual giving that does not correlate with a reduction in the power of those acted upon, a giving that does not diminish the selfhood of others or one's own? Does Ricoeur have to hold power-in-benevolent-abeyance because power would otherwise always degenerate into power-over? If this is indeed the case, then *homo capax* should live no more, and Ricoeur's ontology of power (*conatus*) ought to be left behind.

Identifying Selfhood

What then does Ricoeur's philosophy of the "capable man" bring to language? As I have shown, Ricoeur's attempt to move beyond the philosophies of the *cogito* is part of his own struggle against Husserlian idealism. Through his hermeneutical reorientation of phenomenology Ricoeur has tried to purge consciousness from self-grounding radicality. For him, and unlike Husserl, consciousness is not absolute, transparent, and self-present; rather, the self is linguistically mediated through "all the objectivities . . . in the [reflective] process of the self" (OA 187). By focusing on this linguistic recovery of selfhood, Ricoeur tries to close the difference in Husserl's phenomenology between a self "situated in the world" and another self, "its transcendental double" (RH 57).

For Ricoeur, however, selfhood is situated within the semantic world of the text. In this sense, Ricoeur does indeed close the Husserlian difference between the life-world and its foundation in absolute consciousness. Over the course of my investigation of Ricoeur's hermeneutical philosophy I have shown how metaphor and narrative have recast idealistic concepts of subjectivity into polysemic sonorous images in front of consciousness, where selfhood is understood as a task to be accomplished rather than as an originating source of world accomplishment. Ricoeur is not in search of a transcendental double that secures knowledge of selfhood prior to the act of interpretation. However, Ricoeur's proposal for polysemic selfhood opens a new difference within language itself between first-order and second-order discourse. By placing variations of identity in juxtaposition to the unity of selfhood, Ricoeur begs the question of structural similarity between Husserl's phenomenological idealism and his own position. Although Ricoeur vigorously opposes "the ambition of placing [the self] in the position of ultimate foundation" (OA 18), he still wants to "secure . . . the analogical unity of acting on a stable ontological meaning" (OA 20). Even though Ricoeur qualifies such stability of meaning as inherently polysemic, a relation is established between this source of stability and phenomenological diversity in

need of unification and stabilization. Ricoeur refers to such ontological meaning as second-order discourse, and thereby implies its derivation from a primary
source of mediated meaning. Does not this stability of meaning entail a transformation of second-order discourse into something foundational for that which
is mediated? By formulating the stability of selfhood as *conatus* or productive
power, does not this qualify the objectivities of the reflective process of selfhood
as variations of what is primary, that is, variations of power? While this may be
evidence not so much of a failing of Ricoeur's philosophy of selfhood as it is of
the impossibility of the complete deconstruction of the self or the subject,[18]
what cannot be avoided is a degree of structural similarity between Husserl's
and Ricoeur's understanding of the relation between meaning and unity of
meaning. The argumentative structure remains the same in spite of the change
of topic from a self-grounding ego to a polysemic understanding of selfhood.

Further evidence of such structural similarity can be seen in Ricoeur's
struggle to reconnect the semantic world of the text with the world of experience. Kathleen Blamey explains that "Husserl's most remarkable achievement,
arriving at the *eidos* ego, is at the same time his downfall, for as a result of
reducing all otherness to the monadic life of the ego, he confronts the impossible task of integrating the subject back into the world of things and of people,
into the course of history" (PPR 583). While Ricoeur has developed the concept of a "broken *cogito*" that is always open to involuntary otherness, the path
that interpretation takes is that of linguistic and literary distance from the direct
and intimate experience of belonging. Not to be equated with Husserl's phenomenological reduction, Ricoeur's hermeneutics nevertheless assumes that
the literary process of distanciation and identity formation is necessary for understanding the fundamental experience of belonging, and as I have shown,
becomes virtually synonymous with selfhood itself.

"Appropriation" and "refiguration" become Ricoeur's battle cry in the
struggle to close "the gap . . . between fiction and life."[19] Taking distance from
experience should still be part of the experience of belonging. But why does
Ricoeur, when faced with what he perceives to be the gap[20] between language
and life, either describe the "phenomenon of reverberation"[21] or "something
like *allégorèse*"[22] to close this difference without giving any significant elaboration of how these phenomena function? If this gap "is taken so seriously that
it becomes a very thorny problem to reconnect literature to life by means of
reading" (TN 3:159), then why are these pivotal concepts simply declared essential without further substantial development?

This is why Ricoeur's philosophy of the "capable man" can only bring the
question of identity to language. Selfhood is the source of identity, not in the
sense of foundation, ground, or *archê*, but rather as the living response of self
to self, to otherness, others, and the Other, which can only be given a narrative
identity after the fact, and then, as Ricoeur has made abundantly clear, only

polysemically. As the condition of possibility for responding reflexively, the self, as Ricoeur has quite rightly observed, is reflected in metaphor and narrative language, in action and the ethical prescription for action. But can these identifications of self, these stories we tell about ourselves, about our histories, our children, our deepest commitments, and the like, be equated with the intimacy of the selfhood? I can tell you stories about my children (and given half the chance, I do so for several hours), but such stories can never replace the lived experience of intimacy that I have with them. These stories tell something about me, they may in fact tell a great deal about me, and they can be taken as representative of who I am, but they can never be equated with the living relationship that I have with these word models that I identify with. Hence, the subject matter of *Oneself as Another*, by virtue of this semantic entanglement of the pragmatics of self, is never able to move the question of selfhood beyond the problem of semantic identifications of various models of selfhood. In other words, Ricoeur's call to exchange the ego, master of itself, for a self discipled by the text, cannot escape the semantic world constructed by the linguistic imagination.

This is indeed a "thorny problem" (OA 159) which seems to counter Ricoeur's quest to "attack" and overcome "the paradox we are considering here: stories are recounted, life is lived," by being unable to "cross . . . [this] unbridgeable gap [that] seems to separate fiction and life."[23] Therefore, Ricoeur's assertion that the "whatness" of the text is overshadowed by who is revealed in the text may indeed be correct; but, if in the end the question "who?" ends up being collapsed into the question "what?" then the semantic reference of metaphor and narrative to the self and the world which makes that mode of existing in selfhood possible, is a reference to a variation of identity within the text. Narratives propose alternative models of identity which, if appropriated, will indeed have a significant effect on the reader, but this semantic reference to variations of identity cannot be equated with the living relationship users or interpreters have with these texts. While the ego is certainly enlarged and broken open by the dialogue of exchange with the textual other, and selfhood is certainly discipleship in conjunction with the other (otherness, others, the Other), the intimate reflexive response to oneself and the other can never be accounted for beforehand by the referential world of the text. While I identify with the characters of many texts and incorporate them into the ever-changing landscape of my identity, they can never be equivalent to the intimate reflexive structure of my selfhood that reflects itself in polysemic storytelling.

Narrative identity is a form of testimony or attestation of selfhood, which the reader can either affirm or reject. If the story rings true, the reader identifies with its meaning and receives its textual world as a validation and expansion of his or her conviction concerning the task of selfhood. The inverse is also possible: the world of the text can be rejected as counterintuitive to one's convictions about the task of becoming a self. In this sense, Ricoeur's philosophy of selfhood is deeply rooted in his formulation of the hermeneutical circle. Here he reaffirms his understanding of the relation between belief and understanding, the reception of the gift and the wager of faith. Although originally formulated in the *Symbolism of Evil* in terms of primitive symbols and speculative religious discourse, this circle can now be formulated as follows: I believe in narratives which identify selfhood as the dialectic of the self, the same, and the other, in order to understand selfhood; and, I understand selfhood identified as the dialectic of the self, the same, and the other, in order to believe in these narratives of selfhood.

The conviction that narratives can indeed speak truthfully about selfhood (OA 300) is "set in opposition to . . . the notion of *episteme*, of science, taken in the sense of ultimate foundation" (OA 21). The kind of certainty that Ricoeur wants to advocate is "reliable attestation," "a kind of belief" and "trust" belonging "to the grammar of 'I believe-in' " (OA 21–22, 299). This "assurance of being oneself acting and suffering" is "self-attestation" that takes "impregnable refuge" in the question "who?" (OA 22–23). For Ricoeur, attestation is at once the conviction that selfhood is a dialectic of the self, the same, and the other, and the proof that this is indeed the intimate reflexive structure of selfhood. Even though Ricoeur states that such belief can never be taken as the "ultimate foundation" for the philosophy of selfhood, and that "suspicion is also the path *toward* and the crossing *within* attestation" (OA 302), the impregnability of the question "who?" safeguards its doubt. Ricoeur's hope to give testimony of selfhood beyond the philosophies of the *cogito* and *anticogito* turns back on itself by placing the assurance of self within the analysis of the semantic network of intersignification, that is, within the narrative identifications of selfhood. On the one hand Ricoeur wants to say that selfhood is such a fundamental experience that its full philosophical account is impossible and therefore calls for some kind of attestation; but, on the other hand, he locates this belief or credence within his philosophical analysis of the question "who?" and thereby makes the attestation of selfhood a topic for investigation alongside any other philosophical topic. It is almost as if Ricoeur wants to have an opening to move beyond the stability of philosophical universality and necessity, but at the same time limit the destabilizing effect this might have.

If, as Ricoeur claims, selfhood is linked to the other, then the reception of the other, be that other persons, other narratives, or the Wholly Other, can never be abstract. It is the particular other that I now face, or the moment of crisis, or the confrontation with the text I am now reading, that shapes selfhood. It is the alterity of the immediate other that calls what I affirm into question, that can make myself suspicious of what I attest to, and that invites me to listen. If true "listening excludes founding oneself" (FS 224) and claims to move beyond the mastery of the identifying circle of the self-same, then attestation must be more than "impregnable . . . self-attestation" (OA 22–23); it must be an act of surrender, of giving oneself to the other, and a willingness to be receptive to a destabilizing transformation that the testimony of the other may bring. In other words, contrary to Ricoeur's claim that a philosophy of selfhood can be an "autonomous, philosophical discourse," agnostic with regard to his own "convictions that bind me to biblical faith" (OA 24), the language of attestation transgresses this presumed limit of philosophical discourse through its connection to the immediacy and particularity of the Other. Ricoeur's understanding of selfhood as a "mandated self" is a "respondent" to a call that does not come from an anonymous other, but from a summons to listen to "the propositions of meaning issuing from the symbolic network" of biblical faith (FS 262). Even though Ricoeur claims that "the philosopher as philosopher has to admit that one does not know and cannot say whether this Other, the source of the injunction, is another person whom I can look in the face or who can stare at me, or my ancestors for whom there is no representation . . . , or God—living God, absent God—or an empty place" (OA 355), Ricoeur himself does not refrain from naming this Other as the Other of "the Jewish and Christian tradition" (FS 262).[24]

It is not that Ricoeur needs to exclude such particularity of commitment from his philosophical investigations of selfhood; rather, as he himself admits, his formulation of selfhood is already deeply interconnected with his commitment to hear the summons of the Other within the textual world of biblical faith (OA 24). But what does Ricoeur's commitment to the biblical narrative contribute to his understanding of the perceived necessity of the narrative structure of selfhood? Surely his commitment to biblical narratives, which he believes to identify selfhood as the dialectic of the self, the same, and the other, contributes something to "thinking, which aims at what is universal and necessary"? For more than forty years Ricoeur has insisted that symbol, myth, and narrative give rise to thought, that the "primacy of the gift,"[25] although beyond the construct, is nevertheless inescapably interconnected with the production of thought. Rather than separating the uniqueness of my own narrative tradition from philosophical reflection, shouldn't I think along with and in the narrative texture that gives me my sense of self-direction and orientation? If conviction and certainty of self cannot be produced by rational analysis, shouldn't Ricoeur articulate how the particularity of his own religious tradition stimulates the production of an imaginative vision that affects what appears to him as philosophically necessary; that seeing selfhood as . . . is indeed inseparable from being as . . . ? Ricoeur seems to make just such a claim: "I boldly stay within this circle in the hope that, through the transfer from text to life, what I have risked will be returned a hundred fold as an increase in comprehension, valor, and joy" (FS 217). Not to give consideration to that which can only be received as gift and is worthy of risking one's whole life, excludes too much. Philosophical reflection is embarrassed by what can never be deemed necessary and universal: the radical particularity of the reflexive self who finds herself or himself confronted by the immediate other.

> Shall I tolerate the fact that thinking, which aims at what is universal and necessary, is linked in a contingent way to individual events and particular texts that report them? Yes, I shall assume this contingency, so scandalous for thinking, as one aspect of the presupposition attached to listening. For I hope that once I enter into the movement of comprehending faith, I shall discover the very reason for that contingency, if it is true that the increase in comprehension that I expect is indissolubly linked to testimonies to the truth, which are contingent in every instance and rendered through certain acts, lives, and beings. (FS 217–218)

I too share Ricoeur's commitment to the narratives of biblical faith. But if I hope to find the "very reason" for what I accept in faith, will I ever hear a voice that is other than my own, other than that demanded by philosophical necessity? If the risk of faith expects a return of a hundredfold is it really a wager or simply insider trading, a sure bet for someone skilled on the floor of the exchange of the same? Is this really what Ricoeur hopes for, or has he rightfully carried philosophical reflection to the threshold of faith, acknowledging that in the end a philosophy of selfhood can only recognize the self and others as subjects of testimony? Is this the meaning of hope, crossing over the threshold of faith without crossing out the interpretations of selfhood, only their metaphysical guarantee? Attestation is the recognition of radical contingency at the heart of the experience of selfhood, and that philosophical "critique is still always linked to powers that I master, whereas this giving of meaning seems to constitute me both as receptive subject and as a critical subject."[26] Without the safety of *episteme*, attestation is a polysemic confession of not-knowing or perhaps knowing-otherwise,[27] a confession of love that knows through intimacy and risk, a confession of the impossibility to master the "superabundance" (FS 302) of the gift of the other and the self, and a confession "that there is a call to love that comes from farther and from higher"[28] that delights in a response from *soi-même avec et pour l'autre*.

NOTES

Introduction

1. See OA 297–356. In "My Relation to the History of Philosophy," in the context of Gabriel Marcel's ontological investigations, Ricoeur affirms that "the desire for this concrete ontology has never left me" (p. 5). He qualifies his indebtedness to Marcel by the lessons in systematization learned from Husserl, and he maintains that even though "Husserlian idealism did run counter to Marcel's concrete ontology" (p. 6), ontology is not in principle antithetically opposed to phenomenology, but only the idealistic interpretation thereof.

2. Ricoeur's major publications can be classified into three different historical periods: (1) early phenomenological work: *Truth and History* (1955), *Freedom and Nature* (1950), *Fallible Man* (1960), *Husserl* (1967); (2) early hermeneutical studies: *Symbolism of Evil* (1960), *Freud and Philosophy* (1965), *Conflict of Interpretations* (1969); (3) hermeneutical phenomenology: *Interpretation Theory* (1976), *Rule of Metaphor* (1975), *Hermeneutics and the Human Sciences* (1981), *Lectures on Ideology and Utopia* (1986), *Time and Narrative* (1983–1985), *Oneself as Another* (1990).

3. Augustine, *De libero arbitrio* I, c. 2, § 4; II, c. 2, § 5.

4. Ricoeur makes numerous references to his philosophical and theological commitments. For explicit self-conscious evaluations of such commitments, see: OA 1–25; "On Interpretation," in *Philosophy in France Today*, ed. A. Montefiore (New York: Cambridge University Press, 1983), 175–197 (reprinted in FTA 1–20); "A Response by Ricoeur," in HHS 32–40; "My Relation to the History of Philosophy," in *Iliff Review* 35.3 (1978): 5–12; "From Existentialism to the Philosophy of Language," *Criterion* 10 (Spring 1971): 14–18, reprinted in *Paul Ricoeur: An Anthology of His Work*, ed. Charles E. Reagan and David Stewart (Boston: Beacon Press, 1978), 86–93; "Intellectual Autobiography," in *The Philosophy of Paul Ricoeur*, ed. Lewis Edwin Hahn (Chicago: Open Court, 1995), 3–53.

5. We will examine this in greater detail below, 1.3 and 1.4.

6. "It seemed, therefore, that direct reflection on oneself could not go very far without undertaking a roundabout way, the detour of a hermeneutics of symbols." P. Ricoeur, "From Existentialism to the Philosophy of Language," in *The Philosophy of Paul Ricoeur: An Anthology of His Work*, ed. Charles E. Reagan and David Stewart (Boston: Beacon Press, 1978) 87 (OI 17).

7. For further discussion on Ricoeur's distinction between reflection and reflexive (*réflexif* and *réfléchi*), or the reflective process and reflexive structure, see below, chapter 5 n. 1.

8. The contrast between Ricoeur's philosophy of the subject and the tradition of modernity is not directly comparable with the so-called contrast between modernism and postmodernism. Although Ricoeur does advocate a hermeneutic of selfhood that is supposed to be beyond the philosophies of the *cogito* and *anticogito*, Ricoeur is certainly not an advocate of the end of philosophy and all things modern. Further, designating Ricoeur's hermeneutic of selfhood as a variation of philosophical postmodernism is not particularly helpful given the present state of "temporal disjunction" that seems unable to define postmodernism in the first place (Jean-François Lyotard, 1984, 3. See also Joseph C. McLelland, "Via Postmoderna: Toward Modal Theology," in *ARC*, The Journal of the Faculty of Religious Studies, McGill 23 [1995]: 47–58). As Gary Madison points out, the question "Just what is postmodernism?" offers endless plurality of reply. "There seems to be no canonical answer to this question. As one writer pertinently observes: 'Every student of modern culture is evidently required to state a position of modernism and postmodernism, even though it is not clear what these words denote. They mean, it appears, what ever we want them to mean' " (HP x).

However, Madison does go on to offer a definition, by way of contrast with modernism, that does help to limit some of the ambiguity of the term *postmodernism*. " 'Modernism' denotes what the traditional term 'modern philosophy' denotes: that movement of thought which originates with Descartes and which has perpetuated itself up to and into the twentieth century. . . . What above all characterizes that form of the logocentric metaphysics of presence known as modern philosophy is that it seeks to realize philosophy's traditional goal of achieving a basic, fundamental knowledge (*episteme, Wissenschaft*) of what is (*ta onta*) by turning inward, into the knowing subject himself (conceived of either psychologistically or transcendentally), where it seeks to discover grounds which will allow for certainty of our 'knowledge' of what, henceforth, is called 'the external world'. . . . The two great theoretical by-products of modern, epistemologically centered philosophy which places all the emphasis on method (as opposed to insight [*noesis*], as in the case of the ancient metaphysics of presence), are the notions of subjectivity and a fully objective, determinate world—the essential business of the 'knowing subject' ('man') being that of forming true 'representations' of so-called objective reality. The end of modernism means, accordingly, the end of epistemologically centered philosophy (as Richard Rorty has remarked). It means the end of what modernism understood by 'the subject,' and it means as well the end of the 'objective world' (a world which is fully what it is in itself and which simply waits around for a cognizing subject to come along and form a 'mental representation' of it)" (HP x).

Essential to this way of describing philosophical postmodernism is the deconstruction of the philosophical core of modern philosophy. However, such critical description is not without thetical content. Madison points out that "many of the deconstructions of modernism . . . point only in the direction of relativism and, even more, of nihilism, the kind of nihilism which Nietzsche prophesied and which he and his philosophical heirs have sought—vainly—to conjure away by means of a joyful affirmation of the pointlessness of our effective history" (HP xiii). The story Madison wishes to tell is not without a plot. Life is purposeful and full of meaning, even if such meaning can be only spoken of through partial stories haltingly told. Perhaps the fragmented movement beyond the subject and the project of foundationalism is still predicated on a metaphysic of a new kind not yet made fully conscious. But that does not mean, as Ricoeur points out, the dissemination of all meaning. The story of the self is one in which "I exchange the *me, master* of itself, for the *self, disciple* of the text" (PH 113). For those whose lives are marked by the narratives of biblical faith, philosophical reflection is not one guided by some sort of Hegelian consummation of the Absolute or nihilistic despair, but by a hope for some kind of final restoration and forgiveness that acknowledges the primordiality of goodness over suffering and evil.

9. Ricoeur's understanding of hermeneutic self-disclosure is similar to John Caputo's formulation of the hermeneutical inquiry: "For hermeneutics in the broadest sense means for me coping with the flux, tracing out a pattern in a world in slippage. Hermeneutics is the latest form of the philosophy of becoming, the latest response to the Heraclitean challenge" (RH 37).

10. OA 187 n. 22. Here the English translation talks about "the reflexive process of the self," whereas the French original has "*le procès réflexif du soi*" (SA 219), not *le procès réfléchi*. See below, chapter 5 n. 1, for clarification of the terms *réflexif* and *réfléchi*.

11. Paul Ricoeur, "A Response by Paul Ricoeur," trans. David Pellauer, in *Paul Ricoeur and Narrative: Context and Contestation*, ed. Morny Joy (Calgary: University of Calgary Press, 1997), xxxix.

12. OA 20. In this context Caputo's assertion that all desire for stability of ontological meaning is in fact an attempt to bring metaphysical peace to the anxiety generated by the original difficulty of living, merits careful consideration. Caputo explains that Gadamer "and *a fortiori* Ricoeur" attempts "to block off the radicalization of hermeneutics and to turn it back to the fold of metaphysics" (RH 5).

13. OA 148, 132–133, 159, 164, 170, 264, 276, 288.

14. TDI 181, 183; OA 121.

15. See above, Introduction n. 21.

16. RM 7, 255; TN 1:64; TN 3:157; FM 124; OPR 171.

17. RM 213, 246; TN 1:xi; TN 3:151–152, 181; IDA 8.

18. OA 187 n. 22; SM 219 n. 1. See also below, chapter 5 n. 1.

19. Paul Ricoeur, "A Response by Paul Ricoeur," trans. David Pellauer, in *Paul Ricoeur and Narrative: Context and Contestation*, ed. Morny Joy (Calgary: University of Calgary Press, 1997), xxxix.

20. Ricoeur's most recent bibliography lists a total of 1,241 publications, which includes the various translations of original French and English works. See "Bibliography of Paul Ricoeur: A Primary and Secondary Systematic Bibliography," comp. Frans D. Vansina and Paul Ricoeur, in *The Philosophy of Paul Ricoeur*, ed. Lewis Edwin Hahn (Chicago: Open Court, 1995), 605–815.

21. Ricoeur uses the terms *dialectical* or *dialectic*, as well as *aporia*, in a less than precise manner to indicate a relation between two terms, phenomena, features of experience, or movements within language, and so on, which work together through the creative power of the imagination to produce something new: new meaning in metaphorical language, new understanding of the world of the text, new and refigured identity, new visions of selfhood. Usually indicating an impasse, opposition, or tension between terms that are inescapably juxtaposed, Ricoeur does not attempt to overcome their

opposition but thinks through and along with the problems they pose in order to create new ideas and modes of thought. Ricoeur explains that "my thesis is that if there is a place where productive oppositions can be observed, recognized, and identified, this place is human reality. . . . Dialectic can be nothing other than the process of things proceeding by productive opposition" (P. Ricoeur, "What Is Dialectical?" in *Freedom and Morality*, ed. John Bricke [Lawrence: University of Kansas Press, 1976], 174–175).

It is important to note that what is said for the terms *dialectic* and *dialectical* is also true for Ricoeur's use of the term *imagination*. Used in a wide variety of ways, the imagination can be understood as a connecting matrix of activities that accounts for the various forms of creativity. Hence, it can be said that the imagination is dialectically structured, and that dialectic opposition is made productive through the connecting matrix of the power or work of imagination. What is produced can be referred to as the work of imagination: signs, symbols, and texts.

Chapter 1. From Ego to Selfhood

1. See, for instance, Hans-Georg Gadamer, "L' herméneutique philosophique," *Studies in Religion* 5.1 (Summer 1975–1976): 3–13.

2. See Hans-Georg Gadamer, *Truth and Method* (New York: Crossroads, 1975), and *Philosophical Hermeneutics*, trans. David E. Linge (Berkeley: University of California Press, 1976).

3. If we hold to our original periodization of Ricoeur's published works (see above, p. XX n. 2), PH cannot only be placed at the beginning of the third historical period, but is emblematic of the period as a whole.

4. PH 101. See also Ricoeur, "Hegel and Husserl on Intersubjectivity," FTA 234, and Anderson (1993) 15.

5. See below chapter 4, and TN 1:52–87.

6. Paul Ricoeur, "An Introduction to Husserl's *Ideas 1*," in *Husserl: An Analysis of His Phenomenology*, trans. Edward G. Ballard and Lester E. Embree (Evanston, Ill.: Northwestern University Press, 1967), 14. This essay was originally published as the introduction to E. Husserl, *Idées directrices pour une phénoménologie* (Bibliothèque de philosophie). Traduction de *Ideen 1* avec introduction et notes de P. Ricoeur (Paris: Gallimard, 1950). A new translation of this introduction and the interpretive notes can be found in KH.

7. Ricoeur in his commentary on *Ideas 1* explains that "Husserl's method of approach is to extract from methodical doubt, better known than *epochè*, the component which is precisely the *epochè*. This component is more primitive than doubt since the latter adds the exclusion of certainty. The *epochè* consists in a act of suspension rather than negation, conjecture, calculation, or doubt" (KH 89).

8. Since the thesis of the world is not an act of consciousness, it remains on the level of a passive synthesis. Husserl explains that the "fact-world *that has its being out there*, does *not* consist of course *in an act proper*, in an articulated judgement *about existence*. It is and remains something all the time the standpoint is adopted, that is, it endures persistently during the whole course of our life of natural endeavor" (Ideas 96).

Hence the suspension of the natural attitude is the result of a higher conscious act over the lower passive constitution of the world.

9. While Ricoeur points out that Husserl is only offering a " 'first glimpse' of transcendental consciousness and thus [it is] gradually elevated to the level of reduction," and therefore only "half phenomenological psychology and half transcendental idealism," it must not be forgotten that this question of implementation is of considerable debate. Ricoeur does, however, seem to acknowledge that the transcendental reduction has been implemented in part when he further comments that "at this stage, phenomenology is a regional eidetic which is delineated by the exclusion of the region of nature, while consciousness is the region not touched by this exclusion" (KH 93). Hence, the extent to which this "new" found "region of being" has been mapped out is the point in question.

10. Ricoeur confirms the significance of this distinction but is quick to point out that such a division "does bear any cosmological meaning here. It would be wrong to interpret this distinction in the sense of Aristotelian and Medieval ontology in which knowing is a relation within being. Here there are two *modes of intuition*, one immanent and the other transcendent, which, by opposing each other, distinguish the two regions to which they relate" (KH 100).

11. Ricoeur refers to this as "the radical difference which separates the adequacy of immanent perception and the inadequacy of transcendent perception" (KH 102).

12. For all Husserl's protestation of the inappropriateness of metaphysics, what he in fact describes is a variation of what philosophers since Aristotle have dreamed of: that which exists by virtue of its essence, that form of being which gives everything else being, namely, God.

13. Ricoeur formulates his understanding of phenomenology through dialectical concepts that are supposed to reflect a process of mediation that characterizes selfhood. Ricoeur states that the "situation of man" can be found in the contrasts between "being and nothingness," "the infinite and the finite," "discourse and existence, meaning and appearance," "value and presence," and as "the feeling of disproportion of self to itself, of a non-coincidence or an interior 'difference' which attests to the original fragility of human reality." Paul Ricoeur, "The Antinomy of Human Reality," in *The Philosophy of Paul Ricoeur: An Anthology of His Work*, ed. Charles E. Reagan and David Stewart (Boston: Beacon Press 1978), 35. These dialectical formulations will be examined in more detail when in the following chapter I focus on Ricoeur's two books *Freedom and Nature* and *Fallible Man*.

14. Ricoeur goes on to say that "initially I am lost and forgotten in the world, lost in the things, lost in the ideas, lost in the plants and animals, lost in others, lost in mathematics. Presence (which can never be disavowed) is the occasion of temptation; in seeing there is a trap, the trap of my alienation; there I am external, diverted.... For if I lose myself in the world, I am then ready to treat myself as a thing of the world. The thesis of the world is a sort of blindness in the very heart of seeing. What I call living is hiding myself as naïve consciousness within the existence of all things: 'In natural living I live the fundamental form of all 'actual life.' Thus, the spiritual discipline of phenomenology is a true conversion of the sense of intentionality, which is first the forgetting of consciousness, and then its discovery of itself as given.... Through it I apparently lose the world that I truly gain" (HL 20). Also see FP 45.

15. HL 12. For an interesting response to this problem, see M. Boutin, "Relation, Otherness, and the Philosophy of Religion," *Journal of Religious Pluralism* 2 (1992): 61–82; see especially pp. 66–67.

16. HL 205. Ricoeur's intuition about the "world" in this passage is more clearly and fully expressed by Gordon D. Kaufman in "A Problem for Theology: The Concept of Nature," *Harvard Theological Review* 65:3 (July 1972): 337–366, particularly pp. 343–344: "*World* is never an object of perception or of experience: it can never 'come into view' or be in any way directly experienced. It is, rather, the backdrop against which or context within which we have all our experience and within which we know ourselves to be situated. . . . If we treat the concept of world as fundamentally like other concepts which refer to or represent objects (identifiable in experience), we get into insoluble antinomies. . . . 'World' is a concept for which no object (in that sense) exists (at any one time) at all. The notion of world is a construct created by the human imagination as a heuristic device to make possible the ordering and relating of all our other concepts of objects and events. It is thus indispensable to our thinking and even to the orderliness of our experience—and in every culture we find some sort of (often mythical) notions of this widest context within which human life transpires—but it is itself not an object of experience; it is a fundamental presupposition of experience."

17. See below, chapter 2, section 2.2, for more detail on Ricoeur's early employment of the hermeneutic of the drama of existence.

18. PH 107. This dual "rule" of meaning plays a significant role in the development of Ricoeur's own hermeneutic. Referring to Heidegger, Ricoeur explains that "interpretation is above all an explication, a development of understanding which 'does not transform it into something else, but makes it become itself' . . . what is explicated is the *as such* (als) which adheres to the articulations of experience; but 'the assertion does not make the "as such" appear, it only gives it an expression' (SZ 149; BT 190)" (TH 57). For Ricoeur, the "as such" is the imaginative power of language which can see reality "as" the possibility to live otherwise.

19. See 1.2 nn. 5 and 7.

20. "Composition, belonging to a genre and individual style characterize discourse as a work. The very word 'work' reveals the nature of these new categories; they are categories of production and of labor. . . . Discourse thereby becomes the object of a *praxis* and a *techne*" (HFD 136).

21. On occasion Ricoeur uses the metaphor of a "spiral" to clarify the meaning of the dialectical structure of hermeneutical understanding. In *Time and Narrative*, vol. 1, Ricoeur explains that "the hermeneutical circle of mimesis and temporality would resolve into the vicious circle of mimesis alone" if it were not for life's lack of narrative closure. He goes on to say "that the analysis is circular is indisputable. But that the circle is a vicious one can be refuted. In this regard, I would rather speak of an endless spiral that would carry the meditation past the same point a number of times, but at different altitudes. The accusation about a vicious circle proceeds from the seduction of one or the other of two versions of circularity. The first emphasizes the violence of interpretation, the second its redundance" (TN 1:72). Ricoeur also uses the metaphor of the "spiral" to explain the relation between ideological and utopian language: "we cannot get out of the circle of ideology and utopia, but the judgment of appropriateness may

help us to understand how the circle can become a spiral." Paul Ricoeur, *Lectures on Ideology and Utopia*, ed. George H. Taylor (New York: Columbia University Press, 1986), 314.

22. Ricoeur explains that "I cannot accept the irrationalism of immediate understanding, conceived as an extension to the domain of texts of the empathy by which a subject puts himself in the place of a foreign consciousness in a situation of face-to-face intensity. This undue extension maintains the romantic illusion of a direct link of congeniality between the two subjectivities implied by the work, that of the author and that of the reader. However, I am equally unable to accept a rationalistic explanation that would extend to the text the structural analysis of sign systems that are characteristic not of discourse but of language as such. This equally undue extension gives rise to the positivist illusion of textual objectivity closed in upon itself and wholly independent of the subjectivity of both author and reader. To these two one-sided attitudes, I have opposed the dialectic of understanding and explanation. By understanding I mean the ability to take up again within oneself the work of structuring that is performed by the text, and by explanation, the second-order operation grafted onto this understanding which consists in bringing to light the codes underlying this work of structuring that is carried through in company with the reader" (OI 18–19).

23. See below chapter 3, sec. 2. Also IT 45–46, 55, 57; FP 28–31, 496–506; SE 347–357; RM 193–200, 213–215, 239–246. For further discussion, see Richard Kearney's excellent book *Poetics of Imagining: From Husserl to Lyotard* (London: Routledge, 1991), 134–169; additionally, see Leonard Lawlor, *Imagination and Chance: The Difference between the Thought of Ricoeur and Derrida* (Albany: State University of New York Press, 1992), 29–41, 63–72.

24. Jervolino, in his insightful analysis of Ricoeur's method, explains that Ricoeur's transformation of transcendental idealism proposes a new model of "rationality" capable of giving a justifiable interpretation of experience. "Choice in favor of meaning, dialectic between belonging and distanciation, primacy of the totality of experience with respect to its expression in language, temporal and historical nature of living experience: these are the features of a phenomenological and hermeneutical reason capable of countering phenomenological idealism's model of rationality with a different form of rationality, suitable to a historical, incarnate subjectivity. In effect, the 'radicalness' of this phenomenological undertaking can never be carried out by means of a chain of intuitive leaps back toward a presumed 'originary' evidence, but only through an interpretative penetration into the life of the ego" (Jervolino 98).

25. See below, 2.1.

Chapter 2. Imagination

1. Ricoeur goes on to say that "it is essential to show how the different discourses may interrelate or intersect but one must resist the temptation to make them identical, the same. My departure from Husserlian phenomenology was largely due to my disagreement with its theory of a controlling transcendental *cogito*. I advanced the notion of a wounded or split *cogito*, in opposition to the idealist claims for an inviolate absolute

subjectivity. . . . I think that there is a certain 'degree zero' or emptiness which we may have to traverse in order to abandon our pretension to be the center, our tendency to reduce all other discourses to our own totalizing schemas of thought. If there is an ultimate unity, it resides elsewhere, in a sort of eschatological hope. But this is my 'secret,' if you wish, my personal wager, and not something that can be translated into a centralizing philosophical discourse" (Dialogues 27–28).

   2. Ricoeur, in reference to Merleau-Ponty's book *Phenomenology of Perception*, explains that "the project of a phenomenology of perception, in which the moment of saying is postponed and the reciprocity of saying and seeing is destroyed, is, in the last analysis, a hopeless venture." "Négatvité et affirmation originaire," *Aspects de la dialectique* (Recherches de philosophie, II) (Paris: Desclée de Brouwer, 1956). Translated as "Negativity and Primary Affirmation," in *Truth and History*, trans. Ch. A. Kelbley (Evanston, Ill.: Northwestern University Press, 1965), 309. Elsewhere Ricoeur states that "Merleau-Ponty's existential phenomenology thus represents the strictest disagreement with the Platonic conversion of the here-below to the beyond. Placed in the service of a reconversion from reflection to the pre-reflective, existential phenomenology becomes identified with the justification of being-in-the-world. One can only wonder, though, how the moment of reflection on the unreflected, how the devotion to universality and to truth, and finally how the philosophical act itself are possible if man is so completely identified with his insertion into his field of perception, action, and life." Paul Ricoeur, "Phénoménologie existentielle," in *Encylopédie française. XIX. Philosophie et religion* (Paris: Larousee, 1957). Translated as "Existential Phenomenology," in *Husserl: An Analysis of his Phenomenology*, trans. Edward B. Ballard and Lester E. Embree (Evanston, Ill.: Northwestern University Press, 1967), 209–210.

   This early critique of Merleau-Ponty by Ricoeur has to a limited extent been reformulated in *Oneself as Another*. Muldoon points out that "the 'I can' is Merleau-Ponty's summary of how one's own body generates, through its own actions, the possible field of action that 'I' can actualize. Ricoeur incorporates the 'I can' because of his intention to understand narrative identity as that which attests to one's own acting and suffering. Such an attestation is mute if it is impossible to distinguish the intentional intervention of self-reflecting agents in the course of worldly events." Mark S. Muldoon, "Ricoeur and Merleau-Ponty on Narrative Identity," in *American Catholic Philosophical Quarterly* 71.1 (1997): 35–52, especially p. 43. However, contrary to Muldoon's positive assessment of Ricoeur's rethinking of Merleau-Ponty's phenomenology of the "I can," Ricoeur's link between the analogical unity of the self and the "I can" calls into question any fundamental reassessment of the hierarchical priority of the voluntary over the involuntary. See below, 5.3.1; also see TN 3:230–233; OA 109–111; "Initiative" FTA 208–222; "Hommage à Merleau-Ponty (1961)" and "Merleau-Ponty: par-delà Husserl et Heidegger (1989)," in Paul Ricoeur. *Lectures 2: La contrée de philosophes* (Paris: Seuil, 1992), 157–172.

   3. Don Ihde, in *Hermeneutic Phenomenology: The Philosophy of Paul Ricoeur* (Evanston, Ill.: Northwestern University Press, 1971), explains that FN "anticipates Ricoeur's subsequent hermeneutics." In particular, "the diagnostic is the methodological anticipation of a general dialectic which animates all of Ricoeur's thought. It is the technique which after a series of transformations and refinements eventuates in a

radicalizing of reflective philosophy. But its use in *Freedom and Nature* is one which remains limited to a clarifying role" (p. 55).

4. It remains to be seen to what extent the phenomenological remedy is also a "pharmacon." I will argue that the immediate character of the phenomenological appropriation of the essential structures, while it does offer a remedy for anthropological disunity, can never be a cure. This becomes evident when Ricoeur moves from an immediate appropriation within a unifying discourse to a mediated plurality of analogical voices not reduced to the circle of the same.

5. The expression *drama of existence* anticipates the central thesis of Ricoeur's *Time and Narrative*. By referring to the mystery of existence by means of a narrative literary genre, Ricoeur implies that existence is interpreted through narrative, which calls for a literary hermeneutic that he will develop many years later. Further, the contrast between the prefigured opaque experience that calls for interpretation, and hence for meaning and order through configuration by means of a plot, bears a remarkable similarity to the description of essential structures that order the mystery of existence. For further comparison, see below, chapter 4.

6. Jean-Paul Sartre makes a similar evaluation when he writes: "Psychologists have thus resembled in their undertakings those mathematicians who wanted to retrieve the continuum by means of discontinuous elements. Psychic synthesis was to be retrieved by starting from elements furnished by a priori analysis of certain logical-metaphysical concepts." Jean-Paul Sartre, *Imagination: A Psychological Critique* trans. and intro. Forrest Williams (Ann Arbor: University of Michigan Press, 1962), 145.

7. "Every psychic fact is a synthesis. Every psychic fact is a form, and has a structure. This is common ground for all contemporary psychologists, and is completely in accord with the data of reflection. Unfortunately, these contentions have their origin in a priori ideas. In agreement with the data of inner sense, they do not originate there, in inner experience." Jean-Paul Sartre, *Imagination: A Psychological Critique*, trans. and intro. Forrest Williams (Ann Arbor: University of Michigan Press, 1962), 145. Also see pp. 127–143.

8. This initial conception of imagination has not undergone the hermeneutical transformation that places the emergence of meaning on a linguistic rather than on a perceptual level.

9. FN 97–98. The quotation in its entirety reads: "Imagination focuses the double anticipation of project and concern. Imagination which completely 'negates' and carries us 'elsewhere'—into an 'elsewhere' which love of the exotic searches beyond distant seas and which is most frequently presented on a theatrical stage and evoked by characters in novels—this imagination is a luxury won from an imagination beset by concerns which does not depict a pure negation of the present, but rather an anticipated and still absent presence of things from whose lack we suffer. It is a lamp we point ahead to light up lack in terms of an entirely worldly absence, while need in turn tinges the imaginary with corporeal, concerned hue, quite different from aesthetic creations which sever its contact with its actual context." The connection Ricoeur makes between imagination's mediating function and aesthetic creation is quite interesting, particularly in the light of later publications which root aesthetic creations even more deeply in an anticipation of the world into which we project ourselves than in the anticipation of the fulfillment of need.

10. Ricoeur makes reference to the convergence of the vertical and horizontal vectors by explaining that "we shall not forget that this temporal and, so to speak, horizontal paradox of continuity and discontinuity in progress sums up the vertical paradox of motivation and project, that is, finally, of the involuntary and voluntary. The event of choice is precisely the practical reconciliation of the paradox in the moment which simultaneously brings the process to a resolution and bursts forth into novelty" (FN 168).

11. FN 172–173. For Ricoeur's ethical development of self-projection in the analogous mode of selfhood, see 5.3. Note the conceptual similarity between the unifying act of self-creation in *Freedom and Nature* and benevolent spontaneity in *Oneself as Another*.

12. FN 60. This disavowal of two selves for a self that is the subject in the objectivities of selfhood will require further reflection. This is particularly important, since Ricoeur in *Oneself as Another* is engaged in a hermeneutics of selfhood that wishes to reflectively implicate the self within the objectivities of selfhood without equating these objectivities with the reflexive structure of selfhood as such.

13. Already here, in *Freedom and Nature*, Ricoeur is placing the question of identity in a temporal context, the full significance of which will not be addressed until his publication of *Time and Narrative* and *Oneself as Another*. What is interesting to note here is the juxtaposition of temporal identity and the atemporal essential structure of the *cogito*/self which accounts for the temporization of identity.

14. Paul Ricoeur, "Negativity and Primary Affirmation," in *History and Truth* (Evanston, Ill.: Northwestern University Press, 1965), 328. Here Ricoeur reflects on Anaximander's metaphysical grounding principle of reality, a determinate ground in dialectical union with the unlimited or indeterminate, and he states: "being is primordially dialectical: determining and undetermined. It is through this dialectical structure that he [Anaximander] puts an end to interrogation concerning its origin and founds the possibility of interrogating upon all else. If such is the case, we may consider our whole itinerary on the basis of its terminal and founding act. It seems to me that a philosophy of being which is not swallowed up in a metaphysics of essence, and still less a phenomenology of the thing, is alone capable of both *justifying* and *limiting* the pact of human reality with negativity" (*Negativity and Primary Affirmation*, 327).

15. Ricoeur makes reference to the struggle within the heart or *thumos* between knowing and feeling. The "whole of man's fragility" experienced "through that of feeling" is a struggle in which "man appeared to us as a being stretched between the this-here-now, the certainty of the living present, and the need to complete knowledge in the truth of the whole." However, "whatever name this primordial duality is called—opinion and science, intuition and understanding, certainty and truth, presence and sense—it forbids us to formulate a philosophy of perception prior to a philosophy of discourse and forces us to work them out together, one with the other, one by the other" (FM 92). Therefore, the division of the primordial recovery of disproportionate existence into three stages of reflection is a methodological strategy that does not divide existence into three independent levels of consciousness, but simply expands the initial model to include the whole person as if diagrammatic transparencies were laid over top of one another.

16. FM 49–50. This concept of character will reappear and play a significant role in *Oneself as Another*. This kind of "summary" offered in *Fallible Man*, however, will be fortunately dropped by Ricoeur later.

17. " 'Nothing human is foreign to me.' I am capable of every virtue and every vice; no sign of man is radically incomprehensible, no language radically untranslatable, no work of art to which my taste cannot spread. My humanity is my essential community with all that is human outside myself; that community makes every man my like" (FM 60–61).

Chapter 3. Metaphorical Reformulation

1. See David Pellauer, "A Response to Gary Madison's 'Reflections on Paul Ricoeur's Philosophy of Metaphor,' " *Philosophy Today* 21.4 supplement (Winter 1977): 444.

2. See OA 334–335, where Ricoeur still employs the language of "priority . . . of the ego toward the alter ego . . . in the gnoseological dimension."

3. This is not to say that the imaginative tension of presence and absence is postmetaphysical; Ricoeur simply shifts the orientation of presence from behind to in front of consciousness. Yet, fundamental to this shift is an imaginative variability not commonly associated with a metaphysic of prior presence. Ricoeur writes: "the nothingness of absence concerns the mode of givenness of a real thing in *absentia*, the nothingness of unreality characterizes the referent itself of the fiction" (FFSR 126).

4. Bachelard writes: "I always come then to the same conclusion: the essential newness of the poetic image poses the problem of the speaking being's creativeness. Through this creativeness the imagining consciousness proves to be, very simply but very purely, an origin. In a study of the imagination, a phenomenology of the poetic imagination must concentrate on and bring out this quality of origin in various poetic images" (PS xx).

5. Ricoeur writes: "There is no symbolism prior to man who speaks, even though the power of symbols is rooted more deeply, in the expressiveness of the cosmos, in what desire wants to say, in the varied image-contents that men have. But in each case it is in language that the cosmos, desire, and the imaginary achieve speech" (FP 1–6).

6. The dialectic of absence and presence must not be confused with presentation of a phenomenological *eidos*. The presenting of the image by way of the extension of metaphorical attribution, which opens the ego to an intersubjective world where subjectivity is understood analogously (oneself as another), is not a static self-contained presentation. Opening a world of possibility is not an end in itself or a revelation of well-rounded truth. Configured meaning is always tied to the mimetic reconfiguration of experience. Presentation is always a presentation of possibility, a presentation in the imaginative mode of the *as if*, which can only become reality by means of an agent responsible for an action that concretizes the possibility envisioned by the imagination. However, since the imagination is a mediating operation, mediating between absence and presence, any possibility made actual becomes after the fact a sedimentation of meaning or configuration of meaning in need of reconfiguration. The emergence of

meaning is a dynamic process which, on a linguistic or imaginative level, is rooted in the flux of absence and presence, which Ricoeur grounds in the ontological dialectic of potentiality and actuality, or productivity and power (act) (OA 302–317).

7. On the origin of "real" as used in philosophy, see M. Boutin, *Conceiving the Invisible* (1994), 5–8.

Chapter 4. Narrative Imagination and Personal Identity

1. In a footnote to the conclusion of the three volumes of *Time and Narrative* Ricoeur writes that "these conclusions might have been called a Postscript. Indeed, they are the result of a rereading undertaken almost a year after finishing the manuscript of this third volume of *Time and Narrative*. Their composition is contemporary with the final revision to that manuscript" (TN 3:331 n. 1).

2. Ricoeur describes the unifying moment of action as "initiative." Here action forms the identity and being of the agent: "I act (my being is my doing)" (FTA 217). Yet as we shall see, it is unclear what sort of being this description of initiative brings to light: a description of agency, identity, or selfhood? See TN 3:230–233.

3. In particular, David Carr (1986) finds Ricoeur's understanding of narrative to be a literary artifice that subjects experience to narrative rules rather than seeing the temporal features of experience as constitutive elements for narrative composition. For further discussion, see 4.3.

4. Although *Oneself as Another* deals extensively with personal and narrative identity, the somewhat provisional proposals for narrative identity found in several of his articles and in *Time and Narrative* will provide key information with regard to Ricoeur's organizing principle of the relation between narrative and temporal experience.

5. I will take up this point again in 4.3, in discussion with David Carr and Gary Madison's critique of Ricoeur's view of narrative.

6. This is particularly evident in psychotherapy, where the therapist attempts to assist the patient in constructing a cohesive narrative from the discord of partial and/or false narratives. Therapy involves the development of a "true" historical narrative as essential to inner healing, but such a reconstruction is a retelling of the past by means of the power to imagine the past as different than received. Further, it might involve reliving one's life in the "kingdom of the as-if" in such a way as to validate and affirm one's personal worth in spite of a past where such worth was absent. This is not the construction of a false past but an attempt to face one's personal and/or common history with the hope of renewal in the present and future. In this sense Ricoeur is absolutely correct when he states: "Without memory there is no principle of hope" (TN 3:258). However, the inverse is equally true: without hope truthful memory is absent.

7. TN 1:66. This form of semantic resolution of the narrative paradox poses enormous difficulties. A semantic paradox can never be resolved by or within the semantic perspective alone, and this Ricoeur continuously forgets. As I will argue in 5.2, Ricoeur fails to understand that changing from one topic to another does not change the semantic orientation eventually responsible for the difficulties to be resolved.

8. Although Ricoeur often uses the term *application* interchangeably with the term *transfer*, it is important to maintain with the use of the concept of transferability

an objectification of identity that can be transferred to the reader who can then engage in an act of application. The objectification of identity and its transfer in the act of reading are maintained by Ricoeur even in *Oneself as Another*, where he writes: "Reading, as the milieu in which the transfer between the world of the narrative—and hence the world of the literary characters as well—and the world of the reader takes place, constitutes a privileged place and bond for the affection of the reading subject" (OA 329).

9. On the emphasis on reading over the past twenty-five years, see Umberto Eco, "*Intentio Lectoris:* The State of the Art," in *The Limits of Interpretation* (Bloomington: Indiana University Press, 1990), 44–63.

10. These two alternatives of logical sameness or dissipation in difference are taken up again in *Oneself as Another*. However, as M. Boutin explains, Ricoeur expands on the possible variations of the concept of identity. "Dans sa communication de juin 1987, Ricoeur propose quatre sens différents de l'identité-mêmeté auxquels, chaque fois, il donne aussi ce qu'il appelle des 'contraires': 1. l'identité-unicité ou 'identité numérique,' à quoi s'oppose ce que Ricoeur appelle la 'pluralité'; 2. l'identité-similitude, dont le contraire est pour Ricoeur la 'différence'; 3. l'identité-continuité, qui a son contraire dans la 'discontinuité'; 4. l'identité-permanence, dont l'opposé est ce que Ricoeur appelle la 'diversité.'" (Maurice Boutin, *Virtualité et Identité: L'identité narrative selon Paul Ricoeur, et ses apories*, Opening paper, Conference on "La constitution narrative de l'identité du chrétien, de la chrétienne," Laval University, Quebec City, December 1994, 3).

11. The possibility of a fissure, fault (FM), or gap existing between art and life requires a fundamental critique not just of narrative identity but of Ricoeur's understanding of the distinction between semantics and pragmatics, that is, between the relation of words to what they refer to (semantics), and between the relation of words to their interpreters or users (pragmatics) (see Boutin 1993 62). In *Oneself as Another* Ricoeur uses this distinction between semantics and pragmatics to make a connection between "utterance and the speaking subject" (OA 40–55); this opens a vast and complex set of problems, the analysis of which falls outside the scope of this study. Since Ricoeur uses the terminological distinction *narrative art* and *life*, these terms will be used for our critical comments.

12. This debate, while restricted principally to David Carr and Ricoeur during a "Round Table Discussion" (see below, n. 14), in a followup article to the discussion by David Pellauer (see below, n. 15) and by Gary Madison in *The Hermeneutics of Postmodernity* (1988), is not important due to the stature of its participants; rather, this debate is important because it deals with the foundation of Ricoeur's claim that selfhood is ultimately mediated by narrative discourse. If an "unbridgeable gap" does exist between mimesis2 and mimesis3, that is, between the world of the text and the world of the reader, then Ricoeur's philosophy of selfhood might indeed be guilty of either enclosing the self entirely within language or finding linguistic identifications of self that are simply variations of a voluntary *cogito*.

13. David Carr, *Time, Narrative, and History* (Bloomington: Indiana University Press, 1986).

14. David Carr, "Round Table: *Temps et récit*, Volume One," *University of Ottawa Quarterly* 55.4 (1985): 302–303. Also found in *On Paul Ricoeur: Narrative and Interpretation*, ed. David Wood (London: Routledge, 1991), 160–187.

15. In David Pellauer's article, "Limning the Liminal: Carr and Ricoeur on Time and Narrative," *Philosophy Today* 35.1 (1991): 51–72, the problematic character of Carr's own understanding of the phenomenology of temporality is taken to task. Complaining that Carr's understanding of temporality lacks the sophistication of that proposed by Ricoeur, Pellauer writes: "The topic of the aporetics of temporality is a crucial one to any effort to explore the difference between Carr and Ricoeur because in volume 3 Ricoeur takes up the same central text upon which Carr bases his initial move, Husserl's *Lectures on the Phenomenology of Internal Time-Consciousness.* He does so within the framework of a larger argument that in many ways might be seen as directed against the foundation of Carr's own approach, namely, that there has never been and never will be an adequate phenomenology (or philosophy, for that matter) of either time or our temporal experience, and that every such attempt pays for its gains at the price of ever greater aporias." Pellauer concludes that "because we can see in retrospect that Carr is not sufficiently attentive to what Ricoeur calls the aporetics of temporality, we also can see that he does not really address the two other aspects of this aporetics that Ricoeur points to, particularly in his concluding remarks to the third volume. These other aspects are the issue of the oneness of time ... and the ultimate unrepresentability of time" (53–54).

Chapter 5. Identity and Selfhood

1. OA 187 n. 22; SM 219 n. 1. The English translation uses the term *reflexive process* instead of *reflective process*, but the original reads *le procès réflexif* and not *le procès réfléchi*. Throughout *Oneself as Another* the translation of these two terms is often given interchangeable meaning, and even Ricoeur in *Soi-même comme un autre* seems to use them on occasion in an interchangeable manner. Yet, as we shall see, the *reflexive* structure of the self and the *reflective* process that leads indirectly back to the self that is structured reflexively have two different meanings that must be handled with great care and subtlety.

2. OA 18. In "On Interpretation," Ricoeur writes: "Reflexion is that act of turning back upon itself by which a subject grasps, in a moment of intellectual clarity and moral responsibility, the unifying principle of the operations among which it is dispersed and forgets itself as subject. 'The *I think*,' says Kant, 'must be able to accompany all my representations.' All reflexive philosophers would recognize themselves in this formula" (FTA 12).

3. In a paper originally presented as part of the 1986 Gifford Lectures that "formed the basis of the studies published here" (OA ix), Ricoeur explains that "a self that responds is a self in relation, without being an absolute self—that is, outside any relatedness and in this sense the foundation of every relation." See Paul Ricoeur, "The Summoned Subject in the School of the Narratives of the Prophetic Vocation," in *Figuring the Sacred: Religion, Narrative, and Imagination*, trans. David Pellauer, ed. Mark I. Wallace (Minneapolis: Fortress Press, 1995), 262.

4. "There is no self-understanding that is not *mediated* by signs, symbols, and texts; in the last resort understanding coincides with the interpretation given to these mediating terms. ... Mediation by *signs*: that is to say, it is *language* that is the primary

condition of all human experience. . . . And since speech is heard before it is uttered, the shortest path from the self to itself lies in the speech of the other, which leads me across the open space of signs. . . . To understand oneself is to understand oneself as one confronts the text and to receive from it the conditions for a self other than that which first undertakes the reading" (FTA 15–17).

5. OA 19. This reference to an "analogical" unity of selfhood links all of Ricoeur's works together. It is the work of imagination at every stage of Ricoeur's philosophical development that gives continuity to the multiplicity of his philosophical "studies." The work of imagination understood in its twofold function as a synthesis of the heterogeneous and as a temporal dynamic unity mediating between sedimentation and innovation, also characterizes the relation between the various components of self-understanding as well as the ontological response to the question "What sort of being is the self?" (OA 297–356).

6. This reduction of action and the various other objectivities of self to the textual form is given explicit development in Ricoeur's "The Model of the Text: Meaningful Action Considered as a Text," where he writes: "Now my hypothesis is this: if there are specific problems that are raised by the interpretation of texts because they are texts and not spoken language, and if these problems are the ones that constitute hermeneutics as such, then the human sciences may be said to be hermeneutical (1) inasmuch as their *object* displays some of the features constitutive of a text as text, and (2) inasmuch as their *methodology* develops the same kind of procedures as those of *Auslegung* or text interpretation" (FTA 144–145).

7. See the sections "The Cogito is Posited" and "The Shattered Cogito," for Ricoeur's understanding of the central features of this problematic (OA 4–16).

8. Gianni Vattimo also raises this question. "But is a recovery of the Aristotelian conception of the plurivocity of Being, as seems to be underway in today's hermeneutic *koiné*, actually possible without the keel of substance—thus without a hierarchy, without a 'first by analogy' (a 'proper' meaning), without a supreme metaphysical case?" Responding that "if the legitimation of this plurality were underpinned solely by the structural multivocity of Being itself, it would in truth become untenable. One cannot do without substance in Aristotle—even the pure and simple affirmation of the irreducible multivocity of Being would always be the object of a 'unitary' metaphysical affirmation." Gianni Vattimo, *Beyond Interpretation: The Meaning of Hermeneutics for Philosophy*, trans. David Webb (Stanford: Stanford University Press, 1997), 46, 54.

9. Jacques Derrida, " 'Eating Well,' or the Calculation of the Subject," in *Points: Interviews, 1974–1994*, ed. Elisabeth Weber, trans. Peggy Kamuf (Stanford: Stanford University Press, 1995), 255.

10 Pamela Sue Anderson points out that, "Ricoeur's present intention is essentially a mediation between the modern and postmodern, which may appear more like an oscillation between Descartes and Nietzsche. Mediation would uncover unrecognized relations between apparently opposing assertions, while oscillation would shift back and forth without bringing the two sides together" (Anderson 1994 73).

11. For the utilization of Husserl's solipsistic egology as a basis for a critique of Ricoeur's understanding of the inescapable correlation of self and the other, see Albert A. Johnstone, "Oneself as Oneself and Not as Another," *Husserl Studies* 13:1–17, 1996.

12. OA 52–55. Echoing Ricoeur's earlier work in *Fallible Man*, where the process of naming marks an epistemological convergence between the singularity of perception and the universality of language, the recourse here to institutionalized naming bears such remarkable features of similarity that I would be amiss not to make a connection between them. See also OA 120 n. 5; 124 n. 11. Elsewhere Ricoeur writes: "I have never returned, at least not in this form, to the theme of disproportion and of fallibility. The sense of the frailty of all things human reappears frequently, however, in particular in my contributions to political philosophy in connection with a meditation on the sources of political evil. The actual return to the theme of fallible man would have to be sought instead in the last chapter of *Oneself as Another*, in which the theme of otherness (*altérité*) — one's own body, other people, conscience — takes the place of the threefold character of *Fallible Man*" (IA 15–16).

13. See OA 32, 40, 54. — Ricoeur also offers a long and highly critical analysis of the debate within analytic philosophy concerning the domination of the network of intersignification by the pair of questions "what?" and "why?" Through the examination of the work of G. E. M. Anscombe and Donald Davidson, Ricoeur demonstrates how the analytical tradition has lost the question "who?" within a "logical gulf . . . between motive and cause," and "action and event" (OA 63). Although further analysis of the concept of intention "erodes the clear-cut dichotomies of the preceding analysis" (OA 69), it has the unfortunate consequence of capturing the "what?" by the "why?" Ricoeur writes: "In this sense, the 'why?' controls the 'what?' and, in so doing, leads away from any interrogation concerning the 'who?' " (OA 84). Further, the debate rests on an ontology of events that presents the person as "torn between event and substance without being relevant in itself" (OA 84). Although this "chronology" of the eclipse of the question "who?" by the pair "what–why?" is quite interesting, it falls outside my concern with the hermeneutical relationship between the self and the other than self, and therefore will not be addressed beyond these few comments.

14. OA 95. This contrast between the "*terminable* investigation" of who is acting, and the "*interminable* investigation" of the what and why of action is puzzling. To terminate the question of agency with the response "the self," implies a completion and/or closure of self that runs counter to Ricoeur's entire philosophical project (TN 3:207, 248, 249). Therefore, the investigation of action can only terminate in a form of objective identification that is subject to the reidentification of the same, as in the case of legal identification of the one responsible for a crime (OA 99, 107).

15. Ricoeur is quick to recognize that this move beyond "render[ing] something in general a someone" to a self-designating agent, taken *as* representative of one of the analogous terms of *ipse* selfhood, is an aporetic process. In particular he addresses three "difficulties": (1) attributing an action to an agent in relation to the descriptive suspension of the agent of action; (2) the prescriptive force of ascribing an action to an agent requires that an agent be held responsible for his or her actions, thus widening the gap between describing an action and imputing an action to an agent; and (3) action "depends on its agent . . . it is in the agent's power" to act, which opens the question of the causal dialectic of freedom and nature (OA 96–112).

While these aporias are specific to the semantics of action, they repeat Ricoeur's familiar methodological problems: 1) the dialectic of suspicion and affirmation, and/or belonging and distantiation; (2) the hermeneutical dialectic of explanation and under-standing, where the world of the text constitutes an ethical laboratory for the exploration of possibilities for being-as; (3) the dialectic of freedom and nature described as the voluntary and involuntary, the infinite and the finite, transcendence and perspective, or the unity of identity and difference.

Each of these difficulties represents a duality in Ricoeur's hermeneutics of selfhood. Universality of description is set in contrast to the specificity of self-designation, which in turn widens the gap between a self-designating subject responsible for his or her action and the general conditions for describing action through a semantic network of intersignification. However, the juxtaposition of a responsible subject who is the agent of his or her own actions, and a universal description of action that does not have the resources for self-designation, puts the question "who?" not only in the context of agency, but qualifies the meaning of agency by ethical and moral evaluations. Thus, developing the ontological explication of the agent's power to act is further qualified by a deliberative process that comes to light through the ethical and moral conditions for action. The answer to the question "who?" is then presumed by Ricoeur to move beyond the identifying reference of semantic description, to identifying selfhood in terms of an ethico-moral power to act.

Hence, recourse to a pragmatics of language involves significantly more than Ricoeur assumes when he focuses on self-designation in situations of interlocution. Besides, such self-designation can always be considered and treated—also by the self-designating subject—semantically in the first place. Self-designation, according to Ricoeur, entails a concept of selfhood that is a power to act in such a manner that one remains self-constant. It is a free choice that is supposed to constitute selfhood; however, since his initial description of *ipse* identity is bound to that of the other, selfhood is a choice under the rule of morality guided by the ethical aim to live the " '*good life*' with and for others, in just institutions" (OA 172, 180, 330).

16. OA 148, 132–133, 159, 164, 170, 264, 276, 288.

17. OA 159; TN 3:158, 174, 176, 181; TDI 183; LQN 32, 33.

18. Elsewhere, Ricoeur continues to emphasize the objectification of narrative selfhood by explaining that "reading, as the milieu in which the *transfer* between the world of the narrative—and hence the world of the literary characters as well—and the world of the reader takes place, constitutes a privileged place and bond for the affection of the reading subject" (OA 329, emphasis mine).

19. OA 187 n. 22. See above, chapter 5 n. 1.

20. OA 144–145. See also the following pages for more detail with regard to Ricoeur's understanding of suffering in relation to agency: OA 150, 151, 157, 162, 178, 188–191, 192, 193, 213, 215, 219, 220, 222, 223, 225, 229, 251, 315.

21. See above, 2.4.3, and also FM 134–146.

22. Ricoeur places attestation in dialectical relation with suspicion, and in this manner repeats his hermeneutic of belonging and distantiation. "A kind of uneasy bal-ance between attestation and suspicion was then imposed, whenever certainty of self had to take refuge in the inexpungible retreat of the question 'who?' " (OA 302). For further analysis of Ricoeur's hermeneutic of belonging and distantiation, see above, 1.1.

23. This correlation is once again affirmed by Ricoeur when he explains that Heidegger's contrast of *Dasein* and *Vorhandenheit* parallels his own: "Here, we are not

far from the opposition resulting from our notion of narrative identity between character (ourselves as *idem*) and moral constancy illustrated by promising (ourselves as *ipse*)" (OA 309 n. 11).

Conclusion

1. David Rasmussen, in "Rethinking Subjectivity: Narrative Identity and the Self," *Philosophy and Social Criticism* 21:5–6 (1995): 159–172, offers an excellent evaluation of Ricoeur's hermeneutic of intersubjective selfhood, stating that "if Ricoeur's critique is correct, it would follow that the attempted overcoming of the problem of subjectivity through a theory of interlocution is achieved only by undermining an adequate concept of self-identity" (p. 159). Rasmussen goes on to argue that Ricoeur's "attempt to force the 'theory of interlocution' associated with speech-act theory beyond the narrow confines of the 'identity' problematic which characterizes it" (p. 170), points the way to a recovery of intersubjective self-identity through the narrativization of identity.

2. At the end of *Oneself as Another* Ricoeur writes that "perhaps the philosopher as philosopher has to admit that one does not know and cannot say whether this Other, the source of the injunction, is another person whom I can look in the face or who can stare at me, or my ancestors for whom there is no representation, to so great an extent does my debt to constitute my very self, or God—living God, absent God—or an empty place. With this aporia of the Other, philosophical discourse comes to an end" (OA 355).

3. Interestingly enough, Ricoeur recognizes not only the limitation of this duality of action carried out and being acted upon, but also the lack of emphasis in *Oneself as Another* on the suffering self. While not giving up on this dialectic of activity and passivity, Ricoeur states that he wants to give greater weight to the incapacitated self as constitutive of *ipse* selfhood than he previously has done. See Paul Ricoeur, "A Response," in *Paul Ricoeur and Narrative: Context and Contestation*, ed. Morny Joy (Calgary: University of Calgary Press, 1997), xxxix–l.

4. This is precisely Jacques Derrida's point in *The Gift of Death*, trans. David Wills (Chicago: University of Chicago Press, 1995). For an even better critique of the economy of the gift, see Jacques Derrida, *Given Time: I. Counterfeit Money*, trans. Peggy Kamuf (Chicago: University of Chicago Press, 1992).

5. James H. Olthuis, "Face to Face: Ethical Asymmetry or the Symmetry of Mutuality?," in *Knowing Other-wise: Philosophy at the Threshold of Spirituality*, ed. James H. Olthuis (New York: Fordham University Press, 1997), 146.

6. Lévinas states that: "'I think' comes down to 'I can.'... Ontology as first philosophy is a philosophy of power." *Totality and Infinity: An Essay on Exteriority*, trans. Alphonso Lingis (Pittsburgh: Duquesne University Press, 1969), 46. If this is true, then in spite of Ricoeur's best intentions and careful analysis of mutuality and reciprocity, the presumption of the 'I can' as the core of voluntary power sets his understanding of selfhood on a collision course with the power of others.

7. Olthuis 146.

8. Ibid.

9. Robert C. Solomon, *Continental Philosophy since 1750: The Rise and Fall of the Self* (Oxford: Oxford University Press, 1988), 1.

10. "Ricoeur is not sufficiently suspicious concerning the identity of the Other and so leaves his account to selfhood open to a feminist critique. To what degree is the Other different? Is there a difference of gender, or even one of race and ethnicity, implied? In fact the abstract—and nonspecific—nature of Ricoeur's account of otherness—for example, his account of one's own body is clearly gender neutral—may be his way of avoiding the devalorization of universal human experience. But such abstraction, as it tends to traditional biases, may be questioned." Pamela Sue Anderson, "Agnosticism and Attestation: An Aporia concerning the Other in Ricoeur's *Oneself as Another*," *The Journal of Religion* (1994): 74. Elsewhere Anderson states that Ricoeur's understanding of "the rational subject is thought to be exclusively homogeneous and hopelessly male." See Pamela Sue Anderson, *Ricoeur and Kant: Philosophy of the Will* (Atlanta, Ga.: Scholars Press, 1993), 3.

11. See above, 5. 3.1. See also OA 150, 151, 157, 162, 178, 189, 190–191, 192, 193, 213, 215, 219, 220, 222, 223, 225, 229, 251, 315.

12. Here Olthuis, 151, quotes Emmanuel Lévinas, "Useless Suffering," in *the Provocation of Lévinas: Rethinking the Other*, ed. R. Dernasconi and D. Wood (New York: Routledge, 1998), 159.

13. Olthuis 147.

14. The concept of the absolute involuntary is a puzzling formulation. If there is such a radical involuntary, such absolute otherness, how can I consent to that which is totally other? Does not the act of consent make the absolute involuntary one's own and thereby overcome it as other? Hence, otherness is never something that I can really consent to.

15. Ricoeur reinforces this interchangeability of the self and the other in the tenth chapter of *Oneself as Another*, where he summarizes his understanding of reciprocal power: "Acting and suffering then seem to be distributed between two different protagonists: the agent and the patient, the latter appearing as the potential victim of the former. But because of the reversibility of the roles, each agent is the patient of the other. Inasmuch as one is affected by the power over one exerted by the other, the agent is invested with the responsibility of an action that is placed from the very outset under the rule of reciprocity, which the rule of justice will transform into a rule of equality. Since each protagonist holds two roles, being both agent and patient, the *formalism* of the categorical imperative requires the 'matter' of a *plurality* of acting beings each affected by forces exerted reciprocally" (OA 330).

16. Paul Ricoeur, "A response by Paul Ricoeur," trans. David Pellauer, in *Paul Ricoeur and Narrative: Context and Contestation*, ed. Morny Joy (Calgary: University of Calgary Press, 1997), xxxix.

17. See above, 2.4.3; 5.3.1; also FM 134–136.

18. For a rather remarkable discussion of this topic, see Jacques Derrida, " 'Eating Well,' or the Calculation of the Subject," trans. Peter Connor and Avital Ronell, in *Points . . . : Interviews, 1974–1994*, ed. Elisabeth Weber (Stanford: Stanford University Press, 1995), 255–287.

19. OA 159. See also 4.2 n. 13.

20. In *Oneself as Another* Ricoeur expresses the need to "suture" the gap between the question "who?" and the pair "what–why?" (OA 98, 110). This medical metaphor echoes the theme in *Fallible Man* of the mediating third term that bridges the fault line that runs through the heart of transcendental, practical, and self-consciousness. See above, 2.4.2.

21. RM 215; IDA 8; FFSR 129–130. See also 3.3.

22. TN 3:176. See also 4.2.5.

23. Paul Ricoeur, "Life in Quest of Narrative," in *On Paul Ricoeur: Narrative and Interpretation*, ed. David Wood (London: Routledge, 1991), p. 25.

24. See also "Naming God," 217–235.

25. Paul Ricoeur, "The Golden Rule: Exegetical and Theological Perplexities," *New Testament Studies* 36 (1990): 392–397.

26. Paul Ricoeur, *Critique and Conviction: Conversations with François Azouvi and Marc de Launay*, trans. Kathleen Blamey (New York: Columbia University Press, 1978), 146.

27. For an insightful collection of essays that explore some of the problems of faith and knowledge, see *Knowing Other-wise: Philosophy at the Threshold of Spirituality*, ed. James H. Olthuis (New York: Fordham University Press, 1997).

28. Ricoeur, *Critique and Conviction*, 146.

BIBLIOGRAPHY

Ricoeur's Works

Ricoeur, Paul. *Fallible Man.* Trans. Charles Kelbley. Chicago: Henry Regnery, 1965. *Philosophie de la volonté. Finitude et Culpabilité. I. L'homme faillible* (Philosophie de l'esprit). Paris: Aubier, 1960.

Freedom and Nature: The Voluntary and the Involuntary. Trans. and intro. Erazim V. Kohak. Evanston, Ill.: Northwestern University Press, 1965. *Philosophie de la volonté. I. Le voluntaire et l'involontaire* (Philosophie de l'esprit). Paris: Aubier, 1950.

History and Truth. Trans. Charles A. Kelbley. Evanston, Ill.: Northwestern University Press, 1965. *Historie et vérité* (Esprit). Paris: Seuil, 1955.

Husserl: An Analysis of His Phenomenology. Trans. Edward G. Ballard and Lester E. Embree. Evanston, Ill.: Northwestern University Press, 1967.

"Husserl and Wittgenstein on Language." *Phenomenology and Existentialism.* Ed. E. N. Lee and M. Mandelbaum. Baltimore: Johns Hopkins University Press, 1967, 207–217.

"New Developments in Phenomenology in France: The Phenomenology of Language." *Social Research* 34 (1967): 1–30.

"Philosophy of Will and Action." *Phenomenology of Will and Action.* Ed. E. W. Straus and R. M. Griffith. Pittsburgh: Duquesne University Press, 1967, 7–33.

Symbolism of Evil. Trans. Everson Buchanan. Boston: Beacon Press, 1967. *Philosophie de la volonté. Finitude et Culpabilité. II. La symbolique de mal* (Philosophie de l'esprit). Paris: Aubier, 1960.

Freud and Philosophy: An Essay on Interpretation. Trans. Denis Savage. New Haven, Conn.: Yale University Press, 1970. *De l'interpretation. Essau syr Freud* (L'order philosophique). Paris: Seuil, 1965.

"The Model of the Text: Meaningful Action Considered as a Text." *Social Research* 38.3 (1971): 529–562.

"Creativity in Language: Word, Polysemy, Metaphor." *Philosophy Today* 17.2–4 (Summer 1973): 97–111.

"The Task of Hermeneutics." *Philosophy Today* 17.2–4 (Summer 1973): 112–128. All references taken from reprinted version in *Hermeneutics and the Human Sciences: Essays on Language, Action and Interpretation.* Trans. and ed. John B. Thompson. Cambridge: Cambridge University Press, 1981.

"The Hermeneutical Function of Distanciation." *Philosophy Today* 17.2–4 (Summer 1973): 129–141. All references taken from reprinted version in *Hermeneutics and*

the Human Sciences: Essays on Language, Action and Interpretation. Trans. and
   ed. John B. Thompson. Cambridge: Cambridge University Press, 1981.
The Conflict of Interpretations: Essays in Hermeneutics. Ed. Don Ihde. Evanston, Ill.:
   Northwestern University Press, 1974. *Le conflit des interprétations/Essais
   d'herméneutique* (L'ordre philosophique). Paris: Seuil, 1969.
"Phenomenology and Hermeneutics." *Nous* 9.1 (1975): 85–102. All references taken
   from reprinted version in *Hermeneutics and the Human Sciences: Essays on
   Language, Action and Interpretation.* Trans. and ed. John B. Thompson. Cam-
   bridge: Cambridge University Press, 1981.
"Philosophical Hermeneutics and Theological Hermeneutics." *Studies in Religion/Sci-
   ence Religieues* 5 (1975–1976): 14–33.
"Biblical Hermeneutics." *Semeia* 4 (1975): 27–148.
"History and Hermeneutics." *Journal of Philosophy* 73.19 (1976): 683–695.
"Ideology and Utopia as Cultural Imagination." *Philosophic Exchange* 2.2 (1976): 17–28.
Interpretation Theory: Discourse and the Surplus of Meaning. Forth Worth: Texas Chris-
   tian University Press, 1976.
"What is Dialectical?" *Freedom and Morality.* Ed. and intro. John Bricke. Lawrence:
   University of Kansas, 1976, 173–189. "Le 'lieu' de la dialectique." *Dialectics.
   Dialectiques* (Entretiens de Varna, 1973). Édité par Ch. Perelman. La Haye: M.
   Nijhoff, 1975, 92–108.
*The Rule of Metaphor: Multi-Disciplinary Studies of the Creation of Meaning in Lan-
   guage.* Trans. Robert Czerny with Kathleen McLaughlin and John Costello.
   Toronto: University of Toronto Press, 1977. *La métaphore vive* (L'ordre
   philosophique). Paris: Seuil, 1975.
"Writing as a Problem for Literary Criticism and Philosophical Hermeneutics." *Philo-
   sophical Exchange* 2.3 (Summer 1977): 3–15.
"History and Hermeneutics." *Philosophy of History and Action.* Ed. Y. Yovel. Dordrecht:
   D. Reidel Publishing Company, 1978, 3–25.
"Imagination in Discourse and Action." *Angelica Husserliana* 7 (1978): 3–22.
   "L'imagination dans le discours et dans l'action." *Savoir, faire, espérer: les limites
   de la raison I.* Bruxelles: Facultés Universitaires, Saint-Louis, 1976, 207–228.
"The Metaphorical Process as Cognition, Imagination, and Feeling." *Critical Inquiry* 5
   (1978): 143–159.
"My Relation to the History of Philosophy." *The Iliff Review* 35 (1978): 5–12.
"Myth as the Bearer of Possible Worlds: Interview with Paul Ricoeur, With R. Kearney."
   The Crane Bag 2.1–2 (1978): 260–266.
Main Trends in Philosophy. New York: Holmes & Meier Publishers, 1978.
The Philosophy of Paul Ricoeur: An Anthology of His Work. Ed. Charles E. Reagan and
   David Steward. Boston: Beacon Press, 1978.
"The Narrative Function." *Semeia* 13 (1978): 177–202. "La fonction narrative." *Études
   théologiques et religieuses* 54 (1979), n. 2, 209–230.
"Epilogue: The 'Sacred Text' and the Community." *The Critical Study of Sacred Texts.*
   Ed. W. D. O'Flaherty. Berkeley: Graduate Theological Union, 1979, 13–29.
"The Function of Fiction in Shaping Reality." *Man and World* 12 (1979): 123–141.
"The Human Experience of Time and Narrative." *Research in Phenomenology* 9 (1979):
   17–34.

"Narrative Time." *Critical Inquiry* 7 (1980): 169–190. "La function narrative et l'expérience humaine de temps." *Archivio di Filosofia* (Esustenza, mito, ermeneuticca. Scritti per Erico Castelli. I) 80 (1980), n. 1, 343–367.

" 'Ways of Worldmaking,' by Nelson Goodman." *Philosophy and Literature* 4.1 (Spring 1980): 107–120.

"Sartre and Ryle on the Imagination." *The Philosophy of Jean-Paul Sartre* (The Library of Living Philosophers, 16). Ed. P. A. Schilpp. La Salle: Open Court, 1981, 167–178.

"The Bible and the Imagination." *The Bible as a Document of the University*. Ed. H. D. Betz. Chino: Scholars Press, 1981, 49–75. "La Bible et l'imagination." *Revue d'histoire et de philosophie religieuses* (Hommage à Roger Mehl) 62 (1982), n. 4, 339–360.

Hermeneutics and the Human Sciences: Essays on Language, Action and Interpretation. Trans. and ed. John B. Thompson. Cambridge: Cambridge University Press, 1981.

"Mimesis and Representation." *Annals of Scholarship* 2.3 (1981): 15–32. "Mimesis et représentation." *Actes de XVIII Congrès de Sociétés de Philosophie de langue française* (Strasbourg 1980). Strasbourg: Université des Sciences Humaines de Strasbourg, Faculté de Philosophie, 1982, 51–63.

"Phenomenology and the Theory of Literature: An Interview with Paul Ricoeur," by E. Nakjavani. *MLN Modern Language Notes* 96.5 (1981): 1084–1090.

"Poetry and Possibility." *Manhattan Review* 2.2 (1982): 6–21.

"Action, Story, and History: On Re-reading 'The Human Condition.' " *Salmagundi* 60 (1983): 60–72.

" 'Anatomy of Criticism' or the Order of Paradigms." *Center and Labyrinth: Essays in Honour of Northrop Frye*. Ed. E. Cook. Toronto: University of Toronto Press, 1983, 1–13.

"Can Fictional Narrative Be True?" *Angelica Husserliana* 14 (1983): 3–19.

"Narrative and Hermeneutics." *Essays on Aesthetics: Perspectives on the Work of Monroe C. Beardsley*. Ed. John Fisher. Philadelphia: Temple University Press, 1983, 149–60.

"On Interpretation." *Philosophy in France Today*. Ed. A. Monteriore. Cambridge: Cambridge University Press, 1983, 175–197.

"From Proclamation to Narrative." *The Journal of Religion* 64.4 (1984): 501–612.

Time and Narrative. Vol. 1. Trans. Kathleen McLaughlin and David Pellauer. Chicago: University of Chicago Press, 1984. *Temps et récit. Tome I* (L'ordre philosophique). Paris: Seuil, 1983.

"Toward a 'Post-Critical Rhetoric'?" *Pretext* 5.1 (Spring 1984): 9–16.

"History as Narrative and Practice." *Philosophy Today* 29 (Fall 1985): 213–222. "L'histoire comme récit et comme pratique. Entretien avec Paul Ricoeur (porpos recueillis par P. Kemp)." *Esprit* (1981), n. 54, 155–165.

"The History of Religions and the Phenomenology of Time Consciousness." *The History of Religions: Retrospect and Prospect*. Ed. J. M. Kitagawa. New York: Macmillan, 1985, 13–30.

"Narrated Time." *Philosophy Today* 29 (Winter 1985): 259–272. "Le Temps raconté." *Bulletin de la Société française de Philosophie* 78 (1984), n. 4, 436–452.

"The Power of Speech: Science and Poetry." *Philosophy Today* 29 (Spring 1985): 59–71. "Puissance de la Parole: science et poésie." *La philosophie et les savoirs* (L'univers de la Philosophie, 4). Edité par J.-P. Brodeur et R. Nadeau. Montréal-Paris-Tournai: Bellarmin-Desclée, 1975, 159–177.

Time and Narrative. Vol. 2. Trans. Kathleen McLaughlin and David Pellauer. Chicago: University of Chicago Press, 1985. *Temps et récit. Tome II. :a configuration dans le récit de fiction* (L'ordre philosophique). Paris: Seuil, 1984.

"The Text as Dynamic Identity." *Identity of the Literary Text.* Ed. M. J. Valdés and O. Milko. Toronto: University of Toronto Press, 1985, 175–186.

Lectures on Ideology and Utopia. Ed. George H. Taylor. New York: Columbia University Press, 1986.

Time and Narrative. Vol. 3. Trans. Kathleen Blamey and David Pellauer. Chicago: University of Chicago Press, 1988. *Temps et récit. Tome III. Le temps raconté* (L'ordre philosophique). Paris: Seuil, 1985.

"Humans as the Subject Matter of Philosophy." *Philosophy and Social Criticism* 14 (1988), no. 2, 203–215. All references taken from reprinted version in *The Narrative Path: The Later Works of Paul Ricoeur.* Ed. T. Peter Kemp and David Rasmussen. Cambridge: The MIT Press, 1989, 89–101.

"The Golden Rule: Exegetical and Theological Perplexities." *New Testament Studies* 36 (1990), no. 3, 392–397. "Entre philosophie et théologie: la Règle d'Or en question." *Revue d'histoire et de philosophie religieuses* 69 (1989), n. 1, 3–9.

From Text to Action: Essays in Hermeneutics, II. Trans. Kathleen Blamey and John B. Thompson. Evanston, Ill.: Northwestern University Press, 1991. *De texte à l'action. Essais d'herméneutique. II.* Paris: Seuil, 1986.

"Life in Quest of Narrative." *On Paul Ricoeur: Narrative and Interpretation.* Ed. D. Wood. London and New York: Routledge, 1991, 20–33.

"Narrative Identity." *Philosophy Today* (Spring 1991): 73–81.

"Ricoeur on Narrative." *On Paul Ricoeur: Narrative and Interpretation.* Ed. D. Wood. London and New York: Routledge, 1991, 160–187.

Lectures 2: La contreé de philosophes. Paris: Seuil, 1992.

Oneself as Another. Trans. Kathleen Blamey. Chicago: University of Chicago Press, 1992. *Soi-même comme un autre.* Paris: Seuil, 1990.

"Self as *Ipse.*" *Freedom and Interpretation, The Oxford Amnesty Lectures 1992.* Ed. Barbara Johnson. New York: Basic Books, 1993, 103–119.

Figuring the Sacred: Religion, Narrative, and Imagination. Trans. David Pellauer, ed. Mark I. Wallace. Minneapolis: Fortress Press, 1995.

"Intellectual Autobiography." *The Philosophy of Paul Ricoeur.* Ed. Lewis Edwin Hahn. Chicago: Open Court, 1995.

A Key to Husserl's Ideas 1. Trans. Bond Harris and Jacqueline Bouchard Spurlock, ed. and intro. Pol Vandevelde. Milwaukee: Marquette University Press, 1996. Adapted from: Husserl, E., *Idées directrices pour une phénoménologie* (Bibliothéque de philosophie). Traduction de *Ideen I* avec introduction et notes de P. Ricoeur. Paris: Gallimard, 1950.

"The Crisis of the *Cogito.*" *Synthese* 106 (1996): 57–66.

Critique and Conviction: Conversations with François Azouvi and Marc de Launay. Trans. Kathleen Blamey. New York: Columbia University Press, 1998. *La Critique et la Conviction.* Paris: Calmann-Lévy, 1995.

"A Response by Paul Ricoeur." Trans. David Pellauer. *Paul Ricoeur and Narrative: Context and Contestation.* Ed. Morny Joy. Calgary: University of Calgary Press, 1997, xxxix–l.

"The Self in the Mirror of Scriptures." *The Whole and Divided Self.* Ed. David E. Aune and John McCarthy. New York: The Crossroad Publishing Company, 1997.

———, and André LaCocque. *Thinking Biblically: Exegetical and Hermeneutical Studies.* Trans. David Pellauer. Chicago: University of Chicago Press, 1998.

Secondary Sources

Anderson, Pamela Sue. *Ricoeur and Kant: Philosophy of the Will.* Atlanta, Ga.: Scholars Press, 1993.

———. "Agnosticism and Attestation: An Aporia concerning the Other in Ricoeur's *Oneself as Another.*" *The Journal of Religion* (1994): 65–76.

Arendt, Hannah. *The Human Condition.* Garden City: Doubleday Anchor Books, 1958.

Bachelard, Gaston. *The Poetics of Space.* Trans. Maria Jolas. Boston: Beacon Press, 1964.

Bal, Mieke. *Narratology: Introduction to the Theory of Narrative.* Trans. Christine van Boheemen. Toronto: University of Toronto Press, 1985.

———. *Lethal Love: Feminist Literary Readings of Biblical Love Stories.* Bloomington: Indiana University Press, 1987.

Beardsley, Monroe C. *Aesthetics from Classical Greece to the Present.* Tuscaloosa: University of Alabama Press, 1966.

Benjamin, Jessica. *The Bonds of Love: Psychoanalysis, Feminism, and the Problem of Domination.* New York: Patheon Books, 1988.

Berger, Gaston. *The Cogito in Husserl's Philosophy.* Trans. Kathleen McLaughlin, intro. James M. Edie. Evanston, Ill.: Northwestern University Press, 1972.

Blumenberg, Hans. *Work on Myth.* Trans. Robert M. Wallace. Cambridge: The MIT Press, 1985.

Booth, Wayne. *The Rhetoric of Fiction.* 2nd ed. Chicago: University of Chicago Press, 1983.

Borgmann, Albert. *Crossing the Postmodern Divide.* Chicago: University of Chicago Press, 1992.

Bourgeois, Patrick L. *Extension of Ricoeur's Hermeneutic.* The Hague: Martinus Nijhoff, 1975.

Boutin, Maurice. "Relation, Otherness, and the Philosophy of Religion." *Journal of Religious Pluralism* 2 (1992): 61–82.

———. "Conceiving the Invisible: Joseph C. McLelland's Modal Approach to Theological and Religious Pluralism." *The Three Loves—Philosophy, Theology, and World Religions: Essays in Honour of Joseph C. Mclelland.* Ed. Robert C. Culley and William Klempa. Atlanta, Ga.: Scholars Press, 1994, 1–18.

———. *Virtualité et Identité: L'identité narrative selon Paul Ricoeur, et ses apories.* Opening paper, Conference on "La constitution narrative de l'identité du chrétien, de la chrétienne." Laval University, Quebec City, December 1994.

Bubner, Rudiger. *Modern German Philosophy.* Cambridge: Cambridge University Press, 1981.

Caputo, John. *Heidegger and Aquinas: An Essay on Overcoming Metaphysics*. New York: Fordham University Press, 1982.

———. *Radical Hermeneutics: Repetition, Deconstruction, and the Hermeneutical Project*. Bloomington: Indiana University Press, 1987.

———. *Against Ethics: Contributions to a Poetics of Obligation with Constant Reference to Deconstruction*. Bloomington: Indiana University Press, 1993.

———. *Demythologizing Heidegger*. Bloomington: Indiana University Press, 1993.

———. *Deconstruction in a Nutshell: A Conversation with Jacques Derrida*. New York: Fordham University Press, 1997.

———. *The Prayers and Tears of Jacques Derrida: Religion Without Religion*. Bloomington: Indiana University Press, 1997.

Carr, David. *Phenomenology and the Problem of History: A Study of Husserl's Transcendental Philosophy*. Evanston, Ill.: Northwestern University Press, 1974.

———. "Review Essay: Temps et Recit. Tome 1. by Paul Ricoeur." *History and Theory* 23.3 (1984): 357–370.

———. *Time, Narrative and History*. Bloomington: Indiana University Press, 1986.

Casey, Edward S. *Imagining: A Phenomenological Study*. Bloomington: Indiana University Press, 1976.

Cassirer, Ernst. *Language and Myth*. Trans. Susanne K. Langer. New York: Dover Publications, 1946.

Clark, S. H. *Paul Ricoeur*. London and New York: Routledge, 1990.

Comstock, Gary. "Truth or Meaning: Ricoeur versus Frei on Biblical Narrative." *The Journal of Religion* 66.2 (1986): 117–140.

De Boer, Theo. *The Development of Husserl's Thought*. The Hague: Martinus Nijhoff, 1978.

Descombes, Vincent. *Modern French Philosophy*. Trans. L. Scott-Fox and J. M. Harding. Cambridge: Cambridge University Press, 1980.

Dray, William. *Laws and Explanation in History*. London: Oxford University Press, 1957.

Derrida, Jacques. *Of Grammatology*. Trans. Gayatri Spivak. Baltimore: Johns Hopkins University Press, 1974.

———. *Writing and Difference*. Trans. Alan Bass. Chicago: University of Chicago Press, 1978.

———. *Margins of Philosophy*. Trans. Alan Bass. Chicago: University of Chicago Press, 1982.

———. *Given Time. I. Counterfeit Money*. Trans. Peggy Kamuf. Chicago: University of Chicago Press, 1991.

———. *Memoirs of the Blind: The Self-Portrait and Other Ruins*. Trans. Pascale-Anne Brault and Michael Naas. Chicago: University of Chicago Press, 1993.

———. *The Gift of Death*. Trans. David Wills. Chicago: University of Chicago Press, 1995.

———. *On the Name*. Ed. Thomas Dutoit. Stanford: Stanford University Press, 1995.

———. *Points . . . Interviews, 1974–94*. Ed. Elisabeth Weber. Trans. Peggy Kamuf et al. Stanford: Stanford University Press, 1995.

Eco, Umberto. *Semiotics and the Philosophy of Language*. Bloomington: Indiana University Press, 1984.

————. *The Limits of Interpretation*. Bloomington: Indiana University Press, 1990.

Edie, James M. *Edmund Husserl's Phenomenology: A Critical Commentary*. Bloomington: Indiana University Press, 1987.

Ferry, Luc, and Alain Renaut. *French Philosophy of the Sixties: An Essay on Antihumanism*. Trans. Mary H. S. Cattani. Amherst: University of Massachusetts Press, 1990.

Foucault, Michel. *The Archaeology of Knowledge and the Discourse on Language*. Trans. A. M. Sheridan Smith. New York: Pantheon Books, 1972.

Frye, Northrop. *Anatomy of Criticism: Four Essays*. Princeton, N.J.: Princeton University Press, 1957.

————. *The Critical Path: An Essay on the Social Context of Literary Criticism*. Bloomington: Indiana University Press, 1971.

————. *The Great Code: The Bible and Literature*. Toronto: Academic Press, 1982.

————. *Words with Power: Being a Second Study of The Bible and Literature*. Markham: Viking, 1990.

Gadamer, Hans-Georg. *Truth and Method*. New York: Crossroad Publishing, 1975.

————. *Philosophical Hermeneutics*. Trans. and ed. David E. Linge. Los Angeles: University of California Press, 1976.

————. "Religious and Poetical Speaking." *Myth, Symbol, and Reality*. Ed. Alan M. Olson. Notre Dame, Ind.: University of Notre Dame Press, 1980, 86–98.

————. *Reason in the Age of Science*. Trans. F. G. Lawrence. Cambridge: The MIT Press, 1981.

Glass, James M. *Shattered Selves: Multiple Personalities in a Postmodern World*. Ithaca, N.Y., and London: Cornell University Press, 1993.

Grondin, Jean. *Introduction to Philosophical Hermeneutics*. Foreword by Hans-Georg Gadamer, trans. Joel Weinsheimer. New Haven, Conn.: Yale University Press, 1994.

Habermas, Jurgen. *Knowledge and Human Interest*. Trans. Jeremy J. Shapiro. London: Heinemann, 1972.

Hahn, Lewis Edwin, editor. *The Philosophy of Paul Ricoeur*. Chicago: Open Court, 1995.

Halliburton, David. *Poetic Thinking: An Approach to Heidegger*. Chicago: University of Chicago Press, 1981.

Heidegger, Martin. *Being and Time*. Trans. John Macquarrie and Edward Robinson. New York: Harper and Row, 1962.

————. *The Basic Problems of Phenomenology*. Trans. Albert Hofstadter. Bloomington: Indiana University Press, 1982.

Hirsch, E. D., Jr. *The Aims of Interpretation*. Chicago: University of Chicago Press, 1976.

Hoy, David Couzens. *The Critical Circle: Literature, History, and Philosophical Hermeneutics*. Berkeley: University of California Press, 1978.

Howard, Roy J. *The Three Faces of Hermeneutics: An Introduction to Current Theories of Understanding*. Berkeley: University of California Press, 1982.

Husserl, Edmund. *Cartesian Meditations: An Introduction to Phenomenology*. Trans. Dorion Cairns. The Hague: Martinus Nijhoff, 1960.

————. *Ideas: General Introduction to Pure Phenomenology*. Trans. W. R. Boyce Gibson. New York: Collier Books, 1962.

————. *The Phenomenology of Internal Time-Consciousness*. Ed. Martin Heidegger, trans. James S. Churchill. Bloomington: Indiana University Press, 1964.

Ihde, Don. *Hermeneutic Phenomenology: The Philosophy of Paul Ricoeur*. Evanston, Ill.:
    Northwestern University Press, 1971.
———. "Variation and Boundary: A Conflict within Ricoeur's Phenomenology." *Con-
    sequences of Phenomenology*. Albany: State University of New York Press, 1986,
    160–180.
Ingarden, Roman. "Phenomenological Aesthetics: An Attempt at Defining its Range."
    Journal of Aesthetics and Art Criticism 33.3 (Spring 1975): 257–269.
Iser, Wolfgang. *The Act of Reading: A Theory of Aesthetic Response*. Baltimore: Johns
    Hopkins University Press, 1978.
Jauss, Hans Robert. *Aesthetic Experience and Literary Hermeneutics*. Trans. Michael
    Shaw. Minneapolis: University of Minnesota Press, 1982.
———. *Toward an Aesthetic of Reception*. Trans. Timothy Bahti. Minneapolis: Univer-
    sity of Minnesota Press, 1982.
———. *Question and Answer: Forms of Dialogical Understanding*. Ed. and trans. Michail
    Hays. Minneapolis: University of Minnesota Press, 1989.
Jervolino, Domenico. *The Cogito and Hermeneutics: The Question of the Subject in
    Ricoeur*. Trans. Gordon Poole. Dordrecht: Kluwer Academic Publishers, 1990.
Johnstone, Albert A. "Oneself as Oneself and Not as Another." *Husserl Studies* 13:1996,
    1–17.
Joy, Morny, ed. *Paul Ricoeur and Narrative: Context and Contestation*. Calgary: Univer-
    sity of Calgary Press, 1997.
Kaufman, Gordon D. "A Problem for Theology: The Concept of Nature." *Harvard
    Theological Review* 65.3 (July 1972): 337–366.
Kearney, Richard. "[Dialogues with] Paul Ricoeur." *Dialogues with Contemporary Con-
    tinental Thinkers: The Phenomenological Heritage. Paul Ricoeur. Emmanuel
    Levinas. Herbert Marcuse. Stanislas Breton. Jacques Derrida*. Manchester: Manches-
    ter University Press, 1984, 15–46.
———. *Modern Movements in European Philosophy*. Manchester: Manchester Univer-
    sity Press, 1986.
———. *The Wake of Imagination: Towards a Postmodern Culture*. Minneapolis: Univer-
    sity of Minnesota Press, 1988.
———. *Poetics of Imagining: From Husserl to Lyotard*. London: Routledge, 1991.
Kemp, T. Peter, and David Rasmussen. *The Narrative Path: The Later Works of Paul
    Ricoeur*. Cambridge, Mass.: The MIT Press, 1989.
Kerby, Anthony Paul. *Narrative and the Self*. Bloomington: Indiana University Press,
    1991.
Kermode, Frank. *The Sense of an Ending: Studies in the Theory of Fiction*. New York:
    Oxford University Press, 1967.
———. *The Genesis of Secrecy: On the Interpretation of Narrative*. Cambridge, Mass.:
    Harvard University Press, 1979.
———. *The Art of Telling: Essays on Fiction*. Cambridge, Mass.: Harvard University
    Press, 1983.
Kirk, G. S. *Myth: Its Meaning and Functions in Ancient and Other Cultures*. Berkeley:
    Cambridge University Press/University of California Press, 1970.
Kristeva, Julia. *Tales of Love*. Trans. Leon S. Roudiez. New York: Columbia University
    Press, 1987.

———. *Stranger to Ourselves.* Trans. Leon S. Roudiez. New York: Columbia University Press, 1991.

Lauer, Quentin. *The Triumph of Subjectivity: An Introduction to Transcendental Phenomenology.* New York: Fordham University Press, 1978.

Lawlor, Leonard. *Imagination and Chance: The Difference Between the Thought of Ricoeur and Derrida.* Albany: State University of New York Press, 1992.

Lévinas, Emmanuel. *Totality and Infinity: An Essay on Exteriority.* Trans. A. Lingis. Pittsburgh: Duquesne University Press, 1969.

———. *Otherwise Than Being or Beyond Essence.* Trans. A. Lingus. The Hague: Martinus Nijhoff, 1981.

———. *Ethics and Infinity: Conversations with Philippe Nemo.* Trans. R. Cohen. Pittsburgh: Duquesne University Press, 1985.

———. *Face to Face with Levinas.* Ed. Richard A. Cohen. Albany: State University of New York Press, 1986.

———. *Time and the Other.* Trans. Richard A. Cohen. Pittsburgh: Duquesne University Press, 1987

———. *The Levinas Reader.* Ed. Sean Hand. Oxford: Blackwell, 1989.

Levi-Strauss, Claude. *The Savage Mind.* Chicago: University of Chicago Press, 1966.

Lingis, Alphonso. *The Community of Those Who Have Nothing in Common.* Bloomington: Indiana University Press, 1994.

Llewelyn, John. *Beyond Metaphysics? The Hermeneutical Circle in Contemporary Continental Philosophy.* Atlantic Highlands: Humanities Press International, 1985.

Lowe, Walter James. *Mystery and the Unconscious: A Study in the Thought of Paul Ricoeur.* Metuchen: The Scarecrow Press, 1977.

———. "The Coherence of Paul Ricoeur." *The Journal of Religion* (1981): 384–402.

Lyotard, Jean-François. *The Postmodern Condition: A Report on Knowledge.* Trans. Geoff Bennington and Brian Massumi. Minneapolis: University of Minnesota Press, 1984.

———. *Just Gaming.* Trans. Wlad Gozich. Afterword by Samuel Weber, trans. Brian Massumi. Minneapolis: University of Minnesota Press, 1985.

MacIntyre, Alasdair. *After Virtue.* Notre Dame, Ind.: University of Notre Dame Press, 1981.

———. *Three Rival Versions of Moral Enquiry: Encyclopaedia, Geneology, and Tradition.* Notre Dame, Ind.: University of Notre Dame Press, 1990.

Madison, G. B. *Understanding: A Phenomenological-Pragmatic Analysis.* Westport, Conn.: Greenwood Press, 1982.

———. *The Hermeneutics of Postmodernity: Figures and Themes.* Bloomington: Indiana University Press, 1988.

Marcel, Gabriel Marcel. *Tragic Wisdom and Beyond.* Evanston, Ill.: Northwestern University Press, 1973.

McCarthy, Thomas. *The Critical Theory of Jurgen Habermas.* Cambridge: The MIT Press, 1978.

Michelfelder, Diane P., and Richard E. Palmer, eds. *Dialogue and Deconstruction: The Gadamer–Derrida Encounter.* Albany: State University of New York Press, 1989.

Mink, Louis O. "The Autonomy of Historical Understanding." *History and Theory* 5 (1965): 24–47.

———. "Philosophical Analysis and Historical Understanding." *Review of Metaphysics*
    20 (1968): 667–698.
———. "History and Fiction as Modes of Comprehension." *New Literary History* 1
    (1970): 541–558.
Mohanty, J. N. *The Concept of Intentionality* St. Louis: Warren H. Green, 1972.
Mongin, Olivier. *Paul Ricoeur.* Paris: Seuil, 1994.
Olthuis, James H. *Knowing Other-wise: Philosophy at the Threshold of Spirituality.* New
    York: Fordham University Press, 1997.
Palmer, Richard E. *Hermeneutics: Interpretation Theory in Schleiermacher, Dilthey,
    Heidegger, and Gadamer.* Evanston, Ill.: Northwestern University Press, 1969.
Pellauer, David. "Limning the Liminal: Carr and Ricoeur on Time and Narrative."
    Philosophy Today 35 (1991), n. 1, 51–72.
Prendergast, Christopher. *The Order of Mimesis.* Cambridge: Cambridge University Press,
    1986.
Reagan, Charles E., ed. *Studies in the Philosophy of Paul Ricoeur.* Athens: Ohio Univer-
    sity Press, 1979.
———. *Paul Ricoeur: His Life and Work.* Chicago: University of Chicago Press, 1996.
Rorty, Richard. *Philosophy and the Mirror of Nature.* Princeton, N.J.: Princeton Univer-
    sity Press, 1979.
Rasmussen, David. "Rethinking Subjectivity: Narrative Identity and the Self." *Philosophy
    and Social Criticism,* 21.5–6 (1995): 159–172.
St. Pierre, Paul Matthew. *Quelle heure est-il, Monsieur Ricoeur? A Semiotic Narratology
    of Duration, Term, Tempo, and Rec(oe)urrence, Tol(le)d from the Criticism of Paul
    Ricoeur.* Unpublished manuscript, 1993.
Sartre, Jean-Paul. *The Psychology of Imagination.* Trans. Bernard Frechtman. New York:
    Washington Square Press, 1948.
———. *Imagination: A Psychological Critique.* Trans. and intro. Forrest Williams. Ann
    Arbor: University of Michigan Press, 1962.
———. *Being and Nothingness: A Phenomenological Essay on Ontology.* Trans. Hazel
    E. Barnes. New York: Washington Square Press, 1993.
Scholes, Robert, and Robert Kellogg. *The Nature of Narrative.* New York: Oxford Uni-
    versity Press, 1966.
Schrag, Calvin O. *Communicative Praxis and the Space of Subjectivity.* Bloomington:
    Indiana University Press, 1986.
———. *The Self after Postmodernity.* New Haven, Conn.: Yale University Press, 1997.
Silverman, Hugh J. *Textualities: Between Hermeneutics and Deconstruction.* New York
    and London: Routledge, 1994.
Sinyard, Boyd. "Myth and Reflection: Some Comments on Ricoeur's Phenomenological
    Analysis." *Canadian Journal of Theology* 16.1–2 (1970): 33–40.
Spiegelberg, Herbert. *The Phenomenological Movement: A Historical Introduction.* 2nd
    ed. 2 vols. The Hague: Martinus Nijhoff, 1976.
Stanzel, F. K. *A Theory of Narrative.* Trans. Charlotte Goedsche. Cambridge: Cam-
    bridge University Press, 1984.
Sternberg, Meir. *The Poetics of Biblical Narrative: Ideological Literature and the Drama
    of Reading.* Bloomington: Indiana University Press, 1985.

Taylor, Charles. *Sources of the Self: The Making of the Modern Identity.* Cambridge, Mass.: Harvard University Press, 1989.

Thompson, John. *Critical Hermeneutics: A Study in the Thought of Paul Ricoeur and Jurgen Habermas.* Cambridge: Cambridge University Press, 1981.

Trible, Phyllis. *Texts of Terror: Literary-Feminist Readings of Biblical Narratives.* Philadelphia: Fortress Press, 1984.

Van Den Hengel, John W. *The Home of Meaning: The Hermeneutics of the Subject of Paul Ricoeur.* Washington, D.C.: University Press of America, 1982.

Vanhoozer, Kevin. *Biblical Narrative in the Philosophy of Paul Ricoeur: A Study in Hermeneutics and Theology.* Cambridge: Cambridge University Press, 1990.

Waldenfels, Bernhard. "The Other and the Foreign." *Philosophy and Social Criticism* 21.5–6 (1995): 111–124.

Wallace, Mark I. *The Second Naiveté: Barth, Ricoeur, and the New Yale Theology.* Macon Ga.: Mercer University Press, 1990.

Warnke, Georgia. *Gadamer: Hermeneutics, Tradition and Reason.* Stanford: Stanford University Press, 1987.

Waugh, Patricia. *Metafiction: The Theory and Practice of Self-Conscious Fiction.* London: Methuen, 1984.

Weinsheimer, Joel C. *Gadamer's Hermeneutics: A Reading of 'Truth and Method.'* New Haven, Conn.: Yale University Press, 1985.

———. *Philosophical Hermeneutics and Literary Theory.* New Haven, Conn.: Yale University Press, 1991.

White, Hayden. "The Structure of Historical Narrative." *Clio* 1 (1972): 5–19.

———. *Metahistory: The Historical Imagination in Nineteenth-Century Europe.* Baltimore: Johns Hopkins University Press, 1973.

———. *The Tropics of Discourse.* Baltimore: Johns Hopkins University Press, 1978.

Wood, David, ed. *On Paul Ricoeur: Narrative and Interpretation.* London and New York: Routledge, 1991.

Wright, G. H. von. *Explanation and Understanding.* Ithaca, N.Y.: Cornell University Press, 1971.

INDEX

absence, 18–20, 40, 48–53, 77, 78, 86, 87, 173, 175, 176
absolute consciousness, 9, 13–15, 17, 18, 21–24, 32, 158
absolute self, 4, 22, 125, 178
absurd, 52
action, 5–10, 40, 47–51, 63, 66, 68–69, 91, 92, 95–100, 102, 104, 110–111, 114–115, 117, 126–127, 129, 137–138, 141–149, 152, 154–155, 157, 160, 172, 175, 176, 179, 180–183
    acting and suffering, 41, 105, 111, 145, 146, 157, 161, 172
    conceptual network, 99, 100, 137, 145
    field of motivation, 65
    narrative, 100
    power-to-do, 137
    rule-governed behavior, 99
    semantics, 137
    unity, 5–6
allégorèse, 109, 159
analogical transfer, 8, 66, 78, 81, 95, 96, 102–103, 110, 111, 115, 129, 141, 143, 162, 176, 177, 181
analogical unity, 6, 42, 126, 127, 130, 136, 147–149, 158, 172
analytic-reflective structure, 126
application, 11, 43, 56, 58, 70, 94, 95, 97, 102–104, 107–109, 111, 112, 115, 142, 143, 149, 177
appropriation, 4, 10, 12, 13, 30, 32, 34, 35, 46, 70, 81, 85, 95, 98, 103, 107, 143, 148, 149, 159, 160, 173
Aristotle, 20, 22, 36, 61, 103, 112, 115, 127, 129, 149, 152, 156, 169, 179

art and life, problem of, 94, 112, 116–118, 120, 121, 142, 159, 160, 177
attestation, 1, 5, 8, 42, 75, 125, 128, 135, 136, 147, 153, 154, 160–163, 172, 181, 183
Augustine, 1, 165
authorial intention, 27, 31, 32, 94, 95, 98, 109, 171

Bachelard, Gaston, 85, 175
basic particulars, 131, 132
Beardsley, Monroe, 81, 82
being-in-the-world, 29, 42, 172
belief, 1, 2, 27, 71, 161
benevolent spontaneity, 50, 154, 155, 156, 158, 174
Benveniste, Emile, 79
Boutin, Maurice, 170, 176, 177
Brentano, Franz, 16

call, 29, 39, 69, 74, 77, 78, 86, 89, 104, 119, 120, 155, 160, 162, 169
calling, 40, 155, 156
Carr, David, 94, 97, 116–119, 176–178
Cartesian Meditations, 13–15, 25, 26
Cassirer, Ernst, 99
character, 7, 8, 36, 39, 43, 66, 136, 140–143, 149, 180, 182
circle of the self-same, 9, 41, 44, 55, 184
cogito and anticogito, 4, 13, 124, 129, 161, 166
commitment, 1–3, 51, 90, 94, 162, 163
conatus, 6, 8, 10, 125, 149, 156, 158, 159

197

77, 90, 93, 96, 106–108, 116, 124,
125, 128–129, 133, 135, 144, 151,
157, 159, 160, 169, 179, 181
affective otherness, 47, 53, 76
alterity, 9, 10, 129, 154, 161

Pellauer, David, 167, 175, 177, 178, 183
personal identity, 91, 93, 95–97, 103,
106, 116, 123, 132, 138, 139, 141,
142
phenomenology
descriptive, 2, 43
eidetic description, 28, 44, 45
epoché, 13, 16, 17, 33, 35, 36, 101,
168
existential phenomenology, 28, 42,
172
from the top down, 42, 76
"I can," 43–44, 46, 111, 145–146,
153, 157, 182
"I will," 42, 43, 76, 111, 116
Lebenswelt, 24, 35
life-world, 24, 25, 34, 35, 51, 86, 158
natural thesis, 17, 18
noema and noesis, 18, 31, 34, 61
nonidealistic concept of intentionality, 27
passive synthesis, 17, 24, 168
reduction, 16, 18, 23, 35, 36, 42, 43,
45, 48, 54, 55, 86, 103, 159
transcendental phenomenology, 15,
23, 25, 28
transcendental reduction, 13–18, 22,
24, 42, 169
transcendental subjectivity, 15, 16,
20, 25, 26, 27, 32, 40, 47, 48, 56,
121
transcendental synthesis, 56, 58–63
Wesenschau, 16
philosophical anthropology, 54, 57, 58,
68, 73, 76, 79, 89, 90
philosophical method, 2, 11
Plato, 34, 36, 42, 172
poetry, 113
poem in miniature, 82, 88
poetic image, 85, 175

poetic resolution, 83, 97, 101
poetic text, 10
polysemy of language, 4, 6, 32, 40, 78,
106, 126–128, 130
power, 6–10, 25, 29, 30, 36, 39, 43,
49, 51–53, 55, 60–62, 71–75, 78,
82–88, 91, 93–95, 98, 101, 104–
106, 110, 112, 118–120, 125, 126,
140, 142, 144–158, 167, 168, 170,
175, 176, 181–183
of agency, 144, 147, 150
of language, 29, 30, 170
held-in-abeyance, 10, 153, 157
in-common, 146, 149
objectifications, 144–146
power-over, 146, 153, 156, 158
power-to-do, 137, 138, 145, 146, 149,
150, 152, 157
voluntary power, 42, 140, 145, 153, 182
practical consciousness, 58, 64–67
pragmatics, 116, 130–134, 139, 138,
151, 160, 177, 181
predication, 34, 77, 83, 132, 134
predicative assimilation, 77, 84, 92
predicative impertinence, 78
predicative pertinence, 77, 82
prefiguration, 7, 47, 86, 93, 94, 98, 99,
113, 118, 119, 130, 173
presence, 13, 18–21, 24–26, 34–35,
48–50, 53, 56, 58, 61, 63, 65–67,
71, 77–78, 85–87, 111, 121, 148,
166, 169, 173–176
primary affirmation, 42, 55, 57, 157,
172, 174
primordial spontaneity, 50, 154, 155,
156, 158, 174

rationalism and irrationalism, 23, 106–
112, 171
Reading, 106–112
allégorsè, 109, 159
analogous, 109, 111
application, 107
catharsis, 108, 109
receptive, 103, 106–112
rhetorical affect, 107